A History of Southern Africa

Kevin Shillington

Longman

For Pippa

Longman Group UK Limited,
Longman House, Burnt Mill, Harlow,
Essex CM20 2JE, England
and Associated Companies throughout the world

First published 1987

Set in 9/11 pt Palatino (Linotron)

Produced by Longman Group (FE) Ltd
Printed in Hong Kong

ISBN 0 582 58521 X

Acknowledgments

The Publishers are grateful to the following for their permission to reproduce photographs:-

Africana Museum for figs 1.3, 3.1, 4.1, 4.2, 4.3, 6.4, 7.2, 7.3, 8.1, 8.3 and 12.1; BBC Hulton Picture Library for figs 1.1, 2.5, 3.2, 4.4, 6.1, 7.1, 8.4, 10.2a, 10.4, 11.1, 12.2, 13.1 and 13.4; Cambridge University Press (taken from Journal of African History Vol. 5 No. 3 1964) for fig 2.3; Camera Press for figs 16.4 and 18.5; Cape Archives for figs 8.2, 10.1 and 11.4; Frank Cass and Co. Ltd for fig 1.4; Central Office of Information for fig 17.6b; Compix for figs 17.3, 17.5 and 18.4; De Beers Consolidated Mines for fig 9.2; Mary Evans Picture Library for fig 6.3; William Fehr Collection for figs 6.2 and 10.3; I.D.A.F for figs 9.4, 14.3, 15.1, 15.2, 15.3, 16.1, 16.2, 16.3, 18.1, 18.2 and 18.3; Illustrated London News for figs 10.5, 10.6 and 11.2; Local History Museum for fig 11.3; Dr T. M. O'c Maggs for fig 2.4; Mansell Collection for figs 3.3, 3.4 and 3.5; McGregor Museum for figs 9.1, 9.3, 9.5 and 12.4; Professor Van der Merwe for figs 5 and 2.2; Ministry of Information, Zimbabwe for fig 18.6; National Archives of Zimbabwe for fig 13.2; National Army Museum for fig 13.3; Photo Source for figs 14.1 and 14.2; David Philip Publishers Cape for fig 1.2; Punch for fig 12.3; Rivers Thompson, Lesotho for fig 5.2; I. Schapero for fig 17.1; South African Museum for figs 1.6a and 1.6b; State Archives, Windhoek, Namibia for figs 14.4, 14.5 and 14.6; Swaziland National Archives for fig 17.6a and Topham Photo Library for fig 17.2 and 17.4.

The Publishers regret that they have been unable to trace the copyright holders of photographs 2.1 and 5.1 and would be grateful for any information enabling them to do so.

The cover photographs have been reproduced by kind permission of:- Mary Evans Picture Library for top left; Mansell Collection for bottom and The Slide Centre for top right.

Contents

List of maps

Preface

This History of Southern Africa is intended to provide a clear and simple survey of the region from Stone Age times to the late 1980s. It is aimed primarily at students of senior secondary/high school level, studying for School Certificate ('O level') examinations or their equivalent. At the same time it should provide a useful introduction for students studying Southern African history at a more advanced level. Besides meeting the demands of school syllabuses, it is hoped that this History of Southern Africa will provide the general reader with a clear and easily understood historical interpretation of this region where history is so clearly 'in the making'.

The exercises at the end of each chapter are designed as aids to study and to prepare students for School Certificate examinations. All questions can be answered from the information in the text, at times combined with that of maps, illustrations and documents (see Note for Students). Reading beyond the text is to be encouraged and an introductory reading list is provided just before the Index.

The book covers the history of the modern countries of Botswana, Namibia, Lesotho, Swaziland and South Africa. The colonisation of Zimbabwe in the 1890s is included because of its close connection with events further south. Though periodic reference is made to Mozambique and Angola, the history of these countries, as with that of Zimbabwe, falls outside the general scope of this book.

In writing any broad survey of history over a large area and through a long period of time, it is necessary to be selective in the events one describes. In the interests of brevity and clarity much has had to be left out. I have focussed on the events and developments which I consider to have been most important. It is thus *one* interpretation of Southern Africa's past. Other historians may and do interpret the region's history differently. I have attempted here to break away from the Euro-centric approach common to so many earlier histories of the region. The main emphasis of this book is the history of the majority black population of Southern Africa. As far as possible attempts have been made to interpret events from their perspective. Thus where the history of white settlers and colonial government is discussed, it is mainly in relation to the effects of their presence on the majority population of the region. At the same time I have tried to explain developments and changes rather than swamp and confuse the reader with too much 'names-and-dates'.

I am indebted to the work of many historians in the writing of this History. Some of them are listed in the Recommended Further Reading near the back of the book. My debt to these and many others is incalculable, though the interpretation presented here remains my own. I am grateful to students and colleagues of the University of Botswana and teachers and members of the Historical Association of Botswana from whose enthusiasm for the subject I drew encouragement during long hours of writing. I wish to thank those who read and commented on various parts of the working manuscript, in particular Ngwabe Bhebe of the University of Zimbabwe and I. Lubinda of Lobatse Secondary School. Finally I dedicate this book to Pippa whose everpresent support and encouragement is always an inspiration.

Keven Shillington
London   January 1987

Note for students

Section A. Think, discuss, understand and write
This section will help you develop the skill of writing the 'history essay', which is the main way used by examiners for testing one's knowledge and understanding of history. The exercises in this section raise and question the main issues and themes covered in each chapter. It is not necessary to use each one as an essay exercise, but it will be useful to think about and discuss the issues raised. This should aid understanding and stimulate thought about these and other similar issues in the past or present. You may like to use the questions as the basis for making notes on the chapter. If preparing for an examination then it is recommended that the answer to at least one question per chapter is written as an essay.

Hints on essay writing Thinking, discussion and understanding are all very important before starting to write. The period of discussion will help you form the sentences that will make your argument relevant and persuasive. You may find it useful to take the following steps:

1 Read the question carefully, think about it and use a pencil to underline the key words. If necessary re-read the relevant section of the text and think again about the question.
2 Discuss, in small or large groups, the points raised by the question and try out the arguments you will use in answering it. This is the time to raise any points which you do not fully understand.

3 Now note down in *as few words as possible* the key items which will appear in your answer. In these preparatory notes *do not* write full sentences, only key words.
4 Use the notes to sort your ideas into a good order and see if you have left anything out.
5 Now you are ready to start writing your essay. Keep the question in front of you and answer all parts of it. Do not look back directly at the text while you are writing the actual essay: your notes and preparatory discussion should be enough. Try writing in your own words in the same way as if you were explaining your answer orally.
6 Re-read what you have written, if possible aloud, to see what it sounds like, checking for accuracy, relevance to the question asked and persuasiveness.

B. Imaginative writing This is a very useful way of developing the historical imagination as well as practising your writing skills. Use your imagination to really put yourself in the historical part you are playing. Be true to known historical detail: that is, only write what *could* have or *might* have really happened. Do well in this section and you will get more enjoyment and understanding from your history lessons!

C. Mapwork, document study, group work and discussion Use this section to make the most of the maps and documents in the text. The exercises may prompt you to think more about the importance and relevance of the history you are learning.

<u>CHAPTER 1</u>

From Stone Age to Iron Age in Southern Africa

The Stone Age

Before the introduction of the skill of metal-working, a little under two thousand years ago, man in Southern Africa was dependent for his tools on the natural materials which existed around him. He thus made tools out of materials like wood, bone and stone. Because the tools made of stone are the ones which have most commonly survived, this period, which stretches back for more than a million years, is referred to as the Stone Age. Over this very long period of time man gradually developed the skills of stone tool making, from very primitive, simple, hand-sized choppers and diggers to smaller and more sophisticated tools. According to various stages in this development of tool making, archaeologists normally divide the Stone Age into three main periods: Early, Middle and Late.

By ten thousand years ago the Late Stone Age was well established over the whole of Southern Africa. By then man had reduced stone tool making to a fine art. By the skillful striking of one stone against another, Late Stone Age man had learned to shape stones into tiny sharp discs, crescents and points which we call 'microliths'. These were most commonly used as scrapers. They were held between thumb and forefinger and used for cutting meat, scraping animal skins, sharpening sticks or cleaning vegetables, much as one might use a very small hand-knife today. Other, specially-pointed microliths were fixed with vegetable glue onto long thin sticks to form the heads of spears or arrows.

Late Stone Age hunter-gatherers: the San

The Late Stone Age peoples of Southern Africa are thought to be the ancestors of the modern San, small numbers of whom still live in parts of Botswana, Namibia and southern Angola. Some of these, though very few, still live by hunting and gathering in a way that is probably very similar to that of their Late Stone Age ancestors. Hunter-gatherers are people who do not grow their own food. They depend instead on what plant and animal life they can find growing wild in the country around them.

The evidence   We know about the Late Stone Age San from a variety of sources. Firstly, there is the archaeological evidence, that is the remains of stone tools, bones, sticks, shelters and fireplaces found in their camp sites. These kinds of materials have been particularly well preserved in some of the caves and rock shelters which they used along the southern Cape coast. Secondly, there are the paintings made by the San on the walls of their rock shelters (see Fig. 1.1). These depict people as well as animals, tools, weapons and other objects. Much can be learned from these paintings about the San way of life. Many fine examples of San rock art are to be found in the Drakensberg mountains of South Africa and Lesotho as well as in the hills and rock shelters of Zimbabwe, Botswana and Namibia.

The third source of evidence on the San is the written records of early European travellers, traders, missionaries and colonists who came to the Cape from the seventeenth century onwards. Their writings were often hostile to the San whom they criticised as backward and primitive and referred to as 'Bushmen'. Nevertheless, their writings often provide useful descriptions of the San and tell us how and where they were still living by the seventeenth and eighteenth centuries. Finally, there is the evidence of the way of life of the San's living descendants. Those few who still live a hunting and

1.1 San rock art from Southern Africa. In this picture San hunters (centre) appear to have taken cattle from cattle herders (right).

gathering existence, especially in the remoter desert regions of Botswana, have in recent years been intensively studied by anthropologists. These studies of modern hunter-gatherer communities can tell the historian much about how their ancestors probably lived many hundreds and even thousands of years ago.

The San Archaeologists have found very few skeletal remains of Late Stone Age people, but what little there is suggests they were physically similar to the San of recent times. These had yellowish-brown skin and were small and lightly built – seldom more than 150 cm in height. The evidence of recent centuries describes the San as wearing small aprons, or loin-cloths, of soft, tanned animal skins. Their own paintings, however, suggest that the San of long ago may not have worn anything, at least in the warm summer months. Nevertheless, in times of cold weather they probably wore leather cloaks or karosses.

Hunting and gathering The San have long been famous for their skill in hunting and tracking. Archaeologists have found evidence of animal bones in Late Stone Age camp sites. These belong mostly to small varieties of antelope, rodent and rabbit, probably caught in traps. There is also evidence of larger antelope and even occasionally hippo, rhino and elephant. Bones, however, survive better than vegetable matter which quickly rots away or is eaten by termites. This has perhaps led to an exaggeration of the importance of hunting in the economy of the San hunter-gatherers.

Recent studies of the San in Botswana have led historians to look again at their other sources of evidence. As a result it is now realised that in fact it was probably the regular gathering of plant foods which provided the San with most of their daily diet. They collected a wide variety of roots, bulbs, fruit, berries and nuts. To these were added caterpillars, termites and locusts and in some areas tortoises and honey. An advantage of depending on these kinds of gathered foodstuffs was that they were reliable. The San knew where they could find them and when they were ripe for harvest. What is more, plant food was renewable. Since they only ever harvested a portion of the crop, it was able to regrow in roughly the same place each year. The San were thus able to move around from one place to another according to what foods were in season.

Nevertheless, even though gathering accounted for the bulk of their diet, the San were also hunters and game meat provided an important source of extra protein. Furthermore, at certain times of year those in the south moved down to the coast where they lived off shellfish, birds' eggs, fish and seals. On these occasions this kind of food was so plentiful that plant gathering became less important.

Late Stone Age technology The technology of the Late Stone Age San was related to their needs. Their main gathering tool was the digging stick. This was a fire-hardened stick up to a metre in length which tapered slightly towards one end. A circular stone weight with a hole bored in the centre was slid down over the narrow end of the stick until it stuck fast about half-way down the shaft. The thick end was sharpened to a point. The gatherer then had a very effective weighted tool for digging up roots and bulbs from the hard dry earth. A large number of the bored stones have been recovered by archaeologists though the sticks themselves have not survived (see Fig. 1.2). Most of the gathering was done by the women. They collected their food in bags made of leather or string woven from the stem fibres of reeds.

The main task of the men was the hunting and trapping of wild animals. The smaller animals, which formed the larger part of their meat diet, were mostly caught in traps and snares. These were made of string from plant fibres and animal sinew. From about two thousand years ago domestic dogs were also used for hunting. The most common and best-known San hunting weapon was the bow and arrow. This was used for hunting larger game animals. It was also used with considerable success against any enemy who invaded their hunting grounds. The arrow-shaft was made of light stick or reed into which was inserted the head. This was made of bone up to 10 cm in length on the end of which was fastened a small sharpened tip of stone. The tip was treated with specially prepared plant and snake poison which could wear down even the largest of animals. When the arrow was fired, the shaft fell out leaving the tip safely embedded in the animal's side. The San hunters would then follow

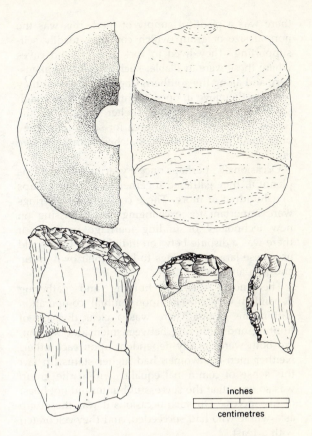

1.2 Stone tools of the Later Stone Age from the Orange Free State, c. 4,000 years old: scrapers and the broken half of a bored stone.

their victim until the poison took effect and the animal dropped. Their meat was usually roasted over a fire which they lit by grinding one stick into another until a spark was created.

San who lived near rivers and the sea used a variety of fishing techniques. Spears were used for hunting fish and seals. In rivers they used funnel-shaped traps woven out of reeds. Although none have survived from Stone Age times, these can be seen in their rock paintings. The same technique is still used in some African rivers today. Rocks were used in rivers to form dams behind which fish could be more easily caught. Along the southern Cape coast there is still evidence of similar tidal traps made of rough stone walls.

Social organisation The San usually lived together in small, family-sized bands of up to twenty or thirty people. Within such a group there would be five or six adult men, a similar number of women and the rest children. Except in special circumstances, where there was a plentiful supply of food, this was the normal size of group which could be readily self-supporting. They lived in rock shelters and caves where these were available, such as in the Drakensberg and along the southern Cape coast. When they were on the move in open country, they built rough screens of brush-wood to shelter them from the wind. When settled in an area for some time, they built small houses of poles thatched with grass (see Fig. 1.3).

Occasionally, perhaps once a year, when food was plentiful, they gathered together into larger groups of a hundred or more. These communal gatherings were important for exchanging news, passing on new technology or finding marriage partners. If there was a dispute between individuals, they could use these large gatherings to leave their own group and join another.

The success of San hunting and gathering depended very closely upon mutual co-operation within the group. There was a clear division of hunting and gathering between men and women, but both were equally dependent upon each other. Neither men nor women had higher status. In fact this sense of communal equality within the group was so great that the successful hunter did not boast of his success. On such occasions it was the group as a whole who had succeeded, and they celebrated with a feast.

Nevertheless, each San group did in fact have a leader, usually the male head of the main family. He made the final decision about things like when to move camp. He was also the guardian of the camp's fire, which was considered to be sacred. It was his duty to start the new fire whenever they moved camp.

Religion The San were an intensely religious people. They believed every valley, hill and stream was inhabited by a guardian spirit. They traced all sickness to the spiritual world though at the same time they were highly skilled in the use of herbal medicines. They believed that each living creature possessed a spirit of its own and thus all creatures should have mutual respect for each other.

San rock paintings The San are perhaps most famous for the beauty, variety and extent of their rock paintings. These have already been referred to as an important source of evidence about their way of life. The San painted on the walls of caves, on rock shelters and sometimes high up on open exposed pieces of rock. They made their paint out of animal fats and vegetable dyes and applied it with sticks and feathers. The most common colours were red, orange, yellow and brown. Many of their paintings still survive in the hills of Zimbabwe and north-western Botswana and in the Drakensberg of

1.3 A modern San camp in the Kalahari.

Lesotho and South Africa. Their paintings are of two types. Some seem to tell a story such as a successful hunt. Others, depicting animals and people, are thought to have religious significance. Among the latter paintings the largest antelope, the eland, occurs most frequently. It was believed to be a sacred animal.

The essence of the San hunter-gatherer way of life was one of co-operation with nature. Thus they neither killed nor took from the environment more than they needed for their daily survival, and their needs were simple as they did not live in comfort or luxury. It was a way of life which had evolved over more than a million years. Then came the advance of new technology which enabled man to control and exploit his environment, his fellow-creatures and, in due course, his fellow-human beings. Faced with such an onslaught, the ancient San hunter-gatherer way of life was to die out within a mere two thousand years.

Stone Age pastoralists : the Khoikhoi

Archaeologists working on sites in Namibia and in the southern and south-western Cape have recently made some important discoveries. The sites have been dated to the last few centuries of the BC era and they contain the remains of pottery and the bones of sheep. These are two items which definitely do not belong to the San's hunter-gatherer lifestyle. And yet the dates are too early to belong to peoples of the Iron Age. In other words, they are evidence of a whole new Stone Age way of life. They belong to a people who were practising a form of pastoralism. A pastoralist is someone who depends for his livelihood wholly or partly upon the herding of domestic animals such as cattle, sheep or goats. The Stone Age pastoralists of south-western Africa are now believed to be the ancestors of a people who called themselves Khoikhoi. The name means 'men of men' and was intended perhaps to distinguish themselves from those who were merely hunters and gatherers.

Origins of the Khoikhoi The Khoikhoi appear to have originated from the dry grasslands of the northern Kalahari desert in Botswana. They were probably a branch of San hunter-gatherers who added pastoralism to their way of life. It seems that in the last few centuries BC they spread out fairly quickly taking their flocks of sheep in search of favourable grasslands in Namibia and the south-western Cape (see Map 1.1). There is the early centuries AD they began to herd cattle as well as sheep.

It is not yet clear exactly how the Khoikhoi obtained their longhorned cattle or their fat-tailed sheep. These animals are not native to Southern Africa and could have come originally from East Africa. They may have been brought from there by Early Iron Age people who, as we shall see, were gradually moving southwards at this time. But exactly when and where the Khoikhoi obtained them is still not known for sure.

The Khoikhoi Most of our knowledge about the Khoikhoi and their way of life comes from descriptions in European writings of the seventeenth and eighteenth centuries. As with the San these early European observers were often highly critical of the Khoikhoi whom they referred to as 'Hottentots'. For instance, Europeans wrongly believed that the Khoikhoi lacked religion. In fact the Khoikhoi were, like the San, an intensely religious people. They had few religious ceremonies as such but they believed in the existence of a supreme God. He was responsible for bringing the thunderstorms which refreshed the pasture. The Khoikhoi also believed that the spirits of their ancestors inhabited natural features of the landscape such as valleys, rivers and mountains.

The Khoikhoi were slightly taller than the San but otherwise they were fairly similar in appearance and spoke related languages. They still hunted and gathered and like the San they used bows and arrows, spears, snares and traps. The main differences between the way of life of the Khoikhoi and the San were related to the Khoikhoi's pastoralism.

The Khoikhoi way of life: changes brought by pastoralism

The adoption of pastoralism by Late Stone Age peoples brought many changes to their way of life. The most obvious of these changes was in diet. For the first time Late Stone Age man had full control over an important new source of food – domestic animals. The Khoikhoi were still heavily dependent upon plant food gathered from the wild and they still trapped and hunted game for their meat. But to these was now added a diet of soured milk from their sheep and cattle. It was perhaps this improvement in diet which led to the Khoikhoi being slightly taller than the San. In addition, when necessary, they slaughtered sheep for meat and melted down fat from the sheep's tail. Cattle were a way of storing wealth and were usually only slaughtered on special occasions.

Compared with the San the Khoikhoi lived in

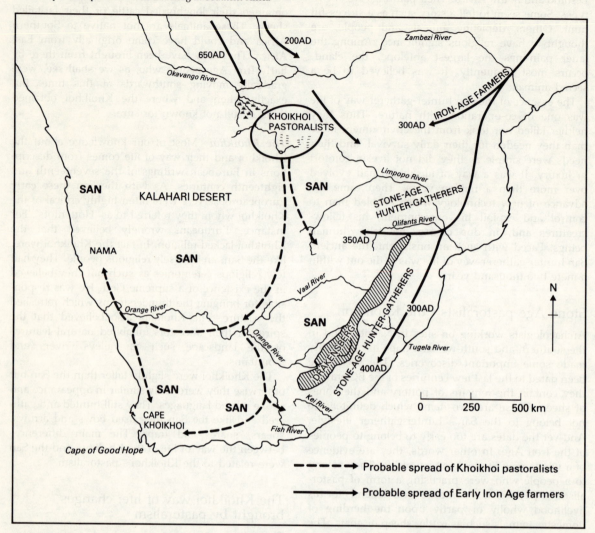

Map labels:
Zambezi River
650AD
200AD
Okavango River
KHOIKHOI PASTORALISTS
IRON-AGE FARMERS
300AD
Limpopo River
SAN
KALAHARI DESERT
SAN
STONE-AGE HUNTER-GATHERERS
Olifants River
350AD
NAMA
SAN
Orange River
Vaal River
SAN
DRAKENSBERG
STONE-AGE HUNTER-GATHERERS
300AD
Orange River
Tugela River
400AD
N
SAN
SAN
CAPE KHOIKHOI
Fish River
Kei River
Cape of Good Hope

0   250   500 km

- - - → Probable spread of Khoikhoi pastoralists
——— → Probable spread of Early Iron Age farmers

larger, more settled communities. They were able to do this because their livestock provided them with a steady supply of food close at hand. Nevertheless it was still necessary for them to move settlement several times a year. As pastures varied from season to season so the Khoikhoi moved their livestock between mountain, valley and coast.

A Khoikhoi settlement consisted of between ten and forty dwellings. These were made of long thin poles driven into the ground to form a circle. They were then bent over and tied to meet in the centre. On this dome-shaped framework were laid woven reed mats. The houses were usually arranged in a circle into which the sheep and cattle were herded at night (see Fig. 1.4).

Khoikhoi cattle were used for riding and also as pack-oxen to carry their possessions such as the poles and mats of their houses. Because they lived a slightly more settled existence and used pack-oxen in this way, the Khoikhoi were able to have far more possessions than the San. As already mentioned, one of these items was pottery. This was made of clay, baked hard in a fire. The pot had pointed bases and lug-handles near the neck for hanging the pot on a stick or from a branch. They were used for storing sour milk or melted fat. The Khoikhoi made milking buckets out of reeds so closely woven that they did not leak. Besides loin-cloths, the Khoikhoi wore leather cloaks, fur caps and leather sandals.

The Khoikhoi's ownership of livestock and other possessions meant that some of the sharing ideal of the San community was lost. The roles of men and

1.4 A Khoikhoi settlement in the early nineteenth century. Note the method of hut construction.

women became more marked and men, who controlled the livestock and hence the wealth of the Khoikhoi community, achieved a position of dominance over women.

Khoikhoi settlements were much larger than those of the San and at times contained up to one or two hundred people. They were able to settle in such numbers because they were only partially dependent upon hunting and gathering. Their livestock provided them with an additional supply of food close at hand. A Khoikhoi settlement usually consisted of a large extended family group or clan. When several of these village clans could trace a common ancestry, they formed a chiefdom, headed by a chief. In practice the individual village clans exercised a fair degree of independence.

As herds of cattle increased in size some clans became richer than others. This often led to disputes over cattle ownership or rights of pasture. One of the principal duties of the chief was to try and prevent or settle disputes of this nature. Much depended upon the personality and strength of the chief as to whether he was able to maintain peace and unity within his chiefdom. Cattle raids between clans and chiefdoms were a common feature of Khoikhoi life. As we shall see in Chapter 3, this was a weakness of which invading European colonists were quick to take advantage in the eighteenth century.

Interaction between Khoikhoi and San

The languages of the Khoikhoi were of the same basic family as those of the San. Their grammatical structure was similar and both contained characteristic consonantal 'clicks'. So it was probably not too difficult for Khoikhoi and San to understand one another and there seems to have been a good deal of interaction between the two. Relations between them were sometimes hostile and sometimes friendly, depending upon circumstances.

On occasions people whom we might linguistically classify as San herded Khoikhoi cattle in return for milk or even acquired some cattle of their own. Similarly Khoikhoi often resorted to full-time hunting and gathering when they had lost their cattle through drought, disease or raid.

Because of this frequent intermixing, historians sometimes prefer to apply the joint-name Khoisan to all those people who spoke the 'click' languages of Southern Africa. Then the only important distinction to make between them is whether they are Khoisan hunter-gatherers or Khoisan pastoralists. As we have seen, whether or not they owned livestock determined the main differences in their way of life.

The coming of the Iron Age

The South African myth of 'Bantu migrations'

Until at least the 1960s South African historians and white politicians had a very distorted view of their region's early history. They believed that black, Bantu-speaking, iron-working farmers were fairly recent immigrants into Southern Africa. Blacks were said to have swept into the region from the north in successive, conquering 'waves of migration'. Furthermore, it was claimed, these 'Bantu Migrations' first crossed the Limpopo between 1500 and 1600 AD, and certainly not earlier than 1000 AD. The idea that blacks had no very ancient roots in the

7

country conveniently suited South Africa's whites who used it to justify their own position of economic and political domination.

Since the 1970s, however, archaeological research and the use of carbon-dating have totally overturned this distorted and biased version of Southern African history. It is now known that Southern Africa has a far more ancient and more complex Iron Age history, stretching back to the first few centuries of the Christian (AD) era.

The importance of iron and agriculture

Two technical innovations were brought into Southern Africa in the early centuries AD: iron and agriculture. The fact that the two came together enabled their rapid spread down through the sub-continent. Iron provided the tools for cutting trees, clearing land and harvesting crops as well as more efficient hunting weapons. Agriculture itself introduced a whole new way of life which was soon to dominate and transform Southern African society.

The new farmers were able to grow much of their own food instead of being entirely dependent upon hunting and gathering. Families no longer had to move from one settlement to another according to season. They could now form longer-lasting settlements, in one place for a number of years. Sturdier, more permanent houses were built and people were able to accumulate more possessions. These included clothing, mats, baked-clay pots for cooking, storage or carrying water, and new tools such as hoes and grindstones.

The better, more regular diet led to an increase in population. Farming families could now grow enough food to support more children. At the same time, children themselves played a role in increasing food production. They weeded fields, chased birds away from ripening crops and helped in the herding of livestock. This in turn both encouraged and enabled people to have larger families.

The nature of the evidence Our knowledge of the early Southern African Iron Age is based virtually entirely upon archaeological evidence. Since people settled for some years in one site, they left behind a fair amount of material in their rubbish dumps when they moved on. And it is from these that today's archaeologist gets much of his information. Fragments of clay pottery show that pots and bowls were fairly thick-sided and decorated by character-istic cuts and simple stamped patterns (see Fig. 1.5). The basic style of manufacture and design seems to have been common to all the early Iron Age

1.5 Samples of Early Iron Age pottery

communities of the region. This suggests that they probably all at one time had some common ancestry and that their spread among non-pot-making peoples was fairly rapid. A particularly fine example of their pottery craftsmanship is a number of clay heads found near Lydenburg and dated to about 500 AD (see Fig. 1.6). These are hollow, about 40 centimetres high and are thought to have had some religious ceremonial purpose.

Vegetable matter does not survive well over long periods, so the main evidence for cultivation has been storage bins and grinding stones. Occasionally sites have contained evidence of grains themselves: finger-millet, bulrush millet and sorghum. Bones

1.6 Two pottery heads recovered from Lydenburg dated about 500 AD.

survive better and these reveal that the earliest Iron Age peoples were still heavily dependent upon hunting for their main supply of meat. Sheep and goats were also eaten and, very rarely, cattle. The latter were to gain in importance over the centuries, especially from the seventh century onwards.

A vital piece of evidence, of course, is that of iron smelting itself. Small circular furnaces were common and it appears that in this early period iron-working was practised in almost every village. A single furnace could be expected to smelt iron from a bucketful of crushed ore combined with three or four times that amount of charcoal. When the furnace had eventually cooled, the block of smelted iron could be reheated in a small forge and beaten into shape to form axes or arrow-heads. But crude iron like this eventually rusts away to nothing and the waste slag from smelting is usually all that remains for the archaeologist to examine.

The people So who were these early Iron Age farmers of Southern Africa? To find the answer we need to look at a combination of archaeological and linguistic evidence. Very few skeletal remains have so far been recovered from early Iron Age sites. But what little evidence there is shows they were larger than the Khoisan and of a definite negroid racial type though with signs of intermixing with local Khoisan populations.

Linguistic evidence further suggests that the earliest Iron Age immigrants into Southern Africa were probably speakers of early forms of the Bantu family of languages.* There are today more than 300 Bantu languages between Cameroun in West Africa and the southern coast of South Africa. By studying similarities and differences between them, linguists have concluded that they probably all stem from an original parent language somewhere in the region of Cameroun. Their subsequent spread southwards across Central and Southern Africa seems to have coincided very closely with the known spread of iron-working as revealed by archaeological evidence and carbon-dating. The early Iron Age farmers, therefore, were almost certainly the earliest ancestors of the black, Bantu-speaking peoples who form the vast majority of the population of Central and Southern Africa today.

* The word 'Bantu' has fallen into disrepute in South Africa since that country's Government began using it in the 1950s to classify and discriminate against the majority black people of South Africa. Thus, for many in South Africa, the very word 'Bantu' is associated with government oppression. The word is, of course, used in this book in its purely linguistic sense.

The spread of the Early Iron Age

The first iron-working farmers seem to have crossed the Limpopo into Southern Africa by about 200 AD. But there is no evidence of large-scale conquering migrations as suggested by earlier historians. They travelled and settled in small, family-sized groups. It is possible that a few may even have reached Southern Africa by sea – sailing along the coastline and venturing up rivers such as the Limpopo. By 300 AD iron-working farmers had pushed south into present-day Natal and by 400 AD their settlements were dotted across the Transvaal highveld (see Map 1.1). The initial spread of Iron Age settlement was fairly rapid. This was probably because population levels were so low. Farmers were thus able to be very selective and chose only the best, most productive sites for their settlements. When, after a few years, soils became exhausted, they moved on.

The early Iron Age peoples were mixed farmers. They grew millets, sorghum, melons, gourds, cow-peas and beans. They kept sheep, goats and cattle. They also hunted a wide range of animals of all sizes and gathered wild plants, especially fruits. From rivers they obtained fish and those near the coast collected shellfish, especially mussels. The relative importance of cultivation, livestock herding or hunting depended upon the varying climate and a region's natural resources.

Prevailing winds blow in off the Indian Ocean so the heaviest rainfall is found in the south-east, between the Drakensberg and the sea. This made it a particularly favourable region for early Iron Age farmers. Early settlement to the east of the Drakensberg was initially concentrated in the fertile and well-wooded valleys and coastal plains. Here, crop cultivation was particularly important and there was plenty of wood for building and smelting. Gradually, over the centuries, more use was made of the drier grassy uplands of the Drakensberg foothills and there livestock became more important. The south-westward range of settlement was restricted by the limits of summer rainfall, needed for their semi-tropical grain crops. Thus early Iron Age farmers do not appear to have settled west of the River Kei.

To the west of the Drakensberg the land flattens out to a highveld plateau. There the summer rainy season becomes progressively shorter and less reliable the nearer one gets to the Kalahari desert. In the drier grasslands, bushveld and thorn scrub regions of the highveld, therefore, cultivation was less productive and Iron Age people depended more upon their livestock. Small villages of six to ten houses were built in a circular pattern, enclosing a cattle kraal in the centre. These were sometimes situated on hilltops, probably for protection from wild animals. Where wood and reeds were scarce, clay became more important for the walls of their circular thatched houses.

Relationships with Stone Age communities

In the early centuries of low population Iron Age farmers and Stone Age hunter-gatherers seem to have lived side by side in relative harmony. The clear economic and social advantages of the iron-working farmers, however, ensured that in due course they would become the dominant population. In areas where the farmers chose to settle, Stone Age hunter-gatherers were probably absorbed into the richer community through a mixture of clientship and intermarriage.

A Khoisan male client might hunt for a farmer or herd his cattle in exchange for food or milk. Khoisan females could be absorbed through the practice of polygamy. Women were either captured or, more probably, obtained by the payment of bride wealth to the woman's family. A greater number of women meant more female and child labour to work the fields. In the long term this strengthened the position of the farmers at the expense of the Stone Age communities.

The characteristic 'click' sounds in some Southern African Bantu languages is further evidence of Khoisan absorption. The spread of Bantu-speaking farmers in Southern Africa was thus a product of iron-working immigrants and indigenous Stone Age populations.

Some well-known examples of San rock art depict scenes of open warfare between San hunters and black cattle herders (see Fig. 1.1). This probably refers to a later period. By then the farmers and herders had come to dominate the grasslands as well as the valleys. The remaining San who had not been absorbed were thus being squeezed out of their traditional hunting grounds. This period is known as the Later Iron Age and will be examined in the following chapter.

Exercises

A. Think, discuss, understand and write

1 Discuss the different kinds of evidence available for studying the history of the Stone Age peoples of Southern Africa. Consider the usefulness and reliability of each.
2 Describe the way of life of the region's Stone Age hunter-gatherers. Consider:
   (a) their food and the relative importance of each kind;
   (b) the manufacture and use of tools and weapons;
   (c) their social organisation and the extent to which it was shaped by environment and the search for food;
   (d) the significance of their religious beliefs.
3 What differences to the hunter-gatherer way of life were brought by the introduction of pastoralism? Consider food, tools, clothing and social and political organisation.
   OR
   Discuss the similarities and differences between the way of life of Khoikhoi and San before the seventeenth century.
4 Discuss the evidence for the study of the history of the Early Iron Age peoples of Southern Africa. Compare your response with that for Question 1.
5 How was the Iron Age brought to Southern Africa? Why has there been disagreement among historians about this topic?
6 Describe the Early Iron Age way of life. Consider how and why people settled where they did. Compare and contrast your response with that for Question 2.

B. Imaginative writing

1 Imagine that you are a Stone Age hunter-gatherer living in Southern Africa in 500 AD. You meet with an Iron Age farmer. Assuming you have learned to speak each other's language, try to persuade the other to join you and your way of life. Write out your arguments.
2 Now swap positions. Do the same thing from the point of view of the Iron Age person.
3 Compare and discuss the differences between the two positions. Which is most persuasive and why?

C. Mapwork

From an atlas trace a modern map of Central and Southern Africa. Put in modern political boundaries. Now transfer onto it the information concerning the positions and movements of Stone Age and Iron Age peoples as revealed in the maps and text of this chapter. Use coloured arrows and shading where appropriate. Now describe (orally or in writing) the information revealed by your map.

CHAPTER 2

The Later Iron Age in Southern Africa, 1000–1800 AD

The period after about 1000 AD is usually referred to as the Later Iron Age. Round about that time a number of distinct changes appear to have taken place in the Iron Age societies of Southern Africa.

Changes in economy and society

After a number of centuries of gradual Iron Age development people began to move their villages away from fertile valley bottoms, riversides and coastal plains. There was a greater emphasis on the raising of cattle and more use was made of the grasslands of the highveld and the foothills of the Drakensberg. Settlement began to expand across these drier areas. Population increased in size, villages became more permanent and people were brought under the closer political control of chiefs and kings. General technology improved and trade expanded. People became specialists in those industries and crafts for which their area was particularly suited. Thus in places like the Tswapong hills of eastern Botswana or Phalaborwa in the eastern Transvaal people became specialist iron smelters as they had plentiful resources of iron ore and charcoal (see Fig. 2.1). In other areas people specialised in copper smelting, gold mining and cotton weaving. Agriculture, too, benefited from an improvement in crops and farming techniques. In a few areas terracing was used to make maximum agricultural use of hillsides. Trade developed between distant communities as people exchanged goods for those they could not produce themselves.

Division of labour As we saw happen in Khoikhoi society, with the increasing importance of cattle in Iron Age communities went an increasing division of labour between men and women. In Stone Age

2.1 A reconstructed working model of a Later Iron Age smelting furnace in Zimbabwe.

societies women had been the gatherers of the basic daily plant-food. In the mixed farming communities of the Iron Age this role extended so that women became the main cultivators of crops. Besides working in the fields, the labour of the woman was centred around the family household. She ground corn, made pottery, fetched and carried water, built and maintained the house, reared children and prepared the daily family meals.

Meanwhile the men were still the hunters in society. But now they added to their role the care of domestic animals, especially cattle. As herds increased in size, those who owned most cattle were able to control and dominate not only women but also other men within their community. This, combined with control of trade, led to an increasing division between rich and poor.

Pottery One of the easiest ways for archaeologists to distinguish between Early and Later Iron Age settlement sites is in the different styles of their

2.2 An example of Later Iron Age pottery. Its style and decoration are important evidence of cultural groupings in Southern Africa.

pottery. Later Iron Age pottery was of much finer quality. It was made of thinner and harder clay and shaped into a wider variety of containers. It was also more elaborately painted and decorated. Archaeologists are able to use the variety of pottery design as evidence of different cultural groupings and periods. The changes in pottery technology and style are thus important as archaelogical evidence, but they are only an outward sign of far more significant changes within Iron Age society itself.

The transition from Early to Later Iron Age

According to the archaeological evidence, of pottery in particular, in many parts of the region Later Iron Age communities seem to have appeared quite suddenly. It is as though the people or the ideas had come from elsewhere, perhaps brought in by new immigrants. In a few areas, however, archaeologists have been able to trace the changeover as a process of gradual transition. One of the keys to this transition appears to have been cattle. The development of mining and trade were probably also important.

The importance of cattle

Although grain crops remained the main source of diet, and hunting was still important, cattle provided Later Iron Age communities with an additional source of food. Milk, collected and soured in leather bags or clay pots, became an important part of the regular diet. In some settlements, where herds were very large, cattle-owners ate more beef than game meat. In many communities, however, cattle were only slaughtered for meat on special occasions. Even

so, cattle remained a useful form of insurance: they could always be eaten in times of drought and hardship when crops failed.

In favourable conditions cattle bred well and herds increased rapidly. This meant that cattle could be an important way of accumulating and storing wealth. During his own lifetime a man starting with a mere handful of cattle might build up a herd several hundred strong. Cows would be kept for breeding while surplus males could be used for either meat or trade.

The owners of large herds of cattle thus had many advantages over others in society. In times of drought and hardship those without cattle came to depend on the cattle-owners for a supply of food. These dependants herded their cattle in exchange for a share in the milk and meat. Furthermore, the wealthy used their cattle to trade with distant communities for more food, iron tools or luxury items such as copper ornaments, beads and cloth. Goods like these could then be used by the wealthy or distributed among loyal dependents.

Two further practices were developed which gave the cattle-owners an advantage over others in society. The first was the lending out of cattle to their poorer dependents. In Setswana and Sesotho these are known as *mafisa* cattle. They could be milked, and, with the owner's permission, the meat of their offspring could be eaten. But the owner could always withdraw the loan whenever he wanted. In this way he controlled the activities and loyalty of large sections of the community.

A second development was the payment of *lobola*, or bride wealth, combined with the practice of male polygamy. *Lobola* was a payment, usually in the form of cattle, made to the bride's family at the time of marriage. A wealthy cattle-owner was able to pay *lobola* for a number of wives. Women, remember, were the key to both the reproduction of the family and the production of agricultural crops. The more wives a man had, the larger his family, the more land he could cultivate and the more wealth he could expect to accumulate for passing down to his descendants.

The wealthy were also able to control the level of bride price to ensure that they had first choice of brides. Furthermore, polygamy among the rich meant there were less women available for poorer men to marry. The latter might have difficulty paying the bride price for only one wife. Many depended on the wealthy to help them pay *lobola*.

As we have seen, therefore, those who controlled large herds of cattle also controlled many aspects of food production, marriage and the reproduction of families within a community. For this reason it is probable that control over cattle was related to the growth of chieftaincy in certain parts of Southern Africa during this period.

The growth of Later Iron Age states

Eastern Botswana Archaeological evidence has recently revealed that a major area for the gradual development of Later Iron Age communities was in the dry grassland districts of present-day eastern Botswana. Small groups of Iron Age farmers first settled this region as early as the fourth century AD. The area was probably too dry for reliable regular crop cultivation, but it was ideal for grazing. From an early stage, therefore, cattle appear to have been

fairly important. Between about 650 and 1300 AD large-scale cattle-owning communities developed within the region.

Settlements were formed on a number of large flat-topped hills. Houses, made of mud, pole and thatch, were built in a circle around the outer edge. In the centre was a huge enclosure where cattle were kept at night. Similar, smaller settlements were built on the many small hilltops found scattered throughout the region. Crop cultivation was done in the valleys below, often some distance from the main large settlements. The hilltops were probably originally chosen for defence against wild animals. There is evidence of continuous occupation on some of these sites for up to two or three hundred years. Society was probably controlled by wealthy cattle-owning chiefs and their families who lived in the larger hilltop settlements. The smaller hilltop

2.1 Later Iron Age Southern Africa, 10th to 14th centuries

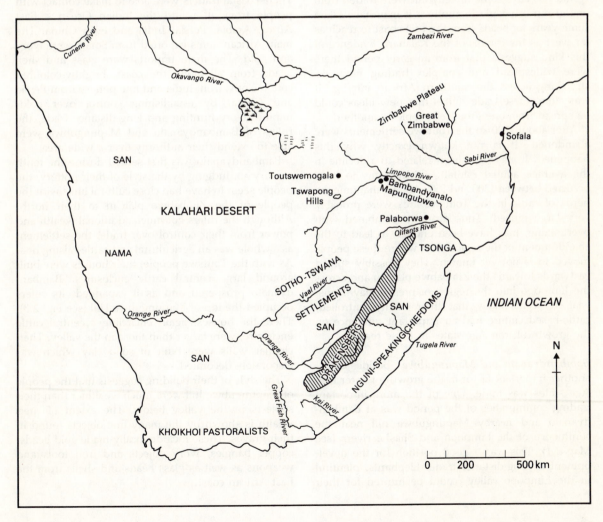

villages were probably occupied by more junior headmen. Poorer people, without cattle, lived in simple, less permanent houses in the valleys. Here they tended crops and herded the cattle which were brought down from the hilltop enclosures during the day.

Modern archaeologists and historians refer to these Iron Age communities as part of the 'Toutswe Tradition'. The name is taken from Toutswemogala, the site of the largest of the hilltop settlements (see Map 2.1). Among the Tswapong hills to the southeast there is evidence of large-scale iron-smelting dating back to at least the seventh century AD. It was probably from here that the Toutswe people got much of their iron. There is evidence too of trade between the Toutswe area and the neighbouring peoples of the northwestern Transvaal and the Zimbabwe plateau. From some Toutswe sites sea-shells and glass beads have been recovered. These originally came from the Indian Ocean coast. They would not have come directly but were traded from one group of people to another. It may have taken some years for beads from the east coast to reach as far west as the fringes of the Kalahari. Evidence of this kind suggests that from an early period there were widespread and complex trading networks stretching across the Southern African interior. It was along these trade routes that new ideas could be spread from one group of people to another.

After about 1300 AD the Toutswe settlements were abandoned. It is not known exactly why this happened. It may have been related to a decline in the average annual rainfall which seems to have occurred between 1300 and 1500 AD. By that time the herds of cattle in the Toutswe area were probably very large indeed. Thus drought, combined with overgrazing, may have been enough to lead to the abandonment of the region. Just where these people moved to is not yet known. They possibly spread eastwards towards the Zimbabwe plateau and across the Limpopo into the region of present-day Transvaal. It seems likely that their chiefly-controlled, cattle-based culture had an important influence on the growth of Iron Age states in these regions.

Bambandyanalo and Mapungubwe Besides cattle, another important factor in the growth of Later Iron Age states was trade. One of the more important trading communities of the period was at Bambandyanalo and nearby Mapungubwe hill near the confluence of the Limpopo and Shashe rivers (see Map 2.1). This was a good position for the development of long-distance trade. Elephants, plentiful in the Limpopo valley, could be hunted for their

2.3 Mapungubwe Hill from the south. The main settlement was on top of the hill.

ivory. To the north and north-west were the gold-bearing regions of Tati and the Zimbabwe plateau. To the east were trade routes down the Limpopo and Sabi rivers to the coastal settlement of Sofala. There coastal traders were able to make contact with people from all round the Indian Ocean – East Africa, Arabia, Persia, India and even China. The main African items exported from Sofala were ivory and gold. The main imports were glass and shell beads from all along the coast, brightly-coloured cotton cloths from India and fine pottery from Persia and China. By establishing control over gold-mining, ivory hunting and long-distance trade, the rulers of Bambandyanalo and Mapungubwe were able to extend their authority over a wide area.

Bambandyanalo was first settled during the tenth century AD. Judging by the style of their pottery, the people seem to have had close cultural links with the people of the Zimbabwe plateau to their north. Although the rulers got much additional wealth and power from their control over trade, the settlement as a whole was an agricultural and cattle-raising one. As with the Toutswe people, their houses were built around large central cattle enclosures. Bambandyanalo prospered and as it expanded, its rulers occupied the top of Mapungubwe Hill (see Fig. 2.3). There the houses, again encircling a central cattle enclosure, were larger than those in the valley. Their circular walls were built of solid clay which was elaborately decorated.

The style of their building suggests that the people of Mapungubwe hill were much wealthier than their subjects in the valley below. The extent of their wealth is shown by the many fine objects found in their graves. These include locally-made gold beads, copper bangles, ivory objects and iron tools and weapons as well as glass beads and shells from the East African coast.

The Mapungubwe community reached the height of its prosperity between about 1100 and 1300 AD. Thereafter its importance as a trading centre declined in favour of Great Zimbabwe. The latter was even better situated for the development of crop cultivation, cattle raising and the control of long-distance trade with Sofala.

The growth of states on the highveld

The Sotho-Tswana The main African population of the Southern African highveld today speak a group of Bantu languages known as Sotho-Tswana. Their origins can be found in the early Iron Age population of the region. Between 1000 and 1400 AD there was a big expansion of cattle-keeping Iron Age communities over much of the highveld. For a long time it was thought that this must have been due to the arrival of new immigrants from north of the Limpopo. It now seems more likely that it was related to developments in the Toutswe region of eastern Botswana. The central, eastern and southern highveld was better watered than the more westerly Toutswe region and so was more reliable for agricultural crops. The natural grasslands were free from tsetse fly and thus suitable for large-scale cattle-keeping. By the fifteenth century large numbers of Sotho-Tswana settlements extended both north and south of the Vaal. All over the highveld archaeologists have found the ruins of an enormous number of stone-walled enclosures and house foundations which can be dated to this period (see Fig. 2.4).

The usual pattern for these settlements was a large centralised town, surrounded by agricultural fields. Beyond these lay extensive grazing lands for their cattle. The towns themselves were divided into wards. Each ward was usually made up of a group of related families. The whole settlement was ruled over by a chief. He was head of the most senior ward and probably the owner of the most cattle. Unrelated groups were readily absorbed simply by being added to the settlement as an additional ward. In this way some communities expanded more rapidly than others. But just as settlements expanded, so they also split and divided. The most common cause of divisions were succession disputes within the ruling family. Then a disappointed claimant would gather his supporters and his cattle and move away to found his own settlement. A large group of related settlements might consider themselves a 'nation' (*morafe*). A community such as this was often named after the founder of the

2.4 The foundations of an early Sotho-Tswana house found in the Orange Free State. In the centre is the paved floor of the house with a paved verandah running two-thirds of the way around it. The outer enclosure was a surrounding wall.

ruling lineage. A lineage is a group of people descended in direct line from a common ancestor. In the case of the Sotho-Tswana this was through the male line.

Religion, chieftaincy, marriage and initiation The Sotho-Tswana believed in the existence of a single supreme being, *Modimo*. He controlled the weather, particularly the rain, and was ultimately responsible for good harvests or famine. But he could only be contacted through the medium of the spirits of the ancestors. The chief, as spiritual leader of his people, had closest contact with the ancestral spirits. In an annual rainmaking ceremony the chief would contact the spirits and get them to ensure sufficient rainfall for a good harvest. The religious and political power of a chief was often judged in terms of his ability to 'make rain'. In practical terms, however, much of the chief's power came from his control over cattle. Furthermore, wealthy Sotho-Tswana families encouraged marriage between cousins. In this way the cattle of bride wealth would remain within the extended family.

Initiation ceremonies marked the transition from childhood into full adult life. Only the initiated could marry. Every few years initiates of about the same age were drawn from families right across the chiefdom. After the ceremonies – *bogwera* for boys, *bojale* for girls – the newly initiated adults were formed into age-regiments (*mephato*). They then disbanded and returned to their villages. But regiments could be summoned together by the chief to perform some public work, to defend the chiefdom or to go on a cattle-raid. The regimental system was thus a useful way of binding the various villages of the chiefdom under the central authority of the chief.

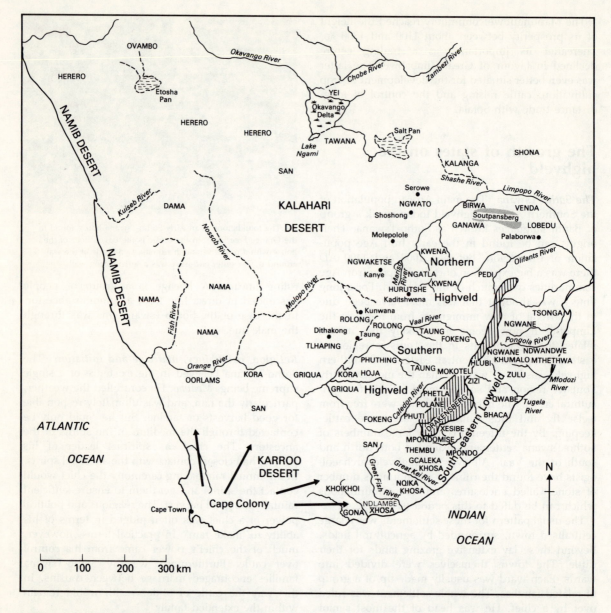

2.2 The peoples of Southern Africa in the 18th century

By the sixteenth century a number of distinct Sotho-Tswana states had emerged under the leadership of powerful lineage chiefs. The most powerful of these owed their strength to their huge herds of cattle combined with the use of polygamy, *lobola* (or *bogadi*) and the *mafisa* system (see above p. 12). Using this strength they controlled access to local resources of iron-ore, fertile land and good grazing and hunting territory. There is only space in what follows to mention a number of the more important Sotho-Tswana lineage groups. The development of

regional language variations places them in three main language sub-divisions: Tswana in the central and western regions, northern Sotho in the north-east and southern Sotho south of the Vaal.

Rolong and Tlhaping   To the west were the *Rolong*, named after their founding ancestor Morolong who may date back to about 1300 AD. Rolong cattle posts and hunting grounds stretched from the Vaal river in the south to the Kalahari in the north-west (see Map 2.2). There was iron ore in the region and they traded cattle from the Nama across the desert. By the eighteenth century the Rolong had built themselves a powerful kingdom. One of their most famous rulers was Tau who is remembered in oral tradition as a great military leader. A new capital called Taung was named after him. During his reign a group of Rolong broke away to the south-west and settled on the banks of the lower Vaal. They became known as baTlhaping because, it was said, during a severe drought they had to eat fish (tlhapi) to survive. There they benefitted from trading connections with the Kora, a group of Khoikhoi living along the Orange and lower Vaal. By the end of the eighteenth century the Tlhaping had become a powerful and independent state with their capital at Dithakong containing 15–20 000 people. Meanwhile the Rolong themselves had split into four main groups, each following one of the sons of Tau: Ratlou, Rapulana, Seleka and Tshidi.

Hurutshe, Kwena and offshoots To the east of the Rolong in the central highveld were the powerful lineage groups of the Hurutshe, the Kwena and the Kgatla. Traditionally the *Hurutshe* are considered the most senior. They controlled the hill country around the headwaters of the Marico and Elands rivers. They became renowned smelters of iron and copper and traded these metals with surrounding peoples. Their capital, Kaditshwena (also known as Kurrechane), described by a European visitor in the early nineteenth century, contained fifty wards and a total of 15 000 people. Groups of houses were encircled by stone-walled enclosures. The town was surrounded by extensive cultivation with huge herds of cattle at its outposts, many of them belonging to the chief. The *Kwena*, however, were the dominant lineage group. Their chiefdoms stretched north of the Hurutshe from the region of present-day Pretoria to as far as Molepolole by the late seventeenth century. One group of Kwena moved south of the Vaal to form part of the southern Sotho. From Molepolole further splits in the eighteenth century gave rise to the *Ngwaketse*, centred at Kanye, and the *Ngwato* who moved northwards through eastern Botswana to the Shoshong hills and Serowe. In the 1790s a further split from the Ngwato established the *Tawana* in the Ngamiland region of north-western Botswana.

Kgatla, Tlokwa and Pedi The original *Kgatla* lineage controlled the north-east of the central Transvaal. They went through a number of splits and divisions between the sixteenth and eighteenth centuries. The most powerful Kgatla lineage to emerge were the Kgafela-Kgatla in the Pilanesberg region of the western Transvaal. An important offshoot from the Kgatla were the *Tlokwa*, who themselves split into several sub-groups, some moving south of the Vaal, others westwards to the Gaborone region of present-day Botswana. Another Kgatla offshoot, the *Pedi*, moved north-eastwards during the seventeenth century to the Olifants river region of the northern Drakensberg. There, centred in the Leolu mountains, the Pedi lineage built up a powerful state through a mixture of marriage alliances, absorption and conquest. By the end of the eighteenth century they controlled a large region made up of numerous smaller lineage groups. Further down the Olifants, on the eastern side of the Drakensberg escarpment, was the iron and copper mining settlement of *Palaborwa*. Copper had been mined here since the tenth century. The region had poor soil, and tsetse fly made it unsuitable for cattle so the Palaborwa people depended heavily for their livelihood on the sale of iron hoes and copper. By 1800 they had been absorbed into the Pedi state. By then the Pedi had set up a regular trade in ivory and cattle with the Portuguese at Delagoa Bay from whom they imported beads, brass and cloth.

Venda and Lobedu In the northern Transvaal between the Soutpansberg and the Limpopo the principal lineage groups were the *Venda* and *Lobedu*. These were not part of the Sotho-Tswana complex. Their ruling lineages had early Shona origins north of the Limpopo. They may also have had links with the later stages of the Mapungubwe settlement. They too were smelters and exporters of copper and ivory.

The southern Sotho The earliest Sotho-Tswana to move south of the Vaal, in about the fifteenth century, were the *Fokeng*, closely followed by groups of Kwena (spelt *Koena* in Sesotho). There is evidence of early links between the southern Sotho and Nguni-speakers from east of the Drakensberg. The *Zizi*, for instance, are known to have made contact through the passes of the Drakensberg, possibly to trade iron for Sotho cattle. Some Nguni groups settled on the southern highveld and were absorbed into southern Sotho lineages. The *Polane*, *Phetla* and *Phuthing* of present-day Lesotho are believed to have Zizi origins. By the late eighteenth century the southern highveld was peopled by a large number of small Sotho chieftaincies, the principal lineages being *Taung* (of Hurutshe origin), *Fokeng*, *Tlokwa*, *Koena*, *Phuthing* and *Hoja*.

Throughout the highveld region there still

remained small bands of San hunter-gatherers. But they were rapidly losing access to the wide open hunting grounds of former times. To this period belong the San rock paintings depicting violent clashes between themselves and large, black cattle-herders armed with iron-tipped spears (see Fig. 1.1).

The growth of states in the south-east: The Nguni

In the south-eastern region of Southern Africa, between the Drakensberg and the sea, the main Bantu language group are the Nguni. Our knowledge of Nguni history before the eighteenth century is not as clear as that of the Sotho-Tswana. There are two main reasons for this. In the first place, there has not been such extensive archaeological work on this period in the Nguni region. This is partly because the Nguni did not build such solid and long-lasting settlements and so there is less left behind for archaeologists to study. Secondly, many of the ancient chieftaincies and guardians of oral tradition were destroyed or scattered by the *mfecane* wars of the early nineteenth century (see Chapter 4).

As with the Sotho-Tswana, the later Iron Age Nguni-speakers appear to have emerged out of the early Iron Age peoples of the region. Until about the tenth or eleventh centuries AD the Iron Age peoples of Southern Africa, both on the highveld and in the south-east, appear to have been culturally fairly similar. The Drakensberg, however, provided a natural though not unsurmountable barrier between them. By at least the fifteenth century a number of distinct cultural and language differences had emerged between the Sotho-Tswana of the highveld and the Nguni of the south-east (see Map 2.2).

Cattle As on the highveld, the expansion of Iron Age settlement in the south-east appears to have been connected with an increasing emphasis on cattle. Settlements moved out of the valleys and onto the uplands and foothills which bordered the steep Drakensberg escarpment. Here the Nguni were able to move their cattle between the varied grasslands of the uplands and the valleys according to season.

It is not known exactly from where the Nguni got their cattle. They may have got them from Khoikhoi pastoralists or from Sotho-Tswana of the highveld. On the other hand they may have simply adopted their *ideas* of milking and cattle-rearing and applied them to their own indigenous, early Iron Age cattle. European survivors from sixteenth century ship-

wrecks reported seeing groups of Khoisan hunters and herders interspersed with Nguni mixed farmers all along the southern and central Nguni coastal regions. In the centuries that followed these were all absorbed into Nguni chiefdoms.

Language A distinctive characteristic of Nguni languages is their use of 'click' sounds. This again suggests close early links with former Khoisan populations. Indeed, something like twenty per cent of southern Nguni vocabulary is believed to stem from Khoisan languages. The amount is only slightly less among the northern Nguni.

Houses and homesteads The houses of the Nguni were more like those of the Khoikhoi than the Sotho-Tswana. A few ruined stone enclosures have been found in the foothills around the headwaters of the Tugela. But the normal Nguni house was constructed of grass and reeds, woven together and secured to a central pole (see Fig. 2.5). A number of these were placed around a circular cattle kraal to form a family homestead. At this stage the Nguni did not live in large, centralised towns like the Sotho-Tswana. Instead, they settled in separate family homesteads scattered over the countryside. The homestead was perhaps the Nguni equivalent of a Sotho-Tswana ward. A group of related homesteads made up a chieftaincy, ruled over by the head of the senior lineage.

Religion, chieftaincy and marriage Like the Sotho-Tswana, the chief was a spiritual as well as a political leader. Religion was based upon belief in a single supreme God, and contact with the spiritual world was achieved through contact with one's ancestors. The chief, descended from the senior

2.5 Nguni style village. Note the method of house construction and central cattle kraal.

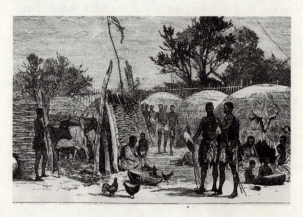

founding ancestors of the lineage, had most direct contact with the spiritual world. It was his role, therefore, to use his spiritual contacts to ensure adequate rainfall, good harvests and healthy cattle.

Succession disputes and splits within the ruling lineages were frequent. Often an unsuccessful claimant would move away, colonise a new bit of land, absorb more dependants and establish a new lineage. Whereas the Sotho-Tswana encouraged marriage between cousins, perhaps to keep the bride wealth within the family, the Nguni were exogamous. That is, they only allowed marriage outside the extended family circle. This meant that bride wealth was more widely spread. It also enabled more thorough absorption of other groups. The Gona chieftaincy to the west of the Great Fish River, for instance, was the product of intermarriage between Khoikhoi and Xhosa (southern Nguni).

Initiation Nguni initiation ceremonies and circumcision were probably adopted from the southern Sotho. The ceremonies marked the transition into adulthood. Since initiates were drawn from all the homesteads within a chieftaincy, the ceremonies were a good way of maintaining close links between the scattered homesteads. Initiates were formed into age-regiments who could be called upon for communal work or for warfare. As chiefdoms increased in size, warfare between them became more frequent and the role of the regiments grew more important.

Nguni chieftaincies By the eighteenth century Nguni chieftaincies stretched from the Usutu in the north to the Sundays River in the south. Most were fairly small but a few larger ones, ruled over by powerful lineages, were beginning to emerge. The southernmost Nguni chiefdoms were those of the Xhosa. In the region of the Sundays River were the Gona, a mixed Khoi/Xhosa group. East of the Kei were the Thembu, Bomvana, Mpondo, Mpondomise and Xesibe. In central Nguniland, between the Mzimkulu and Tugela rivers were the Bhaca and Qwabe and in the foothills, the Zizi, Bhele and Hlubi. Three expanding chiefdoms of the northern Nguni were the Mthethwa, Ndwandwe and Ngwane while among the smaller ones were the Zulu and Khumalo. We shall return to these in Chapter 4.

Tsonga states of southern Mozambique

In the region of southern Mozambique around Maputo Bay, formerly known as Delagoa Bay, lay the kingdoms of the Tsonga. They are a separate Bantu language group from the Nguni though it is possibly from them that the earliest Nguni traced their origins. The basis of Tsonga wealth was agriculture and trade. In the sixteenth or seventeenth century the Portuguese introduced the South American crop maize to the region. With this, food production increased and population expanded. Portuguese and other European ships calling at the bay also provided a market for ivory and copper. Some Tsonga became professional traders, travelling north to Palaborwa and the Venda as well as south along the Nguni coastal region. People captured in warfare between rival Tsonga groups were also sold as slaves to European ships calling at the bay. Between the sixteenth and eighteenth centuries three successive Tsonga kingdoms, Nyaka, Tembe and Maputo, grew powerful from the profits of controlling and taxing this trade.

The peoples of Namibia

We have seen so far that Khoisan were generally hunter-gatherers or pastoralists and that negroid Bantu-speakers were generally iron-working farmers, growing crops and herding cattle. One cannot assume, however, that a people's culture and economy is somehow decided by their language and race. We have already seen how Khoisan joined and were absorbed by Bantu-speaking farmers who themselves may have originally adopted some cattle-keeping practices from Stone Age Khoikhoi. Thus the way people lived was to a large extent determined by their technology and the nature of their environment rather than by their language group or race. Nowhere has this point been more clearly made than among the peoples of present-day Namibia.

In this far western region of Southern Africa the environment is particularly harsh. Rainfall is sparse and bare sandy desert dominates much of the west coast and south of the country. Sparse dry grasslands cover the central highland districts and only in the extreme north is there enough rain to grow tropical cereal crops. The country was too dry to attract early Iron Age farmers. Thus San hunter-gatherers continued to roam uninterrupted over much of the country. In the south were the *Nama*, Khoikhoi pastoralists who had herded their fat-tailed sheep since at least the fourth century AD.

Some time after about 1500 AD Bantu-speaking cattle-herders moved into the northern coastal region. These were the *Herero*, referred to by the Nama as 'Damara'. According to oral tradition they came from the east, which may have been northern

Botswana or southern Angola. Unlike other Bantu-speakers in Southern Africa, the Herero lived entirely from their cattle and grew no crops at all. Clearly this was a local adaption to the demands of the environment. At about the same time another group of Bantu-speakers, the *Ovambo*, moved into the good agricultural land bordering present-day Namibia and Angola. Here they were able to practise crop cultivation. They also exported copper, iron and salt.

Meanwhile, in the central highlands were small numbers of negroid hunter-gatherers, the *Dama*, referred to by the Nama as 'Bergdama' ('mountain Damara'). Their origins are uncertain. They may have originally been related to Bantu-speakers from the north before adopting the Nama language and a way of life normally associated with the San. By the eighteenth century the Dama were metalworkers, mining and smelting copper for the Nama.

Exercises

A. Think, Discuss, Understand and Write

1 What were the main changes brought by the development of the Later Iron Age?
2 Discuss the importance of cattle in the social organisation and growth of Later Iron Age states.
3 Discuss the importance of trade in the social organisation and growth of Later Iron Age states.
4 Describe and account for the distribution of the Bantu-speaking peoples of Southern Africa by about 1750 AD.
5 What were the similarities and differences between the ways of life of the Sotho-Tswana and the Nguni before the mid-eighteenth century? To what extent if any were the different societies shaped by their environment?

B. Imaginative writing

Imagine you are one of the Bantu-speaking people of Southern Africa in about 1700 AD. State specifically which group or nation you belong to and where you live and describe a typical day in your life. Given a choice, which would you prefer: to live then or to live now? Why?

C. Mapwork, Group-work and Class Discussion

From an atlas trace a modern map of Southern Africa. On it place arrows and names of peoples to illustrate the movement of peoples as described in this chapter. Now 'read' your map, that is, describe orally what your map illustrates.

CHAPTER 3

Dutch colonisation of the Cape

The south-western Cape in the seventeenth century

At the beginning of the seventeenth century the Khoikhoi clans of the south-western Cape were organised into a number of loosely-controlled chieftaincies. In the region of Table Bay and the Cape Peninsula were three related groups of clans or 'tribes': the Goringhaiqua, the Goringhaicona and the Gorachouqua. To their north were the cattle-rich Cochoqua and Guriqua while along the eastern coastal regions were the powerful Chainouqua and Hessequa. It has been estimated that by the 1650s there were something like 50 000 Khoikhoi south-west of the Breede and Olifants rivers.

From the 1590s Dutch and English trading ships began calling at Table Bay on their way to East Africa, India and Indonesia. The Cape was about half way between Europe and the Far East and was a convenient place for picking up fresh supplies of meat and water. The Khoikhoi were willing to barter cattle and sheep for copper, iron and tobacco (see Fig. 3.1). Copper was used to make jewellery and to exchange for cattle with other Khoikhoi further inland. Iron was highly valued for making spears and arrows. The Cape, however, was not always a reliable place for passing ships to stop. Because they were only ever passing through, European sailors were not particularly bothered about maintaining good relations with the Khoikhoi. Thus they often stole rather than traded and Khoikhoi retaliated by attacking the next lot of sailors to arrive. Furthermore, the Khoikhoi, as the only suppliers of fresh meat, could demand what they wanted in exchange for their livestock. Thus prices rose steadily during the half-century up to 1650.

3.1 Khoikhoi at the Cape selling livestock to visiting European traders. The picture is taken from a seventeenth-century engraving.

The Dutch East India Company and a refreshment station at the Cape

The Dutch ships were all owned and organised by a private company called the Dutch East India Company. By the middle of the seventeenth century the company's directors in Holland decided to set up their own regular supply station at the Cape. This would have a number of advantages. More regular relations with the Khoikhoi would help stop the violence and so make the supply of fresh meat more reliable. The company would control all trade with the Khoikhoi and so prevent further rises in the price of meat. The company's servants would cultivate gardens and supply their ships with fresh fruit and vegetables. This would improve the health of

21

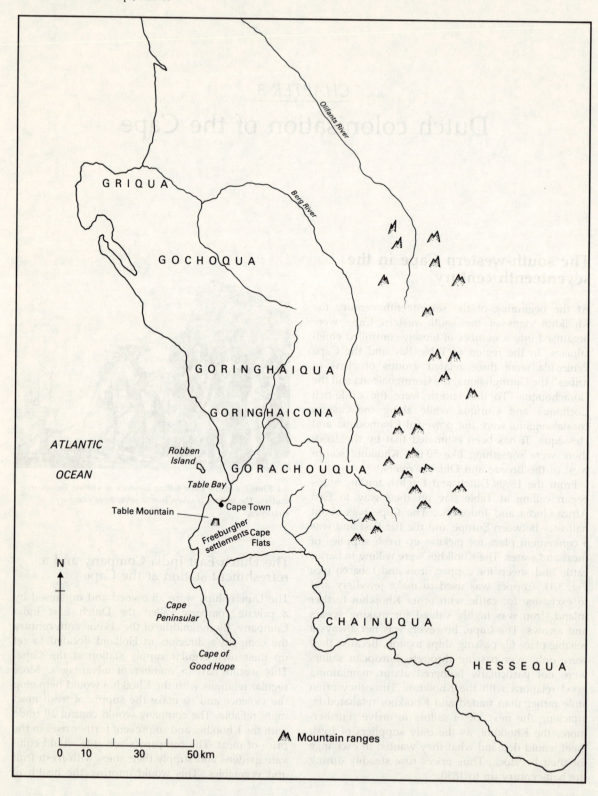

GRIQUA

GOCHOQUA

GORINGHAIQUA

GORINGHAICONA

ATLANTIC

OCEAN

Robben
Island

GORACHOUQUA

Table Bay

Table Mountain

Cape Town

Freeburgher
settlements

Cape
Flats

N

Cape
Peninsular

CHAINUQUA

Cape of
Good Hope

HESSEQUA

Olifants River

Berg River

Mountain ranges

0   10   30   50 km

crews, many of whom died from scurvy, a disease brought on by lack of fresh fruit and vegetables in the diet. A refreshment station at the Cape could also provide a hospital for the sick and repair services for damaged ships. All of these measures would give the Dutch company a clear advantage over its European rivals, such as the British East India Company, to whom it could sell produce and make a profit. As we shall see, however, the Dutch supply station at the Cape did not turn out quite as planned.

Early Dutch settlement at the Cape In 1652 the Dutch East India Company established a small white settlement on the present site of Cape Town under the command of Jan van Riebeeck. They began a vegetable garden and built a hospital and a fort. The latter was to protect the site from rival European ships as much as from Khoikhoi attack. Sheep and cattle were bought from the Khoikhoi and company officials kept strict control over this trade. The market, however, rapidly expanded. There was now a permanent settlement of officials, soldiers and sailors to be fed. And the presence of a supply station encouraged more and more ships to call there for fresh supplies. There were soon complaints that the Khoikhoi were not selling enough of their livestock and the company's servants were not growing enough food. In fact rice had to be imported from Java.

Van Riebeeck decided to expand the farming settlement. In 1657 he released a number of soldiers from their contract with the company and allowed them to set up their own farms on Khoikhoi grazing land south of Table Bay.

As more soldiers, German as well as Dutch, were recruited from Europe, they too applied to become *freeburghers*. Escaping mostly from poverty in Europe, they saw the Cape as a land of opportunity. The number of freeburgher 'Boers', the Dutch word for farmers, thus steadily increased. In the 1680s and 90s, under the governorships of Simon van der Stel and his son Willem, direct immigration was encouraged and a number of orphan girls were imported to provide the settlers with wives. Emigrants from northern Europe were granted free passage in company ships. Among these was a group of 156 French Protestant refugees known as Huguenots who arrived in 1688. By this time settlement had extended across the Cape Flats to the fertile valleys of Stellenbosch and Drakenstein. Immigrants received a free grant of land on which they were only charged a small nominal rent and the company allowed them extensive grazing rights over the surrounding grassland. The main crops were wheat, fruit trees and grapes for making wine. The Boers kept sheep and cattle which they were supposed to buy through the company though most were traded or raided directly from the Khoikhoi. By the turn of the century wheat was being exported. By then there were about a thousand white settlers in the colony, served by a similar number of slaves.

3.2 Ships in the harbour at Table Bay with Cape Town in the background.

Slavery at the Cape From the start slave labour was widely used at the Cape, initially as the personal servants of senior company officials and then as the main source of agricultural labour. The freeburghers in particular were determined not to do the menial tasks of manual labour if there was someone else to do it for them. The Khoikhoi, however, refused to work regularly for the colonists while they still had their cattle on which to depend. Van Riebeeck considered enslaving the Khoikhoi and seizing their livestock, but the company directors feared this would prove too costly and dangerous.

The Dutch were already involved in the trans-Atlantic slave trade and slavery had long been used in their Far Eastern colonies. So when the freeburghers set up their farms in the Cape Peninsula, they were supplied with slaves from Angola and Benin. Thereafter, slaves were mostly brought from Madagascar with a few from Mozambique and Indonesia. Some of the latter, generally referred to as Cape Malays, were highly skilled Muslim craftsmen. As such they were a strong influence on the colonial styles of architecture and furniture which were to become known as 'Cape Dutch'. Most of the imported slaves were men and some took Khoikhoi women as wives, so there was some natural increase in the slave population. But for much of the eighteenth century slaves were imported at the rate of two or three hundred a year. By the 1790s the slave population had risen to 25 000 compared with 21 000 white colonists.

Khoikhoi reaction to early Dutch settlement

As we have seen, at first the Khoikhoi welcomed a certain amount of trade with European ships. They were able to sell off their surplus livestock, especially old and sick animals, in exchange for brass, copper, beads, tobacco and alcohol. Van Riebeeck soon found, however, that there was a definite limit to how many cattle the Khoikhoi would sell. After all, they were being asked to barter away the basis of their livelihood. Furthermore, the items offered in exchange were mostly luxuries, some of which, tobacco and alcohol, were quickly consumed. (Once the company had settled at the Cape, they stopped the trade in iron in case the Khoikhoi turned it into spears to use against them).

With a permanent settlement to feed and more ships calling at the Cape, the market for meat grew rapidly. Thus the company always needed more cattle than the Khoikhoi were prepared to sell.

When persuasion would not work, company officials used force. As a result, there were frequent clashes between them. Whenever Khoikhoi were suspected of any wrongdoing, such as stealing tobacco, company officials seized their livestock. Sometimes they seized chiefs and demanded ransoms of cattle for their safe return. When those nearest the Bay had no more cattle to sell, the company sent trading expeditions inland to buy from Cochoqua and other clans.

Cattle raids between Khoikhoi clans had been common long before the arrival of the Dutch. It was a way of restocking cattle which had been lost by drought, disease or raiding. The company exploited these rivalries by allying themselves with some clans and attacking others. As freeburgher settlement expanded across the Cape Flats, the Boers themselves began trading or raiding cattle from the Khoikhoi despite official company restrictions.

The Khoikhoi/Dutch Wars There were two full-scale wars between Khoikhoi and Dutch during the seventeenth century. The first was prompted by the beginning of freeburgher settlement in 1657. Khoikhoi found themselves cut off from the summer pastures and fresh water of the Peninsula. In 1659 the clans united under a former interpreter, Doman, and attacked the freeburgher farms. The colonists were driven to the safety of their fort which they successfully defended with their guns. After a year of virtual seige Khoikhoi unity fell apart and an uneasy peace was concluded. By the terms of the treaty Khoikhoi had to accept that the freeburghers kept their land. Khoikhoi protests at this injustice are recorded in Document 3.1. From then on the company acted as though any Khoikhoi land was theirs to take. Despite Khoikhoi protests and attacks, as the white population grew, the company gave out land to freeburghers further and further inland.

The Second Khoikhoi/Dutch War, 1673–77, was a series of company raids against the Cochoqua a hundred kilometres to the north. The Cochoqua were accused of attacking white hunters and traders. In the three main raids of the war the company and their Khoikhoi allies took large numbers of Cochoqua sheep and cattle.

The Cape Khoikhoi by 1700 Through a mixture of trade and company raids, the Khoikhoi nearest the Cape had very few cattle left by the end of the seventeenth century. Faced with this loss of their former livelihood, some withdrew to the hills and lived off hunting and raiding sheep and cattle from Boers and other Khoikhoi. Others remained on their

3.3 Work on an early Cape Dutch farm.

former land and survived by working for Boers, alongside their slaves. The Khoikhoi were technically 'free' men and women, but in practice they were treated very harshly. They were paid only with food, old clothing, cheap alcohol and, very rarely, an occasional live animal.

Language and Religion The Dutch East India Company insisted that Dutch should be the only official language at the Cape. A local dialect of Dutch, however, quickly developed. Words were adopted from other European languages as well as from their Malagasy and Indonesian slaves. In this Cape Dutch dialect we find the origins of modern Afrikaans.

The only Christian Church which the company would recognise was the Dutch Reformed Church. This was an extreme Protestant faith, inspired by the writings of the Old Testament. Many remote frontier Boers could barely read or write, but none the less every family owned a Bible. Believing they were God's chosen people, they justified the conquest of 'native' heathens whom they regarded as inferior.

Origins of the 'Cape Coloured' population

The so-called 'coloured' population of the Cape was the result of interbreeding between Europeans and Khoikhoi, and Khoikhoi and slaves. Many of the early white settlers at the Cape were single men and a number took Khoikhoi women as their unofficial wives. Their children were not usually recognised as legitimate and so they did not inherit their fathers' property. On the farms there was also interbreeding between male slaves and female Khoikhoi servants. Gradually there developed a 'coloured' servile population, part slave and part 'free'. They adopted the Dutch language of the colonists and began to lose their African or Asian cultural identities. The same applied to the Khoisan labourers on the more remote farms of the frontier Boers. They too gradually lost their Khoisan cultural identity and adopted the language and dress of the Boers. During the nineteenth century whites began to use the term Cape Coloured to refer to the whole of this Dutch (Afrikaans)-speaking servile population of slaves, mixed race and Khoisan.

The expansion of white settlement in the eighteenth century

Based on the labour of imported slaves, production of wheat and wine expanded in the south-western Cape. There soon developed a marked difference in wealth among the freeburghers of the colony. Wealthy landowners paid for the right to be the company's sole suppliers of wheat, wine or meat. What they could not produce on their own farms they bought at low prices from others. Company officials or their close connections got the most favoured contracts. In this way the former governor Simon van der Stel became one of the wealthiest freeburghers of Stellenbosch: indeed, the town itself was named after him.

As successful arable farming fell into the hands of a minority of wealthy freeburghers, more and more Boers turned towards the interior for their livelihood. Here they took to stock-raising rather than arable farming. The company allowed each adult freeburgher to claim his own 'farm', a huge holding of 2 500 hectares or more. They stocked their farms with sheep or cattle bought or raided from the Khoikhoi. As the pasture of one farm became exhausted they moved on to another.

Trekboers The Boers of the frontier were so often on the move that they became known as *trekboers*, 'trek' being a Dutch word meaning 'to pull (a wagon)'. Occasionally they built houses of stone, but more often of mud and thatch or reed matting like those of the Khoikhoi. They had very large families and each son regarded it as his birthright to go out and claim himself a farm. By the 1750s trekboers had reached the dry sparse grasslands north of the Olifants River. Eastwards expansion was even more rapid reaching the Sundays River and the territory of the Xhosa by the 1760s. The Cape Government kept extending its official boundary to try and keep up with this expansion.

The trekboers lived partly from the products of their livestock, partly from trade with or raid against Khoikhoi pastoralists and partly from hunting wild animals for their meat and skins. Each family was largely self-sufficient though they needed to import guns, gunpowder, tea, coffee, sugar and cotton cloth. These were usually bought from travelling traders in exchange for livestock and the skins of wild animals. Most labour on the trekboer farms was performed by Khoisan servants. Khoisan hunted for the Boers, herded their livestock and joined them in raids against unconquered Khoisan hunters.

3.4 Trekboers on the move with Khoikhoi herdsmen and waggon leaders.

3.2 The expansion of Boer settlement (1660–1800) and conflict with the Xhosa (1779–1803)

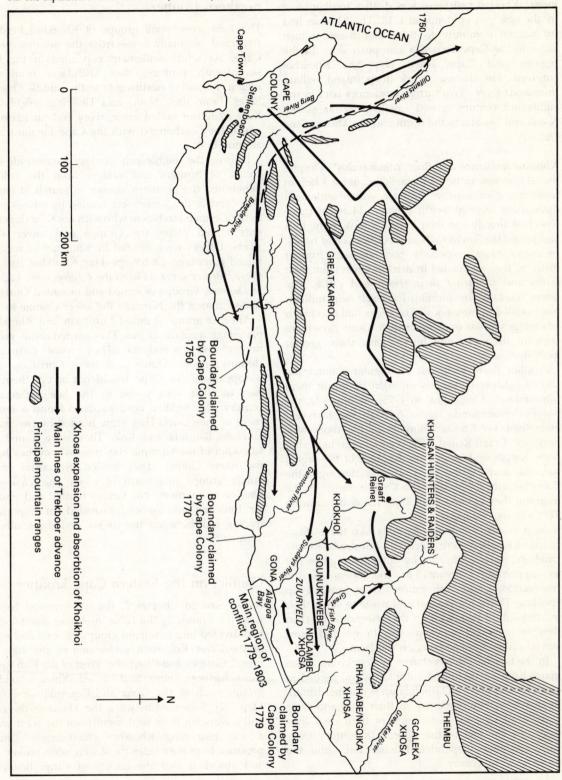

ATLANTIC OCEAN

1750

Oliifants River

Cape Town

CAPE COLONY

Berg River

Stellenbosch

Breede River

GREAT KARROO

KHOISAN HUNTERS & RAIDERS

0

100

200 km

Boundary claimed by Cape Colony 1750

Boundary claimed by Cape Colony 1770

Boundary claimed by Cape Colony 1779

Main lines of Trekboer advance

Xhosa expansion and absorbtion of Khoikhoi

Principal mountain ranges

Graaff Reinet

Gamtoos River

KHOKHOI

GONA

Sundays River

ZUURVELD

GQUNUKHWEBE

NDLAMBE XHOSA

Great Fish River

Alagoa Bay

Main region of conflict, 1779–1803

N

RHARHABE/NGQIKA XHOSA

GCALEKA XHOSA

Great Kei River

THEMBU

27

Khoisan reaction to the expansion of white settlement Khoisan resistance was dealt a terrible blow by the smallpox epidemic of 1713. The Khoisan had no natural immunity to this killer-disease which came to the Cape aboard a European ship. In the regions near Cape Town very few Khoikhoi survived. The disease struck deep inland, killing thousands more. Two further epidemics later in the eighteenth century carried smallpox as far as the Nama and Tswana in the north and the Xhosa in the east.

Khoisan resistance and Boer 'commandos' Despite the destruction caused by smallpox, fierce Khoisan resistance continued to hamper white settlement throughout the eighteenth century. Many of those who had already lost their livestock took to the hills and joined the San in raids on Boer flocks and herds. In many cases, especially the northern frontier districts, they succeeded in driving Boers from their farms and capturing their sheep and cattle. The Boers retaliated by forming local self-help military bands called 'commandos'. The Boers had two major advantages in this ongoing conflict. Guns gave them superior firepower and horses gave them greater mobility.

Frontier Boers went out on regular commando, shooting Khoisan hunters on sight or luring them into ambush. One night, in 1775, for example, the notorious commando leader Adriaan van Jaarsveld ambushed 149 Khoisan hunters in the mountains north of Graaff-Reinet. The commando had shot some hippos and invited the Khoisan of the region to come and eat the meat. During the night the Boers secretly surrounded the Khoisan camp. In the morning they opened fire killing 123 and capturing 21. Only five escaped.

As a result of commando raids like these thousands of Khoisan were killed and hundreds, mostly children, were captured. The latter were given out as 'apprentice' servants to the Boers of the commando. Child 'apprentices' were brought up speaking Dutch (Afrikaans) and made to serve their 'masters' until they were in their twenties. By then they usually had nowhere else to go and most stayed on as 'free' workers on the farm.

In the face of ruthless attacks by Boer commandos many Khoisan submitted voluntarily and agreed to work for the Boers as farm labourers and herdsmen. In this way they remained on their land and were usually allowed to graze some of their own livestock. By the end of the eighteenth century there were very few independent Khoisan left within the borders of the colony.

Hunters, raiders and traders beyond the northern frontier

The *Kora* were small groups of Khoikhoi herders who had originally come from the south-western Cape. As white settlement expanded in the late seventeenth century, they withdrew from the region, migrating northwards to the middle Orange River. From their Nama and Tlhaping neighbours Kora traded or raided cattle, ivory and fur karosses which they exchanged with the Cape for guns and ammunition.

During the eighteenth century commando-like bands of hunters and raiders from the colony penetrated the northern interior in search of ivory, skins and cattle. Some were headed by whites such as the German Jan Bloem who with his Kora dependents raided along the Orange and lower Vaal rivers. Others were headed by Khoikhoi or men of mixed parentage. Dutch-speaking Khoikhoi such as these, former servants from the colony, were known as *Oorlams*. Groups of armed and mounted Oorlams raided among the Nama of the lower Orange River.

Another group of mixed European and Khoikhoi parentage were the *Griqua*. They owned cattle, guns, horses and ox-wagons. They wore European clothing, spoke Dutch and were Christian. But Europeans of the Cape would not accept them as part of their society. So in the late eighteenth century they trekked northwards to found a settlement of their own. They were headed by two main families: Barends and Kok. They were joined by Khoikhoi of the Guriqua clan from whom they took the name Griqua. They settled in several small family groups just north of where the Vaal and Orange rivers meet. The Griqua hunted and traded far into the interior and provided an important trading link between the colony and the southern Tswana.

Conflict on the Eastern Cape Frontier

As we saw in Chapter 2, the westernmost Nguni were the Xhosa. By the 1770s the Xhosa chieftaincies had divided into two main groupings, east and west of the River Kei, each under one of the sons of Phalo, Gcaleka and Rharhabe. West of the Fish River were further Xhosa and mixed Xhosa/Khoikhoi groups such as the Gona and Gqunukhwebe (see Map 3.2). Squeezed between the Xhosa in the east and advancing Boer settlement from the west were a few remaining Khoikhoi chieftaincies. Under pressure from both sides these were soon broken up and absorbed into the society of either Boers or

3.5 A party of huntsmen north of the Orange River.

Xhosa. As we shall see, Khoikhoi such as these were to play an important role in the coming conflict in the region.

Early conflict between Boers and Xhosa Ivory hunters and cattle traders from the colony had been in touch with the Xhosa since the early 1700s. As Boer settlement advanced, contact became more regular. From very early on there was violence in trading relations between colonists and Xhosa. Nevertheless the Xhosa welcomed a certain amount of trade as it brought them copper, iron, beads and tobacco. Furthermore, the Xhosa were much more numerous and more powerful than the Khoikhoi and were not so easily persuaded or forced to part with their cattle.

Initial Xhosa attitudes to the arrival of Boer settlers were not very different from their attitude to other cattle-keeping peoples like the Khoikhoi. Boers were useful trading allies who could perhaps be absorbed into Xhosa society in the same way as the Khoikhoi were absorbed. The Boers on the other hand were not interested in becoming part of a larger Xhosa kingdom. They wanted complete control over both the land and its people.

During the 1770s Boers began to spread their settlements across the Zuurveld between the Sundays and Great Fish rivers. They soon found, however, that it was one thing to *claim* land east of the Sundays, but another matter altogether to prevent Xhosa and Khoikhoi from using it as well. As Boer and Xhosa settlements became more closely interwoven, violence between them became more common.

The First Cape/Xhosa War, 1779–81 Over the next one hundred years there was to be a series of nine 'Frontier Wars' between the Xhosa and the colony. The first started with a cattle raid and developed into war. The others were all deliberate acts of war by one side or the other. In 1779 a small party of Boers crossed the Fish River, killing a Xhosa herdsman and capturing some cattle. The strength of Xhosa retaliation took the colony by surprise. Thousands of cattle were captured before local Boer commandos took to the field.

The war dragged on as Xhosa used the thick forests to evade Boer commandos and hide from their guns, emerging at night to recapture their cattle. And while the Boers were on commando, Xhosa raided their isolated farms. On one occasion the frustrated Boer commander, Adriaan van Jaarsveld, tricked some Xhosa out of cover. Pretending to talk peace he threw tobacco on the ground. As they bent to pick it up his commando opened fire. This act of treachery rankled in Xhosa memory for many years to come. By the middle of 1781 most Xhosa west of the Fish had suffered some defeat and the war ground to a halt.

The Second Cape/Xhosa War, 1793

During the 1780s and early 90s more and more Xhosa crossed the Fish River to the Zuurveld. They were driven partly by drought and partly by the desire of Ndlambe, son Rharhabe, to assert his authority over the Gqunukhwebe. As their numbers grew, the Zuurveld Xhosa ignored Boer protests and grazed their live-stock across Boer farms. Khoikhoi servants began to believe the Boers would soon be driven from the Zuurveld. Some of them deserted their Boer 'masters' and joined the Xhosa. In 1793 a local Boer commando attacked the Zuurveld Xhosa, hoping to drive them across the Fish River. But their action produced the opposite result. In a fierce counter-attack the Xhosa drove the Boers right out of the Zuurveld, capturing thousands of their cattle and destroying many farms. The Graaff-Reinet *landdrost**, H. Maynier, recognised the strength of the Xhosa position and agreed to make peace with them. It was a victory for the Xhosa who remained in possession of the Zuurveld and kept the Boer cattle they had captured.

Boer rebellion against Cape authority, 1795 and 1799

Maynier's peace with the Xhosa was very unpopular with the frontier Boers. So far as they were concerned the company's role in the frontier regions was to recognise their land claims and provide them with military protection. In this Maynier had plainly failed them. Maynier was already unpopular for trying to prevent Boers from ill-treating their servants. He was also trying to collect land rents which the Boers had previously often failed to pay.

In 1795 the Boers of Graaff-Reinet rose in rebellion against the company, expelled Maynier from the district and proclaimed an 'independent republic'. But the rebellion fizzled out during 1796 and 1797 as the Cape Government cut off the supply of ammunition to the eastern districts. Frontier Boers knew that without ammunition they could not survive against continued Khoisan and Xhosa resistance. By then the colony had been captured by the British who were no more sympathetic to the Boers of the Zuurveld. Another brief Boer rebellion in 1799 was only important because it sparked off another major 'Frontier War'.

The Third Cape/Xhosa War, 1799–1803

The British sent an army of British and Khoikhoi soldiers which quickly suppressed this latest Boer rebellion. The Khoikhoi from Boer farms saw it as an opportunity to regain their land and freedom. They attacked Boer farms, seizing horses and guns. Then, as the British withdrew, Khoikhoi allied with the Xhosa of the Zuurveld. Many of these Khoikhoi had themselves been on Boer commandos and were experienced horsemen and marksmen. They greatly strengthened Xhosa armies.

The Khoikhoi-Xhosa alliance defeated a large Boer commando and pushed back European settlement as far as the Gamtoos River. But as the war dragged on the alliance weakened. Many Khoikhoi drifted back to Boer farms or took jobs in Graaff-Reinet. Nevertheless the peace of 1803 left the Xhosa of Ndlambe and the Gqunukhwebe in command of most of the Zuurveld.

Conclusion

So far in their series of wars with the colony the Xhosa had managed to protect and even extend their western frontier of regular settlement. The weakness of the Boers was apparent. Their family farm settlements were spread very thinly over a vast area. In the early 1790s there had been only 150 Boer families in the Zuurveld region compared with some 6000 Xhosa. There was little local unity behind strong Boer leadership. Boers were often reluctant to go out on commando for while they were away their farms were left unprotected.

It was clear that the Boers were unable to defeat the Xhosa and expel them from the Zuurveld without the aid of a large, full-time, regular army. The tiny British force sent to the frontier in 1799 had been enough to arrest a few rebellious Boers but was hopelessly inadequate for dealing with the Xhosa and their Khoikhoi allies. As we shall see in Chapters 6 and 8, even when the British supplied a large, modern army in the nineteenth century it took many more years of warfare before the Xhosa were finally defeated.

* *Landdrost*: local government official whose main job was to register local land claims and collect land rents.

Exercises

A. Think, discuss, understand and write

1 Why did the Dutch East India Company form a settlement at the Cape in 1652? To what extent were their original aims fulfilled?
2 Describe and explain the changing relationship between Dutch and Khoikhoi:(a) before 1650, (b) between 1652 and 1700 and (c) after 1700.
3 In what way and to what extent had Dutch colonisation changed the way of life of the San and Khoikhoi by 1800?
4 Describe and compare San, Khoikhoi and Xhosa resistance to Dutch colonisation between 1652 and 1803. How do you account for the successes and failures of this resistance?
5 Describe the nature and organisation of colonial society in the Cape during the eighteenth century. To what extent was that society shaped by their relationships with other peoples in the region?

B. Imaginative writing

Imagine you are a Dutch colonist at the Cape in the late eighteenth century, a recent immigrant from Europe. Write a letter to some friends in Europe trying to persuade them to join you in the colony. Describe the new country you have arrived in, where you live, the people you have met, the work you do and your prospects for the future.

C. Document study

Read Document 3.1. Bearing in mind the circumstances in 1660, discuss the rights and wrongs of the two points of view as expressed in that interview.

CHAPTER 4

The Mfecane: east of the Drakensberg

During the early nineteenth century a series of terrible wars took place among the northern Nguni peoples of south-eastern Africa. By the 1820s one state had emerged to dominate all others in the region. This was the Zulu kingdom. During the 1820s and 30s armies and refugees from these wars spread warfare and destruction over vast areas of Southern and Central Africa. The period has become known among the Nguni as *Mfecane*, 'the crushing', and among the Sotho-Tswana as *Difaqane* (or *Lifaqane*), 'the scattering'.

Origins of the Mfecane

Economic and political developments   As we saw in Chapter 2, the northern Nguni peoples were mixed farmers. They hunted wild animals, herded cattle and cultivated crops. They lived in a region of reasonably high rainfall and took full advantage of the variety of soils and vegetation between foothills, steep valleys and lowlands. The second half of the eighteenth century was a period of unusually high rainfall. Pastures improved, livestock thrived and herds increased in size. Crop cultivation also became more widespread. This was prompted by the introduction of maize, a South American crop recently brought to the region by Portuguese traders. It yielded heavier crops than the native African sorghum, provided rainfall levels remained fairly high. As more land was brought into regular use, there were larger food surpluses, people were better fed and population grew.

While population levels were low, herdsmen had been able to move their cattle freely between the summer and winter pastures of hills, valleys and lowlands. As population grew and herds increased

in size, however, competition for the best land developed. People needed to control and protect a wide variety of grazing as well as agricultural land. This may have been one reason why Nguni chieftaincies began to co-operate with each other to form larger political units or kingdoms.

Age-regiments   As Nguni states grew in size so the role of age-regiments, *amabutho*, increased in importance. As we saw in Chapter 2, initiation ceremonies and *amabutho* were a way of promoting unity within the state at the same time as providing the chief or king with a large workforce or army. And as competition for land increased the role of this army became more important.

Hunting and trade   The co-operative labour of the *amabutho* was also used for organised hunting parties. Wild animals harboured tsetse fly: carriers of fatal cattle disease. The large-scale destruction of wild game, therefore, made larger areas safe for grazing cattle. The hunting of elephants also provided ivory for trade with the European ships at Delagoa Bay. A chief or king who controlled this long-distance trade was able to increase his wealth and reward his followers. The desire to control the trade with Delagoa Bay may have been a further reason for the growth of larger states in the late eighteenth century.

The Madlatule famine   Around the turn of the century disaster struck. The period of high rainfall came to an end and for about ten years there was a prolonged drought. Crops failed, pasture withered and there was widespread famine. It became known as the *Madlatule famine* from the saying 'Makadle athule': 'Let him eat and be quiet'. Previously prosperous people were brought to the verge of starvation. Competition for scarce resources became severe as people raided each other for their cattle and their meagre stores of grain. The age-regiments were in the field permanently, and circumcision ceremonies were abandoned because young soldiers could not be spared for the necessary six months of initiation rituals. Besides raiding cattle from neighbouring chiefdoms and protecting one's own herds, *amabutho* were needed for hunting wild animals, for meat as well as trade.

Northern Nguni kingdoms: Ndwandwe, Ngwane and Mthethwa By the early 1800s the northern

Nguni region was dominated by three main kingdoms. The Ndwandwe, under the leadership of Zwide, controlled the foothills and valleys between the Mkuze and Black Mfolozi rivers. To their north lay the Ngwane, under Sobhuza of the Dlamini clan, while the south and south-east was dominated by Dingiswayo's Mthethwa. Besides the big three there were numerous smaller chieftaincies with varying degrees of independence, such as the Khumalo, Zulu, Qwabe, Hlube and Ngwane of Matiwane.

The Ndwandwe, being inland, were particularly badly affected by the drought of the early 1800s. This may partly account for the severity of their attacks against their neighbours. Zwide used his

4.1 The northern Nguni in about 1815

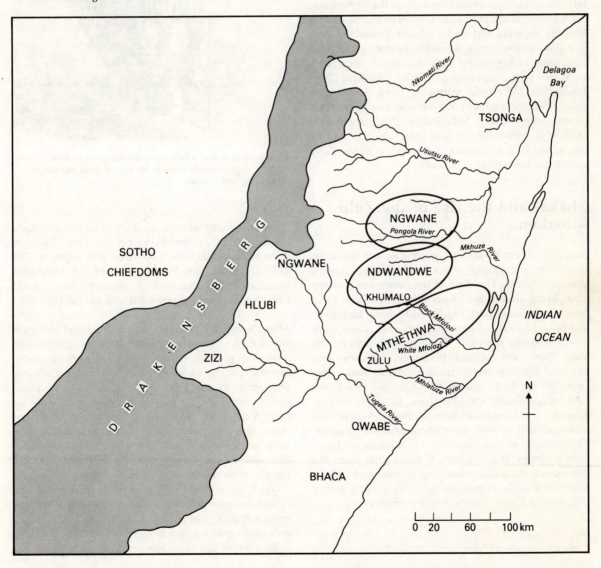

33

army to destroy old chiefdoms, seize their livestock and incorporate young adults into his regiments. In this way he built up a powerful, centrally-controlled kingdom. Dingiswayo's kingdom, on the other hand, was not quite so firmly and centrally controlled. As the kingdom expanded, old chieftaincies were left in place, provided their rulers paid regular tribute in cattle or grain and supported Dingiswayo with regiments. The Mthethwa's great strength lay in their control of coastal hunting forests and the trade with Delagoa Bay.

The beginnings of the Mfecane In 1816 Ndwandwe armies moved into the agricultural valley of the Pongola, expelling the Ngwane and driving them northwards (see below, pages 38–41). Two years later Zwide turned his armies against the Mthethwa, probably in an effort to seize control of Dingiswayo's hunting grounds and trade. What followed seemed like the decisive battle between the two great rival kingdoms. Dingiswayo was somehow separated from his army, captured and killed. Without their leader the Mthethwa regiments were easily scattered. For the moment Zwide was victorious. But almost immediately Ndwandwe dominance was challenged by an entirely new force which rose from the ruins of the Mthethwa: the kingdom of the Zulu under the leadership of Shaka.

4.1 A portrait of Shaka by a European artist, drawn from memory. Certain details, such as the size of spear and shield, may not be very accurate.

Shaka* and the rise of the Zulu kingdom

Shaka was born in about 1787, the son of the Zulu chief, Senzangakhona, and a neighbouring Langeni princess, Nandi. The Zulu at the time were a minor clan, living around the upper Mhlathuze River, and soon to become part of the Mthethwa kingdom. Tradition has it that Senzangakhona and Nandi were never formally married. Whatever the reason, the Zulu chief soon rejected the Langeni princess and she and her son were virtual outcasts. Shaka was brought up first among the Langeni, then the Qwabe and finally the Mthethwa. In due course he joined a Mthethwa age-regiment where he distinguished himself as a brave and able soldier. Dingiswayo soon recognised his abilities and put him in charge of a regiment. It was a time when the Mthethwa kingdom was expanding and Shaka gained valuable experience as a regimental leader and one of Dingiswayo's military advisers.

When Senzangakhona died in 1816, Shaka seized the Zulu throne from his brother Sigujana. This was done with Dingiswayo's approval and support. The Zulu chiefdom was by then part of the Mthethwa kingdom and Shaka, with his military talents, could turn the Zulu into a powerful and useful ally.

Shaka's military changes The old method of Nguni warfare was concerned mostly with cattle raids and a show of military strength. The aim at most was to get the enemy to acknowledge political authority and agree to pay tribute. When two armies faced each other they hurled their long-handled spears until one side gave way. Casualties were not normally very heavy. The victorious side would then retire with a large booty of cattle. The homes of the defeated would sometimes be burned, but the people themselves were usually left in place and allowed to recover. However, as warfare in the region became more common and fighting became more ruthless, this kind of tactical show of strength and cattle raid was no longer sufficient.

Because of Shaka's great military success, he has

* (also spelt Tshaka or Chaka)

often been credited with having invented all his military techniques himself. In fact most of Shaka's military 'innovations' had already been tried to some extent by the Ndwandwe and Mthethwa. Shaka's unique contribution was to bring all the new techniques together, develop and improve them and make them more effective. In doing so, Shaka turned out the most highly trained, disciplined, fit and efficient fighting force the region had ever seen.

Shaka developed the idea of 'total warfare'. This had already been used to some extent by the Ndwandwe. The enemy was to be totally destroyed and so never allowed to recover. Armies were defeated, homesteads burned, women and children killed and all enemy livestock captured. Shaka used the system of age-regiments to build up a permanent standing army. The regimental system had previously been a temporary force following initiation. Its members served the chief for a limited period before being released and allowed to marry. Now initiation ceremonies were abolished and all young men were organised into age-regiments on a long-term basis. They were only disbanded and allowed to marry after they had distinguished themselves in battle or were past their fighting prime.

The regiments were trained regularly until they were extremely fit. Leather sandals were discarded and soldiers ran and fought barefoot to gain extra

4.2 Zulu soldiers in full ceremonial dress.

speed. Young boys were used to carry the soldiers' baggage. Each soldier carried a long shield and was armed with a short-handled stabbing spear. The long shields protected them from the spears thrown by their opponents. They then rushed in close and used the stabbing spears to kill as many of the enemy as possible. For tactics, Shaka developed the 'cow-horn' formation. While the bulk of his army faced the enemy, regiments were sent out on each side like two great horns. While the 'chest' charged forward in the centre, the 'horns' encircled the enemy and prevented their escape. In Shaka's campaigns full use was made of spies, smoke signals and speed of movement to catch the enemy unawares and ensure complete victory. His soldiers developed great pride in their success. Cowardice in battle was punished by execution.

The Ndwandwe/Zulu War, 1818–19 Within a very short time Shaka had turned his regiments into a powerful fighting force. In 1818 he seized the opportunity of Dingiswayo's defeat and quickly brought the chiefdoms of the Mthethwa kingdom under his control. He incorporated the young men into his new regiments and replaced the Mthethwa heir with his own appointee.

Zwide recognised the danger of this new threat to Ndwandwe domination, but the first force he sent against the Zulu was driven off by Shaka's regiments. Determined to defeat this new Zulu kingdom, Zwide launched his whole army across the Mfolozi towards the end of 1818. Recognising the strength of his opponent, Shaka withdrew his entire people in the face of the Ndwandwe advance. As the Ndwandwe marched southwards, they found no livestock, crops or stores of grain to sustain them. Their army was worn down by frequent Zulu night assaults. Then, as the starving and weakened Ndwandwe army turned for home, Shaka launched his attack. The Ndwandwe suffered a terrible defeat. Shaka followed up his victory by sacking the undefended Ndwandwe capital. Ndwandwe refugees fled north of the Pongola. Zwide himself escaped to the region of the upper Nkomati River. Two of his generals, Soshangane and Zwangendaba, led the remnants of their army to the north of Delagoa Bay (see below, page 41). With this victory Shaka was left in command of a vast region from the Pongola in the north to the Tugela in the south.

The expansion of the Zulu kingdom In the years that followed, Shaka's armies attacked chiefdom after chiefdom in the region between the Drakensberg and the sea. Many thousands of men, women and children were killed. Of those who survived, some were incorporated into the expanding Zulu kingdom. Others became refugees, hiding in the forests and hills or leaving the region altogether and fleeing across the Drakensberg. (In this way, as we shall see in the next chapter, the effects of the Mfecane were carried across the highveld west of the Drakensberg). The region south of the Tugela as far as the Mzimkulu River suffered frequent Zulu

raids. Many people were killed, thousands of cattle were captured and all organised chieftaincies in the region were destroyed. Refugees fled into the forests and mountains and much of this region (present-day Natal) was left deserted. In due course Shaka's armies penetrated across the Mzimkulu to attack Faku's Mpondo. The fame of Shaka's army spread wide, and from way beyond the Zulu kingdom chiefs sent tribute to avoid being attacked.

4.2 The Zulu Kingdom and Mfecane, 1818–28

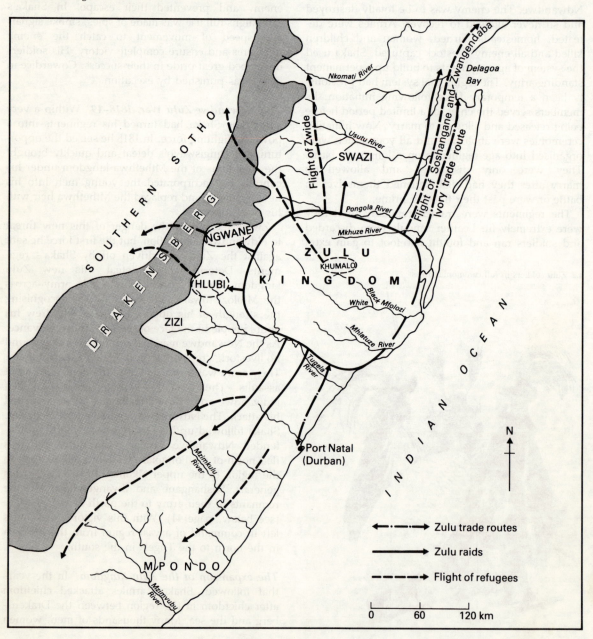

Trade Shaka kept strict control over trade and all ivory hunted in the kingdom belonged to the king. To the north he kept open the trade route to Delagoa Bay where ivory was exchanged for beads and cloth. In 1824 a group of British traders and their Khoikhoi servants from the Cape arrived at Port Natal (present-day Durban) and began ivory trading with the Zulu kingdom. Shaka permitted them to remain and treated them as minor subject chiefs. He was very interested in their muzzle-loading guns, but did not think they would be a match for his regiments as they took so long to reload.

The organisation of the Zulu kingdom

The strength of the Zulu kingdom did not depend solely upon the success of Shaka's new techniques of warfare. Closely connected with his military changes and backing up their success in battle was Shaka's political reorganisation of the kingdom. Shaka converted the loosely controlled chieftaincies and homesteads of the northern Nguni into a single, large, centralised kingdom in which all authority came directly from the king.

The whole kingdom was built along military lines. All young adults between the ages of about eighteen and thirty-five were drafted into male and female regiments. These were housed in a number of large regimental towns carefully placed around the kingdom. Each town encircled a huge cattle enclosure some one hundred metres in diametre. Besides housing the cattle at night, the enclosure was also used for military parades and ceremonies during the day. The male and female regiments lived separately in the houses around the enclosure. Each town was allocated regimental cattle, usually those captured in warfare. The male regiments tended the cattle and fed off their milk and meat. The female regiments cultivated maize and sorghum for consumption in the town. The king appointed a military commander (*induna*) to command the male regiments. A female relative of the king was appointed to take charge of the female regiments of each town. She kept the king informed about the loyalty of the *induna* and his regiments.

Besides the regimental towns the small private homesteads still remained. There the married men and women lived with their young children and elderly relatives. Marriage was only allowed when the king permitted the older soldiers to retire from full-time active service. He then also released a female regiment for them to marry. Even retired soldiers, however, were liable for call-up as a reserve army. The homesteads were still organised into

4.3 The Zulu capital in the 1830s in diagrammatic form. Though the houses look small they were in fact similar to those in Fig. 2.5.

chieftaincies and were expected to pay tribute to the king. But they posed no threat to the central authority of the king for he appointed their chief – often one of his own military commanders – and all the young men were incorporated into the king's own regiments.

Shaka's power was absolute. The indunas formed a central council, but in practice this was of little significance. Shaka's word was law and so great was their respect for or fear of him that his councillors were careful never to offer advice which their king might not want to hear. A sense of unity and national pride within the kingdom was cultivated by the annual *inxwala* or first-fruits ceremony. Held at the capital at the height of the summer rainy season the *inxwala* was attended by regiments and representatives from all over the kingdom. During the ceremony the king's spiritual power as their leader was renewed and his subjects celebrated the prosperity and fruitfulness of the harvest and the kingdom in the year ahead. The centralisation of Zulu authority was so successful and the people so proud of Shaka's victories that all within his kingdom began to refer to themselves as 'Zulu'.

The result of Shaka's political reorganisation, however, was that the whole kingdom was in a perpetual state of war. This was what had enabled the kingdom to expand so rapidly. But at the same time it meant the continued success of the kingdom depended upon continued success in war against its neighbours. As we shall see, this could not always be guaranteed.

The end of Shaka's rule To a certain extent Shaka had always used fear of execution to instil loyalty. For instance, any who lost their spear in battle or were wounded in the back were executed for cowardice. As Shaka became ever more powerful, the rate of executions increased and people were killed for even the pettiest of offences. After the death of Shaka's mother in 1827 many were killed for not showing sufficient grief. It is possible that Shaka's mind became unbalanced. No one, not even his brothers or closest advisers felt safe from his anger or displeasure. The regiments too were tiring of constant campaigns, of having to travel further and further afield to find the enemy, of meeting increasingly better-organised opposition, and of having to return to face Shaka's anger and the inevitable executions.

Shaka had never married though he lived within a royal women's enclosure. Any who fell pregnant were immediately executed, for, it was said, Shaka feared the birth of a son and heir who might one day challenge his claim to the throne. But these precautions did not save him. In 1828 Shaka was assassinated by his half-brothers Dingane and Mhlangane.

The reign of Dingane

At the time of Shaka's death the army was away on a long and unsuccessful campaign against the new Gaza state of Soshangane in the region of Delagoa Bay (see below page 41). By the time the army returned to the Zulu capital, Dingane had proclaimed himself king, having followed the murder of Shaka with that of his co-conspirator, Mhlangane. The army accepted the death of Shaka for they had dreaded his anger at the failure of their recent campaign. In order to win support, Dingane promised an end to war and executions and allowed many regiments to marry.

The new king followed the absolutist principles of his brother. But Dingane was no Shaka. He lacked the inspiration, leadership qualities and military genius which had made the Zulu kingdom great under Shaka. And he did not keep his initial promises of peace for long. He turned on those whose loyalty he suspected and regular executions were quickly re-established. In this respect Dingane was even more despotic than his predecessor. Soon the kingdom itself began to fall apart. As regiments were allowed to return home, regional chieftaincies were strengthened and began to break away. The Qwabe, for instance, defied Dingane's authority and repulsed a Zulu army sent against them. Faced with such open defiance, Dingane quickly re-established the centralised regimental system. And Zulu armies were once more sent out on regular campaigns.

In the 1830s Dingane sent out his armies against the Ndebele on the highveld (see next chapter) and the Swazi to his north (see below page 39). But the Zulu regiments lacked the earlier successes they had achieved under Shaka's leadership. Their opponents were stronger and better organised to resist them.

As Dingane turned on real or imagined opponents within Zululand itself, a number of refugees fled to the protection of the small white settlement at Port Natal. This soured relations between the Zulu and the white traders and in 1833 a Zulu army sacked the port. The white traders fled to the safety of a ship in the harbour and only returned after the Zulu army had dispersed. Nevertheless Dingane continued to be suspicious of white intentions towards his kingdom. And not without reason. In 1834 Boers from the Cape were spying out the land near Port Natal for future settlement. Three years later parties of Boers with their livestock, wagons and servants began to pour down the passes of the Drakensberg and onto the green pastures south of the Tugela. How Dingane and the Zulu faced this new challenge will be examined in Chapter 7.

The turbulence of the Mfecane period gave rise to a number of new and powerful nations. The remainder of this chapter will examine some of those which originated in the region east of the Drakensberg.

Sobhuza, Mswati and the founding of the Swazi nation

As we saw earlier, Zwide's Ndwandwe had driven Sobhuza's Ngwane northwards from the Pongola valley in 1816. The Ngwane retreated to the mountains around the upper Nkomati River. When Zwide himself retreated to this region in 1819, Sobhuza led his people back southwards to the Usuthu valley. It was here that Sobhuza laid the foundations of the nation that was to take its name, Swazi, from his son and heir Mswati. Sobhuza and Mswati built their nation upon a careful mixture of conquest, diplomacy and marriage alliances. By the end of Mswati's reign in 1865 the Swazi kingdom rivalled the Zulu in power and importance.

Marriage as a nation-building policy As Sobhuza absorbed surrounding Nguni and Sotho chieftaincies, marriage was a useful tool for foreign diplomacy as well as for internal control. Sobhuza used marriage alliances to ward off attacks from both Zwide and Shaka. He married one of Zwide's daughters and sent two of his own daughters to Shaka. Though Shaka later had them killed for

4.4 Mswati I (1839–65) and Swazi chiefs in full ceremonial dress.

becoming pregnant, Sobhuza took no action to avenge their death.

Within the kingdom itself Sobhuza allowed the various chiefdoms to remain intact provided they showed loyalty to him by paying tribute. The chiefs of the kingdom were also expected to marry daughters of the royal family. Through their bride wealth Sobhuza received large numbers of cattle. The sons of these marriages would become heirs of the chiefdoms and in due course also marry into the royal family. In this way Sobhuza used marriage to cement close personal relationships between himself and the local aristocracy. At the same time he increased his own personal wealth through receipt of *lobola*.

Sotho influence on Swazi culture As a number of Sotho were absorbed into the growing kingdom, the Ngwane (Swazi) adopted certain Sotho cultural customs. One of these was the marriage of cousins, an important part of the king's marriage policy discussed above. Another was the holding of *libandla*, a nation-wide general meeting summoned by the king: the Swazi equivalent of the Sotho *pitso*. In this way the Swazi king, unlike the Zulu, was answerable to the people for his good government. Further Sotho influence was seen in the importance of the mother of the king, the *Ndlhovukati* ('the Great She-Elephant'). She was the king's closest adviser and ruled for him as regent if the king was under age, as in the case of Sobhuza's heir.

Sobhuza's foreign policy Basically Sobhuza's policy was to avoid conflict with his neighbours. He paid occasional tribute to the Zulu king. If attacked his people retreated to the safety of mountain caves. Nevertheless they suffered a number of Zulu raids, especially from the armies of Dingane. During one of these, in 1839, Sobhuza died. A year later Dingane fled to Swaziland, having been defeated by his brother Mpande and the Boers of Natal (see Chapter 7). In line with Sobhuza's policy, the defeated Dingane was killed and a treaty of friendship was made with the new power in the region, the Boers.

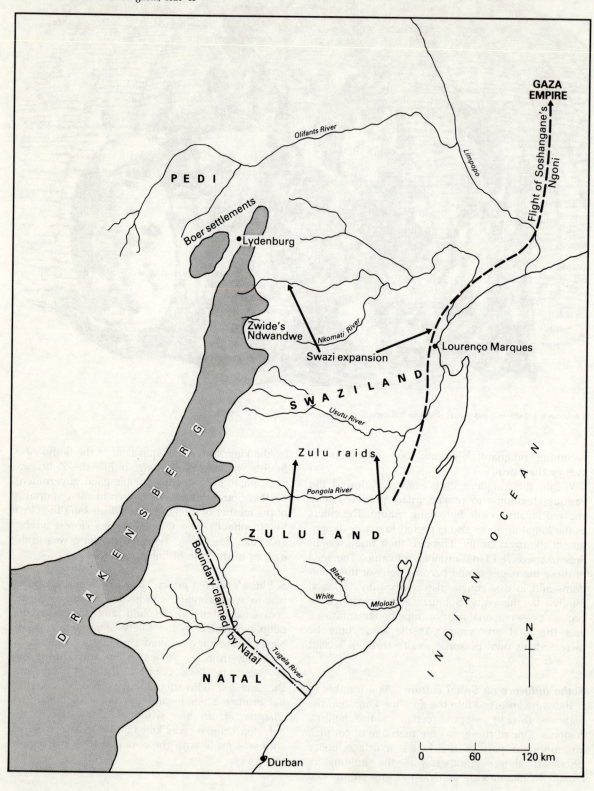

GAZA
EMPIRE

Olifants River

Limpopo

P E D I

Flight of Soshangane's Ngoni

Boer settlements

Lydenburg

Zwide's
Ndwandwe

Nkomati River

Swazi expansion

Lourenço Marques

S W A Z I L A N D

Usutu River

Zulu raids

Pongola River

Z U L U L A N D

D
R
A
K
E
N
S
B
E
R
G

Boundary claimed by Natal

Black

White

Mfolozi

I N D I A N   O C E A N

N

Tugela River

N A T A L

0   60   120 km

Durban

The reign of Mswati, 1839–65 On Sobhuza's death Mswati was only thirteen so his mother, Zwide's daughter, Thandile, ruled as regent. She reorganised the kingdom along more centralised Ndwandwe lines. The annual *inewala* (first-fruits) ceremony was introduced to raise the status of the king as well as unify the kingdom. Age-regiments were formed across the nation and royal villages were set up around the country to control them.

When Mswati took over in 1845 he faced opposition from his older brothers. Fokoti had already led a minor rebellion from the south in 1839. Now, in 1845, Malambule rebelled and sought Zulu help while Somcuba allied with the Boers who had recently settled around Lydenburg. It was to be ten years before Mswati was finally free from threat of foreign invasion. But by a skillful mixture of warfare and diplomacy Mswati emerged with a powerful and relatively independent kingdom. He used a system of alliances to play off one strong neighbour against another. He allied with the Boers of Lydenburg to protect his people from invasion by the Zulu. At the same time he allied himself with the new British authorities of Natal to protect his people from the Boers. But Mswati's foreign policy was not all defensive. In the east his armies conquered as far as Delagoa Bay where he drove the Portuguese to the safety of their fort at Lourenço Marques (present-day Maputo).

Soshangane and the Gaza state

Following the Ndwandwe defeat of 1819, Zwide's centralised state broke apart. The bulk of Nguni refugees fleeing northwards moved into southern Mozambique where they regrouped around former chiefly rulers. There they became known as 'Ngoni'. They reorganised themselves along Zulu regimental lines and raided the local Tsonga and Chopi for grain and cattle. By the 1830s Zwide's former general Soshangane had emerged as the most powerful leader, and other groups were expelled from the region.

In the decades that followed Soshangane built up a powerful military state. His raids extended over a huge area from Delagoa Bay to the Zambezi valley. The state was named after Soshangane's grandfather, Gaza. It was basically a raiding state, organised along strict class lines. All the peoples of the state were known to outsiders generally as 'Shangane'. But the original Ndwandwe, who formed the ruling class and controlled the regiments, considered themselves apart from and above the mass of subject peoples. They referred to themselves as 'Ngoni'. The ordinary 'Shangane' who made up the bulk of the central state, were drawn from conquered peoples who were absorbed into the regiments. The third and lowest class were the mass of Tsonga and Chopi peasants who were never fully absorbed into the state. The regiments lived off raiding these peasant communities and exacting tribute from surrounding peoples. In this way they built up huge herds of cattle. The Portuguese trading settlements of Sofala, Inhambane and Lourenço Marques were also raided and forced to pay tribute for the right to trade.

Further wealth came to the central state through trade. The regiments hunted elephants for their ivory and this was traded in exchange for cloth. War captives were also sold to the Portuguese for export as slaves either for the French sugar plantations of Réunion in the Indian ocean or across the Atlantic to Brazil.

The Gaza state was weakened by four years of civil war which followed the death of Soshangane in 1858. It recovered in the 1860s but thereafter control over the regiments began to decline. Nevertheless the Gaza state of Ngungunyane provided one of the major obstacles to final colonial conquest of southern Mozambique in the 1890s.

The Ngoni of Central Africa

Most notable of those expelled from southern Mozambique by Soshangane in the 1830s were the Jere-Ngoni led by Zwangendaba. They and two other Ngoni groups, the Maseko and Msene, moved north-westwards onto the Zimbabwe plateau. There they attacked the ancient Rozvi and Mutapa kingdoms. Organised along centralised regimental lines, they absorbed conquered peoples into their ranks and lived off raid and forced tribute.

After ravaging the plateau during the early 1830s the Ngoni eventually moved north of the Zambezi. The Msene Ngoni were destroyed by the Kololo (see next chapter) on the upper Zambezi flood plain. The Maseko Ngoni raided up the eastern side of Lake Malawi before returning to settle to the south of the Lake. The Jere-Ngoni reached as far north as south-western Tanzania. After Zwangendaba's death in 1848, his followers split into several groups which eventually settled to the north and west of Lake Malawi. These new Ngoni states still raided their neighbours and used force to exact tribute. But by absorbing local people into their ranks the Ngoni soon found themselves a more stable place in Central African society. They became, in effect, small but powerful, centralised local chieftaincies.

As such they were at the forefront of resistance to colonial conquest in the 1890s.

Other Nguni refugee groups: Mfengu, Hlubi and Ngwane As we saw earlier, one of the results of the rapid growth of Shaka's Zulu kingdom was the destruction of old chiefdoms and the creation of destitute refugees. One of the most devastated areas was the region of present-day Natal. From there people fled southwards to seek refuge among the Mpondo and Thembu. One group of refugees reached the Xhosa. They were referred to as *Mfengu*, meaning 'beggars'. They played an important part in the developing conflict between the Xhosa and the Cape Colony.

Two significant Nguni groups fled westwards across the Drakensberg: the *Hlubi* of Mpangazitha and the *Ngwane* of Matiwane (not to be confused with the Ngwane of Sobhuza). These two chiefdoms had begun the nineteenth century among the foothills of the Drakensberg, on the edge of the expanding Ndwandwe and Mthethwa kingdoms. They suffered attacks from both these powerful neighbours. To recoup their losses in cattle, the Ngwane turned upon the Hlubi. By 1821 they had stripped the Hlubi of virtually all their cattle. That year Mpangazitha led the bulk of the Hlubi across the Drakensberg where they fell upon the unsuspecting Sotho. They were followed a year later by the Ngwane themselves who were driven across the Drakensberg by Shaka's Zulu army.

The destruction caused by these desperate and destitute refugees began a series of wars which raged like a bush-fire across the Southern African highveld. The story of this *Difaqane* will be told in the next chapter which will conclude by considering the overall effects and significance of the *Mfecane/Difaqane* in Southern African history.

Exercises

A. Think, discuss, understand and write

1 Discuss the economic background to the rise of large states among the northern Nguni in the late eighteenth and early nineteenth centuries.
2 Describe the military and political changes introduced by Shaka. How far were these directly responsible for the rise of the Zulu kingdom?
   OR
   Assess the personal role and achievement of Shaka in the rise of the Zulu kingdom. To what extent was he a successful king?
3 What were the results of the expansion of the Zulu kingdom in the period 1818–28?
4 Assess the achievement of Sobhuza and Mswati in the rise of the Swazi nation. How and why did their policies differ from those of Shaka?

B. Imaginative writing

Imagine you are Dingane following the assassination of Shaka in 1828. Make a speech to the returning Zulu army, explaining your action and persuading them to support you as king.

C. Mapwork, group-work and class discussion

Compare and contrast Maps 2.2 and 4.2. Discuss the significance of these changes. As a member of a minor Nguni chiefdom was it better to be incorporated into the Zulu kingdom or to flee the region? What circumstances would affect a decision in this matter?

CHAPTER 5

The Difaqane: west of the Drakensberg

Difaqane ('the scattering'): destruction on the highveld

The scene onto which the Hlubi and Ngwane exploded in 1821–2 was very different from the one they had just left. On the southern highveld (of present-day Lesotho and Orange Free State) the southern Sotho were still loosely organised in a mass of minor independent chiefdoms. Life was relatively peaceful. Young men in search of lobola and the wealth to build up their own following raided cattle from distant neighbours. But the object of warfare was seizure of cattle, not destruction of people. The large expanse of highveld pasture and low population density allowed rival groups to move off and found new chiefdoms.

The southern Sotho were quite unprepared for the total warfare of Nguni regiments. The Nguni invasions of 1821–2, therefore, had a devastating effect. They set off a chain reaction of warfare and destruction which swept right across the highveld, north and south of the Vaal. Chiefdoms were shattered, crops and villages burnt, cattle stolen and consumed. Thousands of people lost their lives, if not in battle, then later, through starvation. Individuals hid in hills and caves, some even resorting to cannibalism to survive. Others fled as refugees, raiding wherever they could find food and so spreading the destruction ever further afield. Seldom had there been a greater need for strong leadership, to restore order out of chaos. And out of that chaos a number of strong leaders did emerge: leaders who built new states, larger and stronger than those that went before. The main focus of this chapter will be on three of those new states, two Sotho and one Nguni in origin.

The Difaqane began with the Hlubi flight across the Drakensberg in 1821. Led by Mpangazitha, the Hlubi fell upon the first Sotho chiefdom they came across. This was the Tlokwa of Mma-Nthatisi, queen regent for the young Sekonyela. Stripped of their livestock and driven from their homes, the Tlokwa followed the example of the Hlubi. Under the energetic leadership of Mma-Nthatisi they devastated the surrounding Sotho chiefdoms. Such was the ferocity of their attacks that far to the west all raiding groups of refugees were referred to as 'Mantatees'. The Hlubi were closely followed across the Drakensberg by Matiwane's Ngwane. Over the next few years the Tlokwa, Hlubi and Ngwane raided up and down the Caledon valley and across the southern highveld. As they went, they scattered groups of destitute Sotho refugees eastwards into the mountains and north-westwards beyond the Vaal.

The two rival Nguni groups met in their final clash in 1825. The Hlubi were defeated and their leader, Mpangazita, killed. The bulk of the Hlubi survivors were incorporated into the growing state of the victorious Matiwane. For a while Matiwane stood alone as the most powerful ruler of the southern highveld. But already, close at hand, a powerful new Sotho kingdom was emerging to challenge Ngwane dominance.

Moshoeshoe and the founding of the Sotho Kingdom

Moshoeshoe* was born in about 1786 at Menkho-aneng, the son of a minor Sotho chief of the Moko-teli clan. From an early age he distinguished himself as a leader of his age-mates and successful cattle-raider. Indeed, 'Moshoeshoe' is a praise-name

* (also spelt Moshweshwe or Moshesh)

5.1 Portrait of Moshoeshoe drawn by a missionary in 1833.

meaning literally, 'the shaver'. It commemorates the time he swept away the cattle of a neighbouring chief as thoroughly as if he had shaved him of his beard. Moshoeshoe's success attracted a small following and in 1820, while his father was still alive, he set up his own village on the slopes of a small mountain called Butha-Buthe.

Birth of a kingdom, 1821–5 Moshoeshoe had been at Butha-Buthe about a year when the chaos of the Difaqane began. Over the next few years Moshoeshoe's Mokoteli suffered a number of attacks from Hlubi, Tlokwa and Ngwane. Though twice driven from Butha-Buthe itself, Moshoeshoe saved most of his cattle by driving them into hiding. In 1822 he bought off further Ngwane attack by sending tribute of cattle to Matiwane. Through able leadership Moshoeshoe held his people together and attracted a number of other Sotho to his side. He increased his herds by raiding weaker Sotho groups and built up his own following by lending out cattle on the *mafisa* system.

The Tlokwa and Ngwane, however, were too close for safety. In 1824, following a major attack by Sekonyela's Tlokwa, Moshoeshoe decided to withdraw from Butha-Buthe. Uprooting his entire people, by now several thousand, he led them to a new mountain home, eighty kilometres to the south. It was a difficult journey. Bandits and cannibals attacked the column, killing stragglers, including Moshoeshoe's own grandfather, Peete. They finally reached their destination on the evening of the second day and called it 'Thaba-Bosiu' ('the Mountain by Night').

Thaba-Bosiu was carefully chosen. It was a large, flat-topped mountain rising steeply one hundred metres from the valley. The top, five square kilometres in extent, was covered by good pasture and contained springs of fresh water. It could only be reached by six narrow passes, easily defended from the top. In the valley below was extensive ground for cultivation. It was a natural fortress and Moshoeshoe placed his villages overlooking the narrow passes. The idea of hilltop settlements was nothing new. Thaba-Bosiu, however, was particularly well suited, both for defence and for establishing control over the surrounding countryside.

The growth of the Sotho kingdom

Once at Thaba-Bosiu Moshoeshoe's reputation and following grew rapidly. Moshoeshoe presented a chance for peace and security. People were attracted to his side by his offers of protection, his increasing wealth in cattle and his ability to defend his mountain stronghold. Refugees from the surrounding country quickly joined him and were lent *mafisa* cattle. Even the cannibals were drawn out of the mountains by offers of forgiveness and were persuaded to mend their ways. Refugees who had fled to the Cape Colony were welcomed back. They brought valuable new technology, including horses and guns. As his kingdom grew whole chiefdoms joined him and requested his protection.

Administration Moshoeshoe's government was built on a loose confederation of semi-independent chiefdoms. Age-regiments were summoned for defence, but there was no centralised standing army. Each chiefdom retained its own regiments for its own defence. Chiefs and headmen were allowed to remain in post with relative freedom of authority over their own people. Moshoeshoe strengthened his ties with his people by a system of marriage alliances and positioning royal villages at various points throughout the kingdom. The *pitso* was widely used for decisions of major importance, both

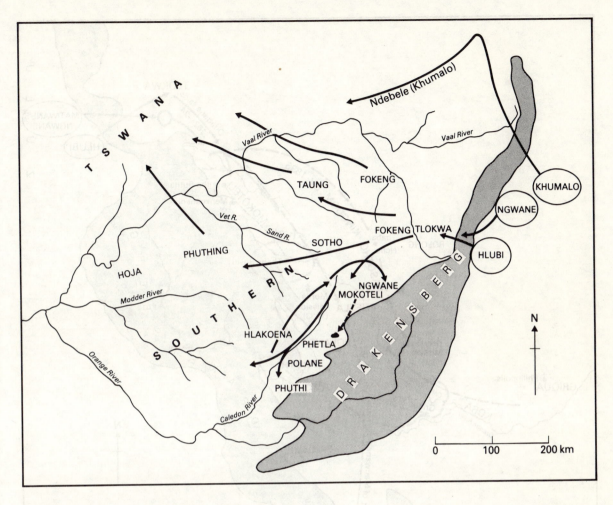

5.1 The Difaqane on the southern highveld, 1820–25

5.2 A modern aerial photograph of Thaba Bosiu, the flat-topped hill on which Moshoeshoe built his capital in 1824.

within the local chiefdoms and at Thaba-Bosiu itself. Unity was maintained and the system of loosely-controlled co-operation worked for two main reasons. Firstly there was the strong personal leadership and peaceful inspiration of Moshoeshoe himself. Secondly there was a continual threat of external danger and a strong general desire for peace and order.

Foreign policy In his relations with other peoples Moshoeshoe followed three main lines of policy. He paid tribute to the powerful, used defensive warfare when attacked, and restricted his cattle raids to distant peoples. Moshoeshoe sent regular cattle tribute to his most powerful neighbour, Matiwane of the Ngwane. He also sent tribute of feathers and furs to Shaka. The latter policy paid off. In 1827 Shaka helped Moshoeshoe by attacking and

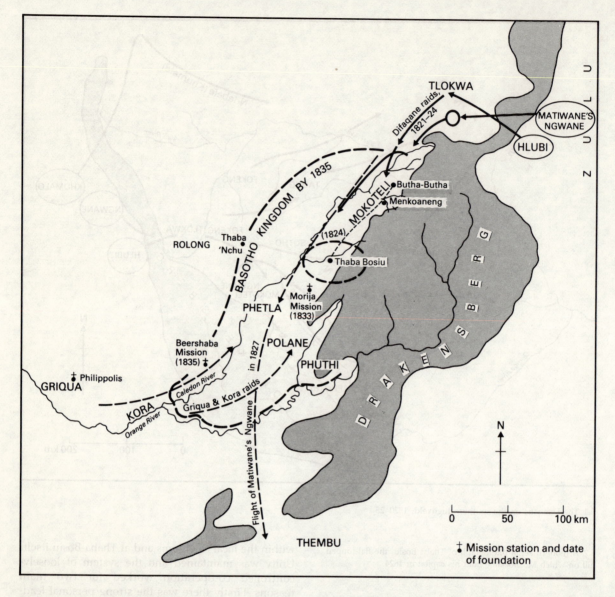

Difaqane raids, 1821-24

BASOTHO KINGDOM BY 1835

MOKOTELI

(1824)

in 1827

Griqua & Kora raids

Flight of Matiwane's Ngwane

TLOKWA

MATIWANE'S NGWANE

HLUBI

Z U L U

Butha-Butha

Menkoaneng

ROLONG

Thaba 'Nchu

Thaba Bosiu

PHETLA

Morija Mission (1833)

POLANE

Beershaba Mission (1835) †

PHUTHI

GRIQUA

† Philippolis

KORA

Caledon River

Orange River

D R A K E N S B E R G

N

THEMBU

0   50   100 km

† Mission station and date of foundation

5.2 The rise of the Sotho kingdom, 1820–35

defeating the Ngwane. Moshoeshoe was then able to drive the weakened Ngwane southwards into Thembuland where they came up against a British army and were scattered. The defeat of Matiwane left Moshoeshoe's kingdom the strongest in the southern highveld. More chiefdoms joined him, including Moletsane's Taung in the north-west and Moorosi's Phuthi in the south.

Moshoeshoe's most famous defensive war of this period was against the Ndebele in 1831. By rolling rocks down the mountain passes, the Sotho beat off the invading Ndebele army. Moshoeshoe increased

his reputation still further by sending the retreating Ndebele a herd of fat cattle for the journey home. When Moshoeshoe's regiments went on the offensive, he ensured that their cattle raids were far from home. His most successful raid was in 1829 against the southern Nguni Thembu far to his south.

The most serious threat to Sotho security in the early 1830s came from the raids of armed and mounted bands of Griqua and Kora. Moshoeshoe was determined to learn about their new technology and began buying horses and guns from the Cape Colony. In due course the Sotho became highly skilled with both gun and horse. When Moshoeshoe heard about European Christian missionaries, he sent two hundred cattle to the Griqua town of Philippolis to 'buy one'.

The arrival of missionaries In 1833 Casalis and Arbousset of the Paris Evangelical Missionary Society arrived in Lesotho. Moshoeshoe welcomed them for a number of reasons. They were, like himself, men of peace. He appreciated their learning and wanted them to educate his people. He believed their presence might control the Griqua and Kora, many of whom were professed Christians. They would also provide a useful link with the Cape Colony which he recognised as a powerful state and the source of guns. Moshoeshoe used the missionaries to set up new centres of control along the Caledon valley. He sent his sons to be educated at mission schools and to each mission centre he sent members of his family to establish new villages. The missionaries became important allies of the Sotho and their writings provide valuable evidence for the history of the kingdom.

By the mid-1830s there were 25 000 people in Moshoeshoe's kingdom with up to 2 000 settled on Thaba-Bosiu itself. Theirs was the most important Sotho state on the southern highveld and they had begun referring to themselves as 'BaSotho', meaning simply, '*the* Sotho people'. It was at this moment that large numbers of Boers from the Cape Colony began to pour onto the southern highveld. Chapters 7 and 8 will discuss how the Sotho coped with this and will make an of assessment of Moshoeshoe's overall achievement.

Sebetwane and the Kololo

Origins of the Kololo The Tlokwa, Hlubi and Ngwane raids of 1821–3 had driven several southern Sotho groups north of the Vaal. Fokeng, Phuthing, Hlakoena and Taung raided the northern highveld in search of food and cattle. Hearing of the large herds of southern Tswana cattle, they began to converge on the Tlhaping capital of Dithakong. By then Sebetwane, the young chief of the Patsa clan, had emerged as the main leader of the Fokeng. In a clash between Fokeng and Phuthing Sebetwane captured a woman of the Kololo clan. Sebetwane's followers adopted her as a mother-figure and thereafter referred to themselves as 'Kololo'. While the Kololo rested nearby, the Phuthing and Hlakoena descended upon Dithakong in a vast starving throng of some 40 000 people.

The battle of Dithakong (26 June 1823) The Tlhaping deserted their town and appealed for help to Robert Moffat, the Christian missionary at nearby Kuruman. Moffat persuaded a hundred armed and mounted Griqua to come to the aid of the Tlhaping. After a battle lasting seven hours this small band of Griqua managed to defeat the huge enemy host which faced them. They were able to ride up, fire their guns and then ride out of range to reload. 500 Sotho were killed but not one Griqua. The battle of Dithakong is historically important for a number of reasons. It was the first major battle of the *Difaqane* for which we have written eye-witness accounts: from Robert Moffat and from an English traveller, George Thompson. More importantly, it proved the military effectiveness of guns and horses. This greatly enhanced the reputation of the missionaries. From now on Moffat and the missionaries of Kuruman were known as the friends of the men

5.3 The Kololo in Southern Africa, 1823–50

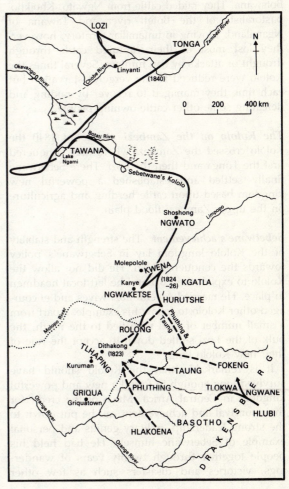

with guns. This helped ensure their welcome among the Tswana further north as well as among other peoples such as the Ndebele and, in due course, the Kololo.

The Kololo and the Tswana.   Following the battle of Dithakong the Hlakoena were scattered. The Phuthing and Taung raided the Tswana for a few more years before moving back south of the Vaal. Sebetwane meanwhile held his Kololo together as a compact and effective raiding force. Between 1824 and 1826 the Kololo inflicted severe defeats on all the major Tswana chiefdoms they encountered: Rolong, Hurutshe, Kwena, Ngwaketse and Kgatla. Then in 1826 the Ngwaketse chief Sebogo retaliated with a surprise dawn attack. They were helped by two English hunters whose guns added to the element of surprise. The Kololo panicked and fled, abandoning their large herds of captured cattle.

Over the next fourteen years the Kololo travelled across much of the northern part of present-day Botswana. They raided cattle from Ngwato, Khoikhoi pastoralists of the Boteti river and Tawana of Ngamiland. Moving in unfamiliar territory, however, they lost most of their captured cattle through drought or attacks by San hunters. Several times the Kololo were reduced to the verge of starvation but each time they managed to recover by raiding and defeating some other cattle-owning people.

The Kololo on the Zambezi   In about 1840 the Kololo crossed the Zambezi where they conquered first the Tonga and then the Lozi. There Sebetwane finally settled and established a powerful new kingdom based upon cattle herding and agriculture on the upper Zambezi flood plain.

Sebetwane's achievement   The strength and stability of the Kololo kingdom lay in Sebetwane's policy towards the conquered Lozi. He did not allow the Kololo to exploit the Lozi and he left local headmen in place. He married several Lozi wives and encouraged other Kololo to follow his example. Apart from a small number of Lozi who fled to the north, the bulk of the Lozi settled down to accept the rule of their new Kololo king.

It is remarkable that the Kololo should have survived long enough to found a new and powerful kingdom in Central Africa. Much of the credit for their survival and achievement can be put down to the strong leadership, military genius and personal example of Sebetwane himself. He had held his people together through twenty years of wanderings, victories and disasters such as few other

Difaqane groups had been able to survive. From 1826 to Sebetwane's death in 1851 the Kololo suffered no other major military defeat. Furthermore, once on the Zambezi Sebetwane adopted new military tactics appropriate to the river environment. Using canoes, islands and floodwaters he was able to defeat one attack from the Msene Ngoni and two from the Ndebele.

The extent of the dependence of the Kololo kingdom on the personal strength and ability of Sebetwane is shown by the kingdom's steady decline following his death in 1851. The Lozi northern exiles were able to reorganise, stage a revolution and regain their independence in 1864.

Mzilikazi and the founding of the Ndebele kingdom

Origins   Mzilikazi was chief of the Khumalo, a northern Nguni chiefdom in the hill country between the Black Mfolozi and Mkhuze rivers. Formerly part of the Ndwandwe kingdom, the Khumalo changed sides and supported Shaka in the Ndwandwe-Zulu war of 1818–19. Grateful for this help, Shaka allowed Mzilikazi to remain both traditional chief and military leader of the Khumalo regiments. This was unusual within the Zulu kingdom and left Mzilikazi in a powerful position among his own Khumalo people. In 1821 Mzilikazi tried to assert his independence. He refused to hand over to Shaka some cattle he had captured from the Sotho. This led to two Zulu attacks against the Khumalo who were forced to flee across the Drakensberg in 1822.

Ndebele on the highveld   The Khumalo entered the highveld with only 2–300 fighting men. Women, children and livestock had been killed or left behind. At first they did not settle and for a year they raided north among the Pedi of the Olifants River region. They consumed local food supplies, collected cattle and absorbed new people. The Sotho referred to these invaders as 'Matabele', the name they gave to all Nguni-speaking strangers from the east. The Khumalo soon adopted this name for themselves, the Nguni version being 'Amandebele' or 'Ndebele'. During the 1820s the Ndebele were joined by further Nguni refugees fleeing from warfare with the Zulu.

The building of the Ndebele state   Once he had gathered together livestock and a larger following, Mzilikazi looked for a place to settle and create a new kingdom on the highveld. Over the next fifteen

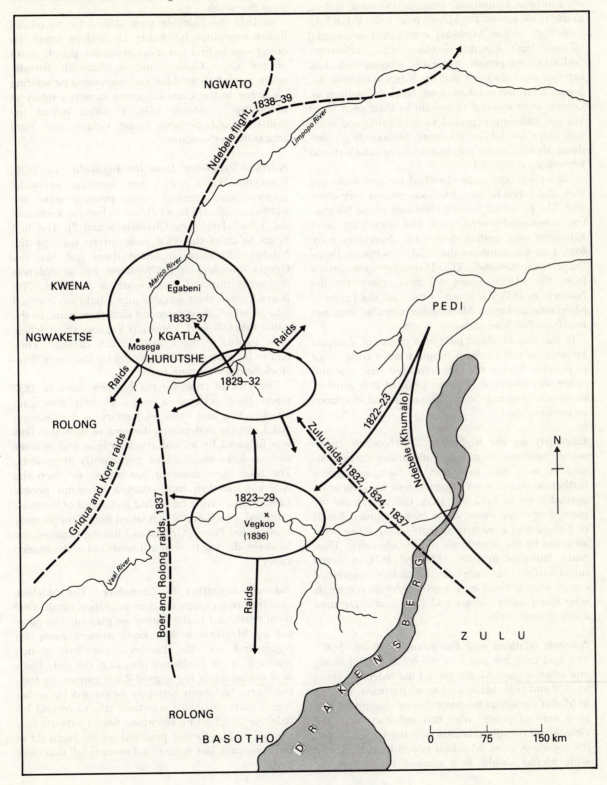

NGWATO

Ndebele flight, 1838–39

Limpopo River

Marico River

Egabeni

KWENA

1833–37

KGATLA

Mosega

NGWAKETSE

HURUTSHE

Raids

Raids

1829–32

ROLONG

Griqua and Kora raids

Vaal River

Boer and Rolong raids, 1837

1823–29

Vegkop
(1836)

Zulu raids

PEDI

1822–23

1832, 1834, 1837

Ndebele (Khumalo)

N

Raids

ROLONG

BASOTHO

D R A K E N S B E R G

ZULU

0   75   150 km

49

years he established three main settlement areas in the southern, central and western Transvaal, ending in the 1830s around the Marico river basin (Map 5.4).

In each region Mzilikazi established regimental villages built around circular cattle enclosures. Sotho-Tswana people, especially women and child captives were absorbed into the Ndebele community. Some men were taken into Ndebele regiments. Others were allowed to remain in their own small villages but were expected to tend cattle and cultivate crops for the Ndebele state. Surrounding chiefdoms that failed to pay tribute were attacked and sometimes destroyed.

Ndebele tribute raids stretched far and wide and their Zulu-style fighting methods proved very effective. The powerful Tswana chiefdom of the Ngwaketse was raided several times. The Rolong capital of Kunwana was destroyed in 1832. Survivors were forced to flee south of the Vaal to settle at Thaba 'Nchu near Lesotho. The Hurutshe were driven from the Marico valley to make room for the Ndebele in 1833. Far south of the Vaal the Taung of Moletsane and even Moshoeshoe's Sotho were not free from Ndebele raids.

In this way Mzilikazi built up a powerful, compact kingdom which received tribute from a wide range of peoples. Within the kingdom itself strict law and order was observed. But the price of this achievement was large numbers of Tswana killed, displaced or impoverished.

Insecurity on the highveld The Ndebele themselves, however, were frequently under attack. This may be why they kept moving their settlements further north and west. Dingane sent his Zulu army against them in 1832 and 1834. But potentially the most dangerous threat came from mounted bands of Griqua and Kora armed with guns. These were attracted by the large herds of Ndebele cattle. Their raids, launched in 1828, 1831 and 1834, achieved initial success. But each time the raiders' unguarded camps were overrun by vengeful Ndebele regiments who killed many Griqua and Kora and recaptured most of their cattle.

Ndebele relations with Europeans, 1829–36 Mzilikazi had probably heard of the battle of Dithakong and at his request Moffat visited the Ndebele capital in 1829 and 1835. Mzilikazi had no particular interest in Moffat's religious teaching. But he recognised him as a man of peace, who had influence with the Griqua and friendly relations with the Cape Colony, the source of guns. Mzilikazi hoped that friendship with Moffat would help control the actions of

Griqua, Kora and European hunters and raiders from the south.

In 1835 the Ndebele were visited by an official British expedition headed by Dr Andrew Smith. Its object was to find out more about the people north of the Cape Colony and to establish friendly relations with them. Mzilikazi responded by sending an envoy to the Cape Governor to sign a treaty of friendship in March 1836. Mzilikazi hoped the British would prevent future Griqua and Kora attacks from the south.

Ndebele expulsion from the highveld By 1836, however, Boers with their families, servants, wagons and livestock were pouring onto the southern highveld in what was to become known as the 'Great Trek' (see Chapters 6 and 7). The first Boers to cross the Vaal were driven back by the Ndebele. Mzilikazi regarded them just like the Griqua: invaders of his territory. But as Ndebele regiments pursued them south of the Vaal, fifty Boers formed their wagons into a tight circle called a *laager* which they defended with their guns. In the battle that followed, known as Vegkop, the Ndebele were unable to break through this defence. They had to be content with rounding up the Boers' livestock before returning home.

The year of crisis for the Ndebele came in 1837 when they suffered a series of four damaging attacks. The first came in January, a Boer/Rolong attack on the Ndebele settlement of Mosega. This was followed by a Zulu attack in June and another Griqua, Kora and Tswana raid shortly afterwards. The final blow came in November. By then the Ndebele had lost more than a thousand people killed, houses were burnt and thousands of livestock captured. In a battle which lasted nine days an army of mounted Boers, Griqua and Rolong pursued the Ndebele, driving them northwards out of the Marico valley.

Ndebele migration to Zimbabwe The Ndebele split into two groups for their migration north. One went north-east to the Zimbabwe plateau. The other led by Mzilikazi took a north-western route via Ngamiland and the Zambezi. The two groups reunited on the Zimbabwe plateau in the early 1840s near the capital of the ancient Rozvi empire. By then the Rozvi had been seriously weakened by earlier Ngoni raids. Mzilikazi was thus able to rebuild his Ndebele kingdom by absorbing Shona subjects in a manner similar to that practised on the highveld of the Transvaal. But there is not room to tell that story here.

Mzilikazi's achievement Mzilikazi created the only large, independent Nguni state founded on the Sotho-Tswana highveld. He combined elements of Nguni and Sotho-Tswana culture and custom to build his own original state. Zulu-style fighting methods were used and the Nguni language was retained. But the large number of Sotho-Tswana women who were absorbed had their influence in, for instance, the building of houses out of pole, mud and thatch instead of reeds. Regiments were based in regional villages rather than at large central capitals. Mzilikazi's rule was not as harsh as that of Shaka or Dingane. Executions were not so frequent and regiments were freer to marry. For ten years, 1825–35, the Ndebele kingdom dominated the highveld north of the Vaal. Law and order was established within the kingdom though those beyond who failed to pay tribute were harshly dealt with. After the disasters of the late 1830s Mzilikazi succeeded in rebuilding the most powerful kingdom north of the Limpopo. Under his successor Lobengula it was recognised as a major power, even by the European colonists who sought to conquer it in the 1890s.

Effects of the Mfecane/Difaqane

The *Mfecane/Difaqane* had begun with the Ndwandwe/Zulu war of 1818–19. It lasted for nearly twenty years though the main effects were felt in the first ten years. The Nguni and Sotho names for it, meaning 'crushing' and 'scattering', aptly describe what the period meant to so many people. The widespread warfare left thousands dead: killed in battle, assaulted by bandits or died of starvation. Old chiefdoms were destroyed and thousands of individuals fled as destitute refugees. Some went to the eastern frontier regions of the Cape Colony where they became known as Mfengu. Others hid among the forests and mountains on either side of the Drakensberg. A few took to banditry or even cannibalism. As peace gradually returned, refugees reemerged to seek the protection of the new strong powers in the region.

During the *Mfecane/Difaqane* livestock were captured and recaptured. Thousands of cattle, sheep and goats were slaughtered for their food, many more than would normally be the case. In many areas cultivation stopped altogether. Crops were only grown in those areas protected by some powerful state. In at least two areas whole regions were largely depopulated. The Zulu created a depopulated zone south of the Tugela in present-day Natal.

The Ndebele did likewise on their southern flank, around the middle Vaal. The idea in both cases was to create a sort of 'no-man's-land' as a protective buffer against enemy attack. Nobody was allowed to enter those areas without the permission of the Zulu or Ndebele king.

Perhaps the most significant effect of the *Mfecane/Difaqane* was the creation of new states and the redistribution of people. At the beginning of the nineteenth century both the Nguni and the Sotho-Tswana were reasonably evenly spread over the south-east and the highveld. The normal political pattern was a large number of semi-independent chiefdoms of varying sizes, the weaker paying tribute to the stronger. By 1835 this population pattern had been transformed. People were now concentrated in certain compact areas under new political leadership. Elsewhere large regions were underpopulated or temporarily deserted as refugees and minor chiefdoms fled to the protection of the more powerful new states.

The largest and most powerful new state was the Zulu kingdom itself. To its north was the Ngwane/Swazi kingdom of Sobhuza and further north Soshangane's Gaza empire and the Ngoni states of Central Africa. The most powerful on the highveld was the Sotho kingdom of Moshoeshoe. Nearby was the rival Tlokwa state of Sekonyela though this was to be absorbed by the Sotho in 1853. The Ndebele still dominated the northern highveld until 1837 while the Kololo left a trail of destruction through the Tswana before settling on the Zambezi in the 1840s. The Rolong were driven to regroup on the southern highveld under the shadow of Moshoeshoe. The northern Tswana re-emerged as more compact states with strong military leaders as their chiefs. Meanwhile the battle of Dithakong had demonstrated the effectiveness of guns and stimulated a desire for trade with the Cape Colony.

Some of the newly created African states were to provide future European settlers with their strongest opposition. Initially, however, the underpopulated areas of the middle highveld and 'Natal' provided emigrant Boers from the Cape Colony with new opportunities for settlement in the late 1830s. African reaction to this movement will be examined in Chapter 7.

Exercises

A. Think, discuss, understand and write

1 Describe the way in which Moshoeshoe built the Sotho kingdom between 1820 and 1835. Compare and contrast his methods with those of Shaka of the Zulu.

2 Assess the importance and achievement of Sebetwane of the Kololo.

3 Describe the rise of the Ndebele state and assess the importance and personal achievement of Mzilikazi.

4 What were the effects of the Mfecane/Difaqane in Southern Africa as a whole? To what extent did it affect the distribution of peoples in the region? What was the result of this redistribution of people?

B. Imaginative writing

You are a Sotho refugee at the battle of Dithakong (26 June 1823). Describe what you saw and did on that day.

OR

Imagine a meeting between Moshoeshoe, Shaka, Mzilikazi, Sobhuza and Sebetwane in 1828. What would they discuss? Draw up an agenda for such a meeting.

C. Mapwork, group-work and class discussion

Use the maps in this chapter to describe what happened to the peoples shown in Map 2.2. Draw a map to show the region in 1835.

CHAPTER 6

The Cape Colony under British rule, 1806–36

British occupation of the Cape

By the early 1800s the number of British ships sailing to and from their colony of India had increased enormously. Like the Dutch before them, the British needed a supply station for their ships. They also wanted a naval base from which to protect their shipping from possible attacks by rival European navies. The British had already seized control of the Cape in 1795. They handed it back to the Dutch Government (known as the Batavian Republic) in 1803. The Dutch East India Company had by then become bankrupt. But war soon broke out again in Europe and the Dutch allied with the French against Britain. Once more the safety of British shipping was threatened. Following victory over the French navy in 1805 the British seized control of the Cape again in 1806. This time Britain was determined to keep the colony and at the European peace conference of 1814 their possession of the Cape was confirmed.

To maintain the safety of their shipping route to India the British Government was determined to make the Cape into a secure British colony. They hoped it would become a place for British settlement like Canada or Australia. Britain at the time was in the midst of its industrial revolution. Her factories were producing more and more manufactured goods. They needed larger markets to sell them overseas. If the Cape economy was made more efficient and exported more goods, then it could become a prosperous market for British manufactured goods. Also, as it became more prosperous, the colony could pay for its own government, from its own taxes and customs dues.

In line with these aims, the British introduced many economic and social changes at the Cape. A number of these changes were unpopular among Dutch colonists, especially the trekboers of the eastern Cape. Indeed, as we shall see, the changes brought by British rule prompted large numbers of Boers to trek northwards from the Cape in the late 1830s.

Economic development

The British occupation gave a great stimulus to the Cape economy. More ships called at Cape Town and there was now a permanent armed force of several thousand soldiers to be fed. Demand for beef increased and prices rose. Wine production expanded, helped by low import tariffs into Britain. Trade with the African interior also expanded, especially after 1815. This was stimulated by Europe's increasing prosperity which demanded luxury items like ivory for ornaments, cutlery handles, piano keys and billiard balls. British and other European merchants set up trading warehouses at Cape Town and the new eastern Cape port of Port Elizabeth. The introduction of Merino sheep soon provided the colony with a further export. Merino sheep were bred specially for their heavy coats of wool which could be cut off and exported each year to Britain's expanding clothing factories. Though it started slowly at first, sheep farming expanded rapidly in the 1830s, especially in the eastern Cape. By the 1840s wool had become a major Cape export.

The 1820 Settlers When the British took over the Cape in 1806 there were about 25 000 whites in the colony, mostly of Dutch origin. Gradually British settlers began to arrive: soldiers, government officials, traders and merchants, but their numbers were still very small. The Government wanted to stimulate farming settlement and make the white popu-

6.1 By the 1850s Grahamstown had become a major market for hunting produce from the African interior. Many of the original 1820 settlers ended up working here as traders and merchants.

lation more British. There were also large numbers of unemployed people in Britain. So the Government sponsored the emigration of 5 000 British settlers to the eastern Cape in 1820. They were given plots of forty hectares each, much smaller than the huge pastoral farms of the trekboers.

The aim was to stimulate crop cultivation and, as we shall see later, to help the security of the eastern frontier. But soil and climate were unsuitable for wheat and the farms were too small for successful pastoral farming. Within two years most of the new settlers had left their farms and become craftsmen and traders in the new small towns of the eastern Cape (see Fig. 6.1).

Land policy The land policy of the Dutch authorities had been inefficient and brought in very little income. Under their 'loanfarm' system trekboers simply 'borrowed' land from the government, paying a very low rent. Huge farms were claimed, they were never properly surveyed and rents were often not paid. Since the land did not belong to them, trekboers wasted it by overgrazing before

moving on to a new 'loan-farm'. The British were determined to introduce a more efficient, more profitable system. They raised rents and began surveying farms, restricting them to slightly smaller areas. They introduced a 'quit-rent' or freehold system. Land could now be treated like private property, to be bought and sold. The aim was to make people value their land more highly because they had paid for it. Trekboers of the eastern Cape opposed the changes. Apart from higher rents, they feared they would lose their 'loan-farms' and have to buy their land in future.

Labour policy The increased agricultural activity – wine, wheat, cattle and sheep farming – created a demand for more farm labour. But an increase in slave labour was no longer possible. For reasons discussed below (p. 57), the British officially banned the trade in slaves in 1807. This ended the importation of new slaves into the Cape. So there was soon a shortage of labour. Besides slaves, the other main sources of farm labour were Khoikhoi and 'free-blacks' (that is, released slaves and people of mixed

Khoi/slave ancestry). These were usually treated much the same as slaves. They were paid very little and were often kept on farms by force, 'apprenticeships' or threats of violence.

In order to increase the supply of labour for colonial farmers the Government introduced the so-called 'Hottentot Code' of 1809. This meant that all Khoikhoi and 'free-blacks' had to carry a pass stating where they lived or who their employer was. Any without a pass could be forced to work for a local white farmer. But the Code did at least insist that contracts of employment should be written down. Another law, of 1812, laid down that children born on a colonial farm could be apprenticed for ten years from the age of eight. These laws strengthened Boer control over their farm workers. They prevented Khoikhoi and 'free-blacks' from moving around in search of higher wages or better working conditions.

The role of missionaries

One of the products of Europe's industrial revolution was the rise of missionaries from the nonconformist Churches such as Wesleyans, Moravians and Congregationalists. They opposed slavery and deplored the poverty and suffering produced by the class divisions in Europe's new urban, industrial societies. They believed that a revival of Christianity and the Christian principles of equality and brotherly love would help the poor and deprived to improve their lives. From the early nineteenth century British, German and French missionaries brought these ideas to Southern Africa. They saw their task as the conversion of the heathen 'native' peoples of the region. They believed this would help them find an improved position in colonial society.

Immediately, however, the missionaries faced strong Boer opposition and they soon found themselves in the role of 'defender of native rights'. The Boers believed all black peoples were racially inferior. Boer employers wanted to keep the Khoisan and other blacks in a subservient position. The Boers did not welcome the changes introduced by the missionaries. If their servants became Christian and learned skills, crafts and literacy, they would no longer work as poorly-paid farm labourers.

The two main missionary societies working in the colony in the early nineteenth century were the Moravians and the London Missionary Society. The Moravians established mission stations in the

6.2 Genadendal mission in the western Cape. Missions like this became a centre for Khoikhoi and 'Free Black' peasant farmers.

western Cape, their best-known being Mamre and Genadendal (see Fig. 6.2). The London Missionary Society established missions among the Tswana and Griqua north of the colony and among the Khoikhoi of the eastern Cape. Their most important eastern Cape mission was that of Dr van der Kemp and his successor James Read at Bethelsdorp near the future Port Elizabeth.

The missionaries attracted people to their stations by offering them small plots of land to grow food. There they were taught Christianity, literacy, manual crafts and other skills. The Boers accused the missionaries of 'stealing' their labourers. The mission stations certainly became crowded with unemployed people. It gave them a place of residence which enabled them to escape the 'pass laws'. The missionaries opposed the colony's labour laws for discriminating against the freedom of Khoikhoi to move about and choose their employers. They insisted on the principle of equal laws for everyone – 'equality before the law'. They were also highly critical of the violence used by employers against their servants.

The missionaries had an important influence with the British government, both in Cape Town and in Britain, and the Boers soon regarded them as their bitter enemies. The most influential missionary was Dr John Philip. He came to the Cape in 1819 as local head of the London Missionary Society. He had powerful friends in Britain and became an important influence with the Cape Governor. His book, *Researches in South Africa* (1828), publicised in Britain the plight of the Khoikhoi in South Africa and helped bring changes in the labour laws of the Cape.

6.3 Angry Boers clash with British soldiers as the Slagters Nek rebels are hanged. This picture shows the first attempt to hang the rebels during which the scaffold (in the background) broke.

'Equality before the law': the 'Black Circuit' and Slagters Nek

A number of changes were made in the legal system of the Cape, among them the introduction of English as the official language of the law courts. But perhaps the most important legal change was the development of the idea of *equality before the law*. This meant that if a servant was ill-treated or not paid his wages, he could sue his employer in the law courts. This was intended to make employers treat their servants better. And it was hoped that if servants had the protection of the law, they would be contented and accept their servile position.

In order that everybody, trekboers and farm workers, would be able to take their cases to court, the Government introduced circuit courts. Judges travelled the rural areas bringing the law courts to each district. Missionaries took full advantage of this

opportunity. They helped Khoikhoi servants bring charges of assault against their employers. In fact many of the charges of violence were for incidents that happened a long time ago, and many cases were dismissed for lack of evidence. But the Boers were not used to being challenged by their servants in open court. They greatly resented it. They saw it as interference by missionaries and British officials in their 'freedom' to treat their servants how they wished. For this reason they referred to the eastern Cape circuit court of 1812 as the *'Black Circuit'*.

Some Boers refused to accept this 'interference' in their own affairs. In 1815 a frontier Boer, named Bezuidenhout from Slagters Nek, was summoned on a charge of assaulting his servant and withholding wages. He refused to appear in court and was shot while resisting arrest. His angry brother tried to raise a rebellion against the Government. He got some support from poorer Boers who resented things like higher rents and loss of control over their servants. But better-off Boers supported the government and the rebels soon surrendered. The government treated the Slagters Nek rebels unexpectedly harshly: five of them were hanged (see Fig. 6.3).

The 'freeing' of labour: Ordinance 50 and the abolition of slavery

With the development of industrial capitalism in Europe there was a growing movement against the use of slavery and other forms of forced labour. Humanitarians argued for greater human liberty and equality. Industrial employers argued for 'free labour' and cash wages because then workers could buy more of their manufactured goods. Experience in Europe had also shown that workers were happier and therefore worked better if they were free to move around and choose their employers. Forcing people to work against their will was therefore less efficient.

After considerable prompting from missionaries, especially Dr John Philip, the British Government applied these principles to the labour laws of the Cape Colony. *Ordinance 50* of 1828 abolished the pass laws and apprenticeships of the 'Hottentot Codes' of 1809 and 1812. This was a great advantage for Khoikhoi and other 'free-blacks' in the colony. They could no longer be forced to work on white farms against their will. They were now free to move around and choose whatever livelihood suited them best. The British government believed this would make Boer employers more efficient. They would now have to pay reasonable wages to attract workers onto their farms. For the wealthier Boers this was not a serious problem. But the poorer Boers of the eastern Cape could not pay the wages and they could no longer force unwilling workers to stay on their farms.

As a result of Ordinance 50 there were many Khoikhoi who wanted to farm on their own. In 1829 the Government provided them with 640 small plots of arable land in the Kat River region of the eastern Cape frontier. This *'Kat River Settlement'* was also intended to act as a buffer zone between the Xhosa and the colony.

The other major movement for the 'freeing' of labour was the *abolition of slavery*. The British Government had officially banned the trade in slaves as early as 1807. Slavery itself, however, was not finally abolished in Britain's colonies until 1834. In the Cape former slave-owners were allowed to keep their 'slaves' as apprentices for a further four years.

After that they became 'free-blacks' and, as a result of Ordinance 50, were free to sell their labour wherever they wished. The compensation paid to slave-owners for their loss of 'property' was very small.

The abolition of slavery caused great resentment among slave-owners, especially the richer Boers who were the main owners of slaves. They not only lost the value of their 'property' (the slaves), but it was also a further loss of their control over labour.

The Eastern Cape frontier

A major change which the British brought to the eastern Cape frontier was the introduction of a full-time, regular army, equipped with the latest guns from Europe. This was a great advantage over locally-recruited temporary Boer commandos. Even so it was to be a long time before Xhosa resistance was finally overcome.

The 'Third Cape/Xhosa War' of 1799–1802 (see page 30) had left Ndlambe's Xhosa in possession of much of the Zuurveld. Over the next few years more and more Xhosa crossed the Fish River to occupy the eastern districts of the colony. By 1811 the regular supply of meat to Cape Town was being affected as more and more Boers were pushed out of their frontier farms. Governor Cradock ordered the expulsion of the Xhosa across the Fish River.

The Fourth Cape/Xhosa War, 1811–12 Lt-Col John Graham was sent to the eastern frontier to command an army of over 2000 men. It consisted of local Boers, regular Khoikhoi soldiers of the Cape Regiment and British soldiers from the Cape garrison. In the summer of 1811–12 8000 Xhosa men, women and children were ruthlessly driven out of the Zuurveld and across the Fish River. A string of military forts was built to ensure they did not recross the Fish River boundary. Graham's action changed the whole character of raid and counter-raid of the first three 'frontier wars'. The expulsion of 1811–12 was the beginning of a form of 'total warfare' which the Xhosa had never seen before.

Meanwhile to the east of the Fish the Xhosa were thrown into turmoil. Ngqika, nephew of Ndlambe, had long claimed to be paramount chief of all the Xhosa. The British now recognised this claim. But Ndlambe's Xhosa were crowded in upon the Ngqika-Xhosa by Graham's expulsion of 1811–12 and civil war soon erupted between them. In 1818 Ndlambe's army defeated Ngqika's at the battle of Amalinde. Ngqika immediately appealed to the British for help.

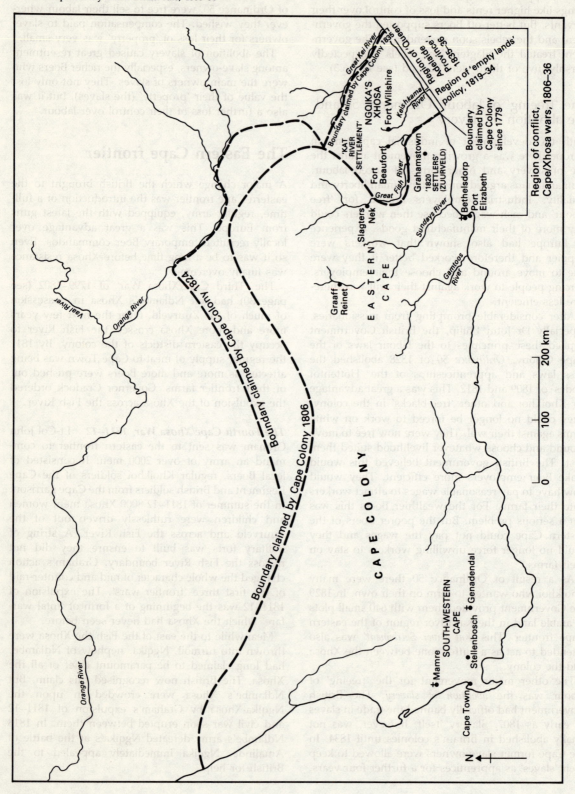

The Fifth Cape/Xhosa War, 1818–19 The British responded to Ngqika's appeal by invading Xhosa territory, attacking Ndlambe's Xhosa and capturing 23 000 cattle. Stripped of their cattle, the Xhosa rallied behind Ndlambe's war-doctor Makana (also known as Nxene). In broad daylight Makana led 6 000 Xhosa in a mass attack on Grahamstown, but the attack was repulsed. The British retaliated by driving Ndlambe's Xhosa as far as the Kei. Makana eventually surrendered. He was imprisoned on Robben Island but drowned in 1820 while trying to escape in a captured boat.

The colonial government then decided to create a barrier of 'empty land' between the Xhosa and the colony. They cleared the land between the Fish and Keiskama rivers and built two fortified towns, Fort Willshire and Fort Beaufort. Two attempts to create a *human* barrier between the Xhosa and the colony both failed. Most of the '1820 Settlers' soon deserted their farms, and the Khoikhoi of the 'Kat River Settlement' proved unwilling allies of the colony. The government used it as a dumping ground for 'coloured' unemployed and the Kat River settlers were eventually driven to rebellion in 1851.

The Sixth Cape/Xhosa War, 1834–5 The 'empty land' policy did not last for long as Boers and Xhosa moved into the region. Clashes between them became common and the shooting of a Xhosa chief sparked off another war in December 1834. The Xhosa swept into the colony killing white settlers and raiding farms as far as the Sundays River.

The colonial forces regathered under Colonel Harry Smith. They invaded Xhosa territory and

penetrated east of the Kei. There they captured and treacherously killed the eastern paramount Xhosa chief, Hintsa. Smith then annexed the whole of the land between the Keiskama and the Kei and called it 'Queen Adelaide Province' after the British queen. Though peace was signed in 1835 the Xhosa in the hills remained undefeated.

The Cape Governor, D'Urban, was unable to prevent the Xhosa from moving back onto their land. Clearly if the new province was to be used for colonial settlement, enormous force would be needed. The alternative was to abandon the territory and sign firm treaties of friendship with the Xhosa chiefs. The Government in Britain decided on the latter course and 'Queen Adelaide Province' was handed back to the Xhosa in October 1836.

Reasons for the Boer Trek

For some years trekboers of the Graaff-Reinet district had been using the grazing land north of the Orange River. But between 1835 and 1841 7 000 Boer men, women and children, with a further 7 000 servants, crossed the Orange River and left the colony permanently. Many reasons have been given for this huge Boer 'trek' and over the years much has been written about it. Modern Afrikaner historians and politicians have glorified it as a great event in Afrikaner history, referring to it simply as 'The Great Trek'.

The most common reason given for the Boer trek was their desire for freedom from British control. But there was much more to it than simply anti-

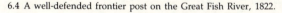

6.4 A well-defended frontier post on the Great Fish River, 1822.

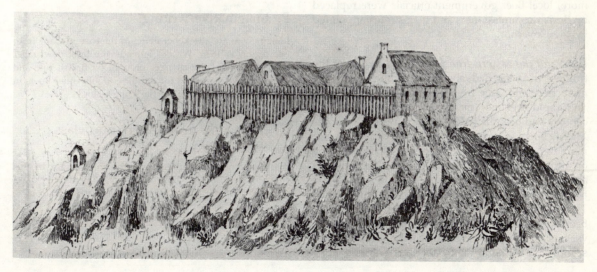

British feeling. There were many things the Boers did not like about British policy changes. But they had been just as anti-government in the period of Dutch Company rule. The British government, however, exerted more effective and direct control than the Company had ever done. Their policy changes could not be ignored and were therefore resented more. In 1795 and 1799 discontented frontier Boers had risen in rebellion. But the British treatment of the Slagters Nek rebels had shown that by 1815 rebellion within the colony was no longer a possibility.

Control of labour and other policy changes The British policy change which the Boers resented most was their loss of control over labour. 'Equality before the law' and the circuit courts allowed servants to challenge their Boer 'masters' in open court. Boers were no longer free to withhold wages or use violence to discipline their servants. The 'freeing' of labour by Ordinance 50 deprived many of the poorer frontier Boers of their only source of labour. The abolition of slavery in 1834 removed the final element of forced labour. Delayed and inadequate compensation was particularly resented by the wealthier slave-owning Boers.

Under the influence of missionaries the British Government appeared to the Boers to be biased towards 'natives' and to deny white racial superiority. This threatened the whole system whereby 'heathen' Khoikhoi and 'coloureds' were automatically of the servant class while Christian Boers were of the land-holding, employer class. The whole approach of British policies seemed foreign to Boer culture. This feeling was increased by the introduction of English in education and the courts. Furthermore, local Boer government officials were replaced by British commissioners and magistrates appointed by the Governor.

Land and the eastern frontier The main aim of the frontier trekboer had always been the search for more free land, free from any government control. The rapid trekboer movement of the eighteenth century had been halted by the firm resistance of the Xhosa. Boers of the eastern frontier districts became more densely settled. Many became landless, living on other people's farms. Then came higher rents and rumours that all 'loan-farms' would be sold. On top of this was the insecurity of the frontier itself. The strong British frontier policy of 1811–12 had been welcomed by the Boers. But the Xhosa invasions of 1819 and 1834 showed the continuing insecurity for Boers on the frontier.

The Boers had heard of the depopulation of vast stretches of country caused by the Mfecane/Difaqane wars of the 1820s. Spies sent out in 1834 returned with glowing reports of 'empty land' around the middle Vaal and south of the Tugela. Drought and another 'frontier war' in the summer of 1834–5 turned more people's thoughts to emigrating. Prospects of new land from the annexation of Queen Adelaide Province in 1835 merely postponed the trek. When the province was abandoned the following year, thousands of Boers packed up their ox-wagons and trekked northwards out of the colony.

Exercises

A. Think, discuss, understand and write

1 Why did the British take control of the Cape in 1806? How and why did they hope to change the colony? To what extent did they achieve their aims?
2 Discuss the work and importance of missionaries at the Cape between 1800 and 1836.
3 What legal changes did the British introduce to the Cape Colony? Who benefitted from these changes and in what way? Who opposed them and why?
4 Discuss the importance of Ordinance 50 (1828) and the Abolition of Slavery (1833–4). Why did the British want 'free labour' at the Cape? What were the advantages and disadvantages of these changes, from the point of view of the employers and from the point of view of the workers?
5 In what way did British rule change relations between the colony and the Xhosa in the period 1806 to 1836?
6 Why did so many Boers decide to leave the Cape in the late 1830s?

B. Imaginative writing

Imagine you are a trekboer living in the eastern Cape frontier region in 1836. Write a letter to the local newspaper protesting about the changes brought by British rule and explaining your reasons for deciding to join other Boers in trekking northwards out of the Cape Colony.

C. Mapwork, group-work and class discussion

With reference to Map 6.1 and the information in this chapter, discuss the aims and achievements of Xhosa policy towards the Cape Colony in the period 1806 to 1836.

CHAPTER 7

The Boer Trek and its results, 1836–54

The Voortrekkers

The Boers who trekked away from the Cape Colony in the late 1830s were known as the Voortrekkers. They packed all their belongings into ox-wagons and set off in large family groups of several hundred. They took with them their Khoikhoi and 'coloured' servants for herding their cattle, sheep and goats and for harnessing and leading the trek-oxen. The Boer men travelled on horseback, their women and children in the wagons which were piled high with household utensils and supplies. They lived from the meat and milk of their livestock. They hunted wild game for meat and where possible they bought grain from local African farmers. They travelled slowly, over rough country, seldom covering more than ten kilometres a day.

Poorer Boers joined the groups of wealthier families and accepted the leadership of the head of the main family. In this way the Voortrekkers travelled northwards onto the highveld in a number of distinct groups, each under its own leader. There was little unity among the various Voortrekker communities. There were disagreements about where they should go and how they should organise themselves. Clashes of personality and personal ambition soon also became apparent.

The direction in which the Voortrekkers should go was determined to some extent by their need to trade in certain goods. Imported luxuries like tea and coffee were considered essential. They also needed new supplies of cloth. But most important of all, they needed a regular supply of gun-powder and lead for their muzzle-loading guns. Some Voortrekkers settled not far north of the Orange and maintained trading contacts with the eastern Cape. Others preferred the well-watered grasslands east of

7.1 Boer trekkers crossing the Drakensberg.

the Drakensberg where they could make contact with the trading settlement of Port Natal. A few had the more ambitious scheme of penetrating to the far north, making contact with Portuguese traders at Delagoa Bay and so breaking away altogether from any form of British control.

Early trek to the northern Transvaal The first Voortrekker group left the colony towards the end of 1835. Led by Trichardt and van Rensburg, this party of about one hundred whites made their way to the Soutpansberg on the northern edge of the

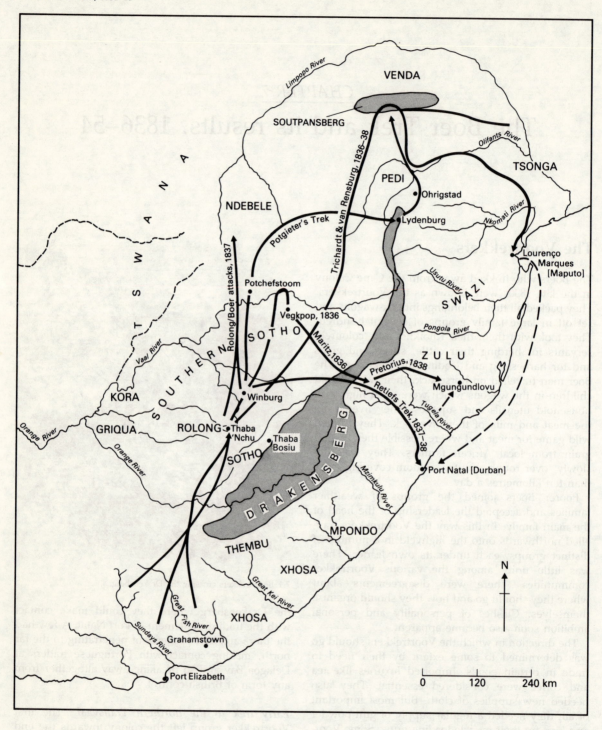

Transvaal highveld. It was good hunting country but infested with tsetse fly and malaria-carrying mosquitoes. Van Rensburg moved down into the Limpopo valley to open up a trade route to Delagoa Bay. There he clashed with local Tsonga and his whole party were killed. They were followed in 1838 by Trichardt and the rest of the group who were running short of ammunition. But they fell victim to malaria and only a handful of women and children finally made it back by ship to Port Natal.

Voortrekkers, Rolong and Ndebele, 1836–7

Early in 1836 a large group of Voortrekkers arrived on the southern highveld and gathered near the Rolong settlement of Thaba 'Nchu. They were led by Potgieter and Cilliers, the heads of two wealthy families from the eastern Cape. It was Voortrekkers from this group who clashed with the Ndebele at the battle of Vegkop in October 1836 (see above, p 50 and see Fig. 7.2). Though they successfully defended themselves, the Boers of Vegkop were stranded with no livestock. They were rescued by Moroka's Rolong who lent them oxen to pull their wagons back to Thaba 'Nchu. The Rolong them-

selves had only recently been driven south of the Vaal by the Ndebele. Moroka and other Rolong leaders regarded the Boers as allies against the Ndebele. They hoped with the aid of the Boers to regain their traditional territory north of the Vaal. As we saw in Chapter 5, the Rolong joined with the Boers in expelling the Ndebele from the Transvaal highveld in 1837. During 1838 Potgieter and others set up the Voortrekker settlements of Potchefstroom and Winburg north and south of the middle Vaal.

Voortrekkers and Zulu, 1837–40

In November 1837, while Potgieter was still engaged in fighting the Ndebele, the majority of Voortrekkers were preparing to leave the highveld and move down into Natal. They had elected as their leader Piet Retief, a wealthy farmer from Grahamstown. Retief visited the the Zulu capital Mgungundlovu to seek permission for a settlement in the partly depopulated zone south of the Tugela.

There can be little doubt that from the start the Zulu regarded the Voortrekkers as a serious threat to their independence. But they were unsure how to deal with them. To test Retief's sincerity Dingane sent him off to recapture some Zulu cattle stolen by

7.2 Inside the Boer laager at the battle of Vegkop. A sketch completed at the time. In the background women are loading guns for the men. In the left foreground a woman is casting new lead bullets and in the right foreground is the 'hospital'.

the Tlokwa. Retief accomplished this task by an act of treachery which must have further worried the Zulu king. Retief tricked Sekonyela into trying on a pair of handcuffs and then held the Tlokwa chief prisoner until the stolen cattle were handed over. In the meantime the Voortrekkers were already moving down from the Drakensberg before Zulu permission had been granted.

The death of Retief

It was probably during the *inxwala* ceremony of December-January 1837–38 that the decision was finally taken to wipe out the Voortrekkers in one swift blow. In February 1838 Retief returned to Mgungundlovu with a party of seventy men. He handed over the stolen cattle and demanded his land concession. Whites later claimed that Dingane signed his mark on a concession granting the Boers free use of all land south of the Tugela. It is unlikely that Dingane would ever have agreed to such a deed. If he did mark a cross on a piece of paper handed to him by Retief, it was only to put the Boers at their ease. What is clear is that Dingane invited the Boers to attend a farewell dance in the central enclosure, but to leave their guns outside. In the midst of the dance Dingane gave the signal, 'Kill the wizards', and Retief and all his companions were set upon and killed.

Zulu regiments were then sent out to kill the rest of the Voortrekkers who were settling around the upper Tugela. They wiped out one group, but others went into laager and survived the Zulu attacks. Trekker commandos who came to their rescue were quickly defeated and for most of 1838 the Zulu remained triumphant. The Zulu tactic of wiping out the Voortrekkers in one swift blow seemed almost to have succeeded.

The Voortrekkers' revenge

The Voortrekkers realised that victory over the Zulu was essential if they were ever to establish a settlement in Natal. In November 1838 a commando of 500 men assembled under Andries Pretorius, an experienced commando leader, newly arrived from the eastern Cape. They crossed the Tugela into the Zulu kingdom and formed a laager of wagons at Ncome river. There on 16th December they successfully beat off a mass attack by a huge Zulu army. Though Zulu regiments repeatedly charged, they failed to penetrate the Voortrekker laager. Three thousand Zulu died in the attempt, mown down by Boer guns while not one Boer was killed. The Boers named it 'the Battle of Blood River' and Afrikaners in South Africa today still celebrate their victory, on 16th December each year.

Pretorius's commando then marched on Dingane's capital, Mgungundlovu, but found it deserted. They buried the bones of Retief and his colleagues before returning to settle in Natal, between the Tugela and Mzimkulu.

The fall and death of Dingane

After such a resounding defeat by the Voortrekkers, Zulu loyalty towards Dingane began to waver. In 1839 Dingane attacked the Swazi in preparation for moving his whole kingdom northwards, further away from Natal. Following defeat by the Swazi, Dingane called for the help of his brother Mpande who was in charge of the southern part of the kingdom. Mpande refused to help his increasingly unpopular and unsuccessful brother and fled south of the Tugela with 17 000 Zulu. There he sought the protection and help of the Boers.

In January 1840, with Boer backing, Mpande returned to Zululand at the head of a large Zulu army. After a fierce battle Mpande's army emerged victorious. Dingane fled northwards only to be captured and killed by the Swazi. Mpande then became king of the Zulu, but had to pay tribute to the Boers.

The Trekker republic of Natal, 1839–43

In 1839 the victorious Boers set up the 'Republic of Natalia' with a *volksraad* (parliament) at Pietermaritzburg (named after Piet Retief and another trek leader, Gert Maritz). They now had access to a trading port, independent of British control, and Dutch and American ships began calling at Durban (formerly Port Natal). But there was soon a shortage of land in their 'republic'. Huge 'farms' of 2 500 hectares each had been so freely given out that soon there was no spare land left. Furthermore, the farms they had were far from vacant. With the defeat of the Zulu and the end of the Mfecane wars Africans began re-emerging from the forests and hills and from south of the Mzimkulu. During 1838–43 the black population of 'Natal' increased from 10 000 to 50 000, compared with only 6 000 whites. The volksraad decided that no more than five African families should be allowed to settle on each farm. In 1842 Pretorius was ordered to expel 'surplus' Africans south of the Mzimkulu. At that point Britain intervened.

British annexation of Natal

For some time the British at the Cape had been anxiously watching the actions of the Voortrekkers in Natal. There were three main reasons for British intervention. Firstly

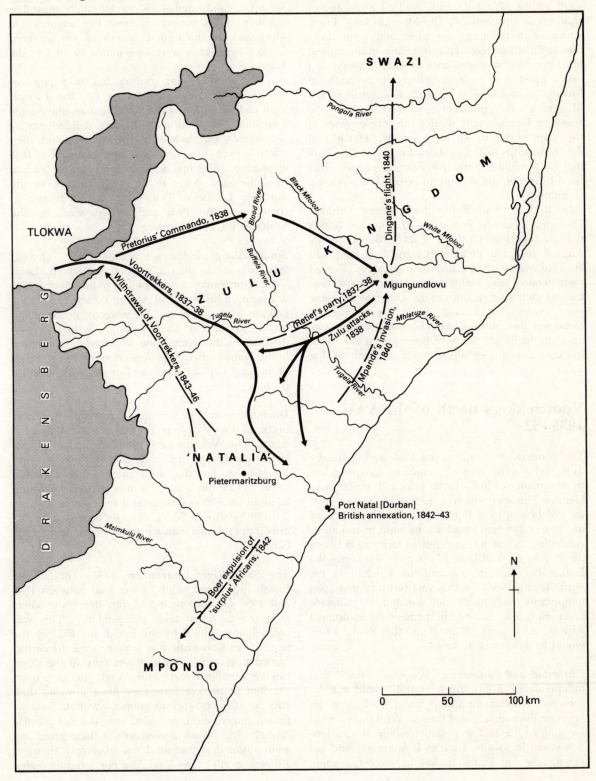

SWAZI

Pongola River

TLOKWA

Pretorius' Commando, 1838

Black Mfolozi

Blood River

Buffels River

Voortrekkers, 1837–38

Withdrawal of Voortrekkers, 1843–46

D R A K E N S B E R G

Z U L U

Tugela River

Retief's party, 1837–38

Z U L U   K I N G D O M

Dingane's flight, 1840

Mgungundlovu

White Mfolozi

Mhlatuze River

Zulu attacks, 1838

Mpande's invasion, 1840

Tugela River

'NATALIA'

Pietermaritzburg

Port Natal [Durban]
British annexation, 1842–43

Mzimkulu River

Boer expulsion of 'surplus' Africans, 1842

MPONDO

N

0   50   100 km

a Boer commando had already raided the Mpondo south of the Mzimkulu and captured a number of children as 'apprentices'. The Mpondo king, Faku, appealed to the Cape for protection from these former British subjects. Humanitarians in Britain and the Cape Colony raised cries of Boer 'slavery' and called upon their government to act. Secondly, if 'surplus' Africans were now pushed south of the Mzimkulu, the resultant overcrowding of the southern Nguni might shatter the fragile peace of the Cape's eastern frontier. Finally, Dutch and American ships calling at Durban raised British fears that Natal might fall into rival European hands. This would threaten the security of British Indian Ocean shipping.

In 1842 a small British force seized Durban. Though besieged by Pretorius's commandos, British reinforcements sent by sea relieved the town. By August 1843 the Pietermaritzburg volksraad had been forced to accept British annexation. Denied their freedom from British control, the Voortrekkers took to their wagons once more. Over the next few years Pretorius and most of the Voortrekkers of Natal left their former 'republic' and trekked back onto the highveld. Many of them joined the Voortrekker communities already settled north of the Vaal.

Voortrekkers north of the Vaal, 1838–52

The Voortrekkers north of the Vaal were generally those who most wanted complete independence from British control. Their principal leader was Hendrik Potgieter who had led them to victory over the Ndebele in 1837. Potgieter claimed the whole of the former Ndebele kingdom, by right of conquest. According to him this covered all territory between the Vaal in the south, the Limpopo in the north, the Drakensberg in the east and the Kalahari in the west. Though some of this vast territory had been temporarily and partly depopulated by Ndebele raids, most of it remained in the hands of its original African inhabitants. With them the Voortrekkers would have to come to terms.

Ohrigstad and Lydenburg Potgieter realised that independence from British control could not be achieved without an independent trading outlet between the highveld and the sea. With this in mind he sought to establish a settlement in the eastern Transvaal. In 1844 he went to Delagoa Bay and got Portuguese and Dutch traders to agree to supply

him with ammunition and other goods in exchange for ivory and animal skins. He then moved a number of his supporters from Potchefstroom to Ohrigstad on the eastern slopes of the northern Drakensberg. They were soon joined by others from Natal.

It was good hunting country, but the region was infested with malaria and tsetse fly. The Tsonga, Pedi and Swazi found the settlement an unwelcome intrusion. The Voortrekkers were divided among themselves and lacked the power to assert their control over their African neighbours. By 1848 elephant hunting had declined and Potgieter led half the Ohrigstad Boers to the Soutpansberg in the northern Transvaal. Those that remained came to terms with the Pedi and moved south to the healthier site of Lydenburg.

Soutpansberg Potgieter's Soutpansberg 'republic' was little more than a hunting settlement. Local Venda huntsmen were employed to hunt ivory. This was sent on the heads of African porters to Delagoa Bay or southwards on the wagons of travelling traders to Natal or Cape Colony. As they were to discover in due course the Voortrekker settlement in the Soutpansberg was dependent on the goodwill of the local Venda population (see following chapter, p 74).

Potchefstroom The strongest Voortrekker 'republic' north of the Vaal was centred around Potchefstroom. The Voortrekkers took advantage of the Ndebele's depopulated zone between the Vaal and the Marico. Here they were able to establish themselves before the region's former African communities had time to re-emerge and re-organise. In 1848 the Potchefstroom Boers were strengthened by the arrival of Pretorius with a party of Voortrekkers from Natal.

The Sand River Convention, 1852 Though the British intervened south of the Vaal between 1848 and 1854 (see below, pp 67–70), the Transvaalers managed to retain their independence. This was officially recognised by the British in 1852. By the Sand River Convention of January 1852 the British agreed to recognise the independence of the Voortrekker 'republics' north of the Vaal. This gave them freedom to behave how they liked towards their African subjects and neighbours without fear of British intervention, provided they did not practise slavery. The British agreed to sell them arms and ammunition but promised not to supply these to Africans north of the Vaal. The Boers rightly feared that if Africans were free to buy guns and gunpowder they would be able to challenge Boer military superiority.

The 'South African Republic' and the Tswana The Potchefstroom Boers now called themselves the 'South African Republic'. They celebrated their freedom from British authority by trying to bring the Tswana more thoroughly under their control. They intended that all Africans within their republic should provide compulsory labour services for the Boers on demand. When the Tswana resisted, the Boers blamed British missionaries and traders based at Kuruman whom they accused of supplying them with guns. In 1852 a Boer commando attacked the Kwena for harbouring fugitives from their forced labour policies. They also sacked the nearby Kolobeng home of the LMS missionary, David Livingstone. The commando then turned on the Rolong who had recently resettled south of the Molopo and had refused to support the Boers against the Kwena. In both of these raids the Boers captured large numbers of cattle and many child 'apprentices'.

The LMS missionaries protested vigorously against the raids, demanding the return of the captured children and accusing the Boers of practising slavery. They begged the British Government to intervene and to lift the ban on arms sales to Africans north of the Vaal so that they could protect themselves. But the British Government, as we shall see, was intent on withdrawing from all involvement north of the Orange. They ignored the missionaries' protests and the Boers retained their independence.

Boers, British and Sotho, 1836–54

South of the Vaal was a very different and more complex situation. To the west were the Griqua of Adam Kok III. Trekboers had been moving into this region and buying or renting Griqua land since the 1820s. North of the Vet River a group of Voortrekkers formed the Winburg republic. In the east the main African states were the Tlokwa, Rolong, Taung and Sotho. Early Voortrekkers had stopped near the Rolong settlement of Thaba 'Nchu. But for most of them this was only a temporary halt before moving on to Winburg, Natal or north of the Vaal. In the south-east, however, Voortrekkers were settling and building permanent houses between the Caledon and the Orange without the permission of Moshoeshoe.

The Napier treaties In 1843 the Cape Governor, Napier, made a treaty of friendship with Moshoeshoe's Sotho and Adam Kok's Griqua. It was part of a general policy of making treaties with the colony's African neighbours. The aim was to get the help of independent African rulers in maintaining peace along the colony's borders. In return the chiefs understood that the colony would stop British subjects, the Boers, from raiding their territory. A British Resident, Henry Warden, was placed at Bloemfontein. He was supposed to settle land disputes in the region.

Meanwhile Moshoeshoe's kingdom was growing in strength. The Sotho were buying horses and guns, and more and more people were being drawn into the expanding kingdom. Sekonyela's Tlokwa and Moroka's Rolong, on the other hand, were both determined to remain independent of Sotho control. They were supported by Warden who saw the powerful Sotho kingdom as a danger to the stability of the region. Perhaps he feared that an all-powerful Moshoeshoe would expel all whites from north of the Orange and threaten the security of the colony itself. But by siding with one side against another, Warden only encouraged conflict. During the 1840s there were frequent raids and counter-raids as Tlokwa, Rolong and Voortrekkers all tried to remain independent of Sotho control. Warden and the 'treaty system' was clearly ineffective in maintaining peace north of the Orange.

British annexation: the Orange River Sovereignty, 1848 In 1848 the new Cape Governor, Sir Harry Smith, annexed the whole region between the Orange and Vaal rivers and named it the 'Orange River Sovereignty'. Smith believed that the way to solve problems beyond the Cape's frontiers was to bring those regions under full British control. This would bring peace to the region, control the Voortrekkers and provide greater security for white settlement in the colony.

Smith, however, had failed to properly consult the Voortrekkers. To those, like Pretorius, who had recently left Natal, Smith's annexation was yet another British challenge to Boer independence. Pretorius led a commando south of the Vaal, occupied Bloemfontein and expelled Warden. Smith reacted promptly. He sent a British army north and defeated Pretorius at Boomplaats.

The Warden Line, 1849 Warden was then ordered to conduct a thorough survey and draw a permanent boundary line for the Sotho kingdom. This, it was hoped, would stop further Sotho expansion, end

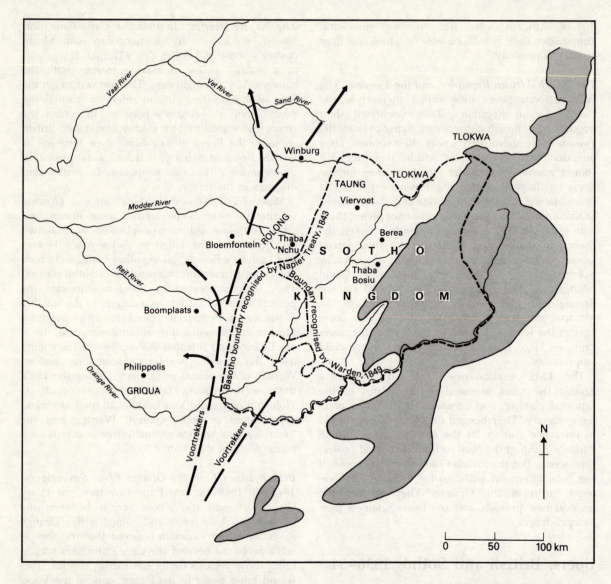

7.3 The Sotho, the Boers and the British, 1843–54

conflict between Sotho, Tlokwa and Rolong and provide whites with secure titles to their land claims.

The 'Warden Line', drawn up in 1849, left the Sotho kingdom with a great deal less land than had been recognised by the Napier Treaty of 1843. In the south Sotho land was given to the Boers. West of the Caledon Warden recognised the independence of Rolong as well as Tlokwa. It was a deliberate attempt to weaken the Sotho kingdom. Moshoeshoe, anxious to avoid war with the British, reluctantly agreed to the Warden Line. But Sotho already living beyond the line refused to move back within the new boundary. Instead of solving land problems, the Warden Line made matters worse. The Sotho felt

betrayed by the British. Though Moshoeshoe tried to keep the peace, raids continued between Sotho, Rolong and Tlokwa, and Boers protested that they were no longer safe upon their farms.

The First Sotho/British War, 1851 In 1851 Warden decided to assert British authority. With 160 British troops and 800 Rolong he attacked the Taung who had been raiding Rolong cattle. The Taung were by then part of the Sotho kingdom and Moshoeshoe sent a huge army to their defence. At the battle of Kononyana (also known as Viervoet) Warden's army was defeated and forced to make a hurried retreat. Moshoeshoe then persuaded local Boers not to support the British, promising that in future Boers and Sotho would live together in peace. Having thus cut off Warden from further white support within the Sovereignty, Moshoeshoe was temporarily safe from another British attack. But he recognised that in due course the British could call upon a huge army from the Cape Colony. So Moshoeshoe appealed for the support of Pretorius and the Boers north of the Vaal.

British withdrawal from the highveld

The British by this time had realised that Smith's policy of annexing territory beyond the Cape Colony had brought more trouble and expense than it was worth. So two special commissioners, Hogge and Owen, were sent north to work out the best way of withdrawing British authority from the highveld. By the time they arrived Pretorius was threatening to invade the Sovereignty in support of Moshoeshoe. Hogge and Owen persuaded Pretorius not to invade by promising British recognition of Boer independence north of the Vaal. This agreement, signed in January 1852, became known as the *Sand River Convention* (see above p 66).

British withdrawal from the southern highveld, however, was not so easily managed without endangering the security of white settlement and trade in the region. Moshoeshoe's unchallenged Sotho power seemed to threaten that security. During 1852

Moshoeshoe continued to expand his kingdom at the expense of Tlokwa, Rolong and Boers.

The Second Sotho/British War, 1852

Towards the end of 1852 the new Cape Governor, Cathcart, finally arrived in the Sovereignty with a large British army. He was determined to humble the Sotho before arranging a British withdrawal. He demanded a fine of 10 000 cattle to be paid within three days. Moshoeshoe paid 3 500 and asked for more time to collect the rest. But Cathcart would not wait and marched on Thaba Bosiu. The Sotho army by this time, however, was well-equipped with guns and horses. At the battle of Berea in December 1852 the Sotho defeated part of Cathcart's army and forced the rest to halt. It looked as though it was going to be a prolonged war, which neither side wanted. Moshoeshoe wisely saved the situation by sending Cathcart a carefully-worded letter offering peace if the British would withdraw. It was an honourable settlement for both sides. The British army withdrew, still largely undefeated; and the Sotho remained 'unhumbled'.

The Bloemfontein Convention, 1854

During 1853 the Sotho finally defeated and absorbed the Tlokwa. Peace then returned to the southern highveld, cattle raiding stopped and the Sotho once again sold grain to white settlers and traders. In 1854 British auth-

7.3 A contemporary engraving showing Boer commandos attacking the Basotho mission station of Beersheba.

ority was formally withdrawn from the Sovereignty. At the *Bloemfontein Convention* government was handed over to the Boers who renamed it the *Orange Free State*. The Boers had regained their independence from the British, but the final boundary between Sotho and Boers remained unsettled.

The results and significance of the Boer Trek

The main result of the Boer Trek of the late 1830s was the rapid expansion of white settlement into the heart of the Southern African interior. Until then white contact in the region had been through individual missionaries and hunter-traders. These had recognised African political authority and were often dependent on the protection of African rulers. The Boer Trek, on the other hand, had brought a new lot of whites who had come to stay, claiming land and political authority for themselves.

British colonial authority too was drawn further into the interior, largely in response to the activities of the Voortrekkers. In Natal they stayed to create a second British colony of white settlement while on the southern highveld their stay was only temporary (1848–54). Nevertheless, as the major power in the sub-continent Britain reserved the right to intervene again in the interior should it become economically worthwhile – as it did in the 1870s (see Chapter 9).

Africans of the highveld and south-eastern interior were permanently affected as a result of the Boer Trek. Two major African kingdoms, Zulu and Ndebele, were severely defeated though not destroyed. The Ndebele went north to rebuild a kingdom that dominated the Zimbabwe plateau for half a century while the Zulu recovered and retained their independence until the 1880s. Other African communities were permanently affected by the presence of the Boer republics. The Voortrekkers recognised no African political or property rights within their republics. In the surrounding territories where Africans were not strong enough to resist they extracted tribute and labour services or 'apprentices'. As a result of Voortrekker activities acquisition of firearms became a major priority for African kingdoms of the interior.

From the viewpoint of the Afrikaner nationalist the Boer Trek was a great achievement. The Voortrekkers had originally set off in search of new land and freedom from British control. By the Sand River and Bloemfontein Conventions of 1852 and 1854 they had apparently achieved both those aims. Furthermore, they had shown their military superiority by their victories over the Zulu and Ndebele.

Afrikaner nationalists look back on the 'Great Trek' as their founding inspiration. In it they can celebrate both freedom from British control and triumph of white over black.

In reality the achievements of the Boer Trek were not so simple or so clear as modern Afrikaner nationalists would have us believe. For a start, there was not *one* 'Great Trek', but several disunited treks, and they did not move into new and empty land. The direction of the treks and the positioning of their 'republics' were in fact determined largely by patterns of African settlement and resistance. Both in Natal and on the highveld the main Boer settlements were in areas temporarily depopulated by the Mfecane/Difaqane wars. Expansion beyond these regions was slow and depended on varying degrees of African co-operation or resistance. Nor were the Voortrekkers ever totally independent of some degree of British control. The Sand River and Bloemfontein Conventions granted them political independence. But they remained economically dependent on travelling traders from the British colonies of the Cape and Natal. From them they got the guns and ammunition so essential to their continued existence as the dominant military powers of the interior.

Document 7.1 *On 15 December 1852 Moshoeshoe, King of the Basotho, met with Cathcart, British Governor of Cape Colony, on the banks of the Caledon River, with Casalis, missionary, acting as Moshoeshoe's interpreter. The following is a record of the meeting*:

Governor – I am glad to see you and to make your acquaintance.

Moshesh – I am glad to see the Governor, as since his arrival in this country I have been expecting a visit from him.

Governor – I will not now talk much, but wish to know whether you received my message yesterday, in which I made the demand of cattle and horses. I have nothing to alter in that letter.

Moshesh – I received the letter, but do not know where I shall get the cattle from. Am I to understand that the ten thousand head demanded are a fine imposed for the thefts committed by my people, in addition to the cattle stolen?

Governor – I demand but ten thousand head, though your people have stolen many more, and consider this a just award, which must be paid in three days.

Moshesh – The time is short, and the cattle

many. Will you not allow me six days to collect them?

Governor – You had time given you when Major Hogge and Mr Owen made the first demand, and then promised to comply with it, but did not.

Moshesh – But I was not quite idle. Do not the papers in the Commissioners' hands show that I collected them?

Governor – They do, but not half of the number demanded.

Moshesh – That is true; but I have not now control enough over my people to induce them to comply with the demand, however anxious I may be to do so.

Governor – If you are not able to collect them, I must go and do it; and if any resistance be made it will then be war, and I shall not be satisfied with ten thousand head, but shall take all I can.

Moshesh – Do not talk of war, for, however anxious I may be to avoid it, you know that a dog when beaten will show his teeth.

Governor – It will therefore be better that you should give up the cattle than that I should go for them.

Moshesh – I wish for peace; but have the same difficulty with my people that you have in the colony. Your prisons are never empty, and I have thieves among my people.

Governor – I would then recommend you to catch the thieves, and bring them to me, and I will hang them.

Moshesh – I do not wish you to hang them, but to talk to them and give them advice. If you hang them they cannot talk.

Governor – If I hang them they cannot steal, and I am not going to talk any more. I have said that if you do not give up the cattle in three days I must come and take them.

(Adapted from *Basutoland Records*, 1883, Reprint Cape Town 1964, Vol I, pp. 618–9)

Exercises

A. Think, discuss, understand and write

1 Why did the Voortrekkers settle where they did? To what extent if any were their choices shaped by African attitudes and policies towards them?
2 Describe the events leading to the establishment of the Voortrekker republic of Natalia. How and why did it end?

3 Describe the events leading to the establishment of Voortrekker settlement north and south of the Vaal before 1852. What factors helped the Voortrekkers establish themselves on the highveld?
4 Why did the British intervene north of the Orange in 1848? Why did they conflict with the Sotho, and why did they withdraw in 1854?
5 What were the original aims of the Voortrekkers? To what extent were these aims achieved?
6 Describe and account for the successes and failures of African resistance to the Voortrekkers between 1836 and 1854. (List the major areas of conflict and assess the success and failure or each).
7 Assess the results and significance of the 'Great Trek' between 1836 and 1854.

B. Imaginative writing

Imagine that the year is 1835 and you are one of the following: Dingane, Moshoeshoe or Mzilikazi. You have heard that Boers of the eastern Cape Colony are planning a huge trek into the interior. Write a letter of protest to the Cape Governor seeking to persuade him to prevent it. Choose your arguments carefully: your aim is to persuade the British Governor to control his subjects and prevent the Boers from leaving the colony. (This is a difficult task and you may find it useful to have group or class discussion first).

Now imagine you are the Cape Governor. Write your reply.

C. Mapwork, group-work and class discussion

Read your answer to question 6 above. Now draw a map to illustrate these events, using colour, arrows and dates where appropriate. Discuss the different military tactics used. Could African resistance have been more effective? If so, how?

Document study Read Document 7.1 and discuss the answers to the following questions:

1 What are the treaties referred to by Moshoeshoe? Why might they lead Moshoeshoe to expect that the Governor of Cape Colony would visit him when he was in the region?
2 To what does Moshoeshoe refer when he says he does not have enough control over his people? Was this to become more or less of a problem in the years ahead?
3 Which of the two adopts the more aggressive attitude, Moshoeshoe or Cathcart? Why do you think he took this attitude?
4 What happened in the week following this meeting?
5 The colonial official who recorded these minutes commented that Moshoeshoe's 'sincerity was doubtful'. Do you agree? From the evidence of this meeting assess Moshoeshoe's sincerity.

CHAPTER 8

From Boer Trek to mineral revolution: Southern Africa before 1870

The British colony of Natal, 1843–70

Following British annexation of Natal most of the Voortrekkers left the region and returned to the highveld where they hoped to escape from British control. The British, however, were just as determined to create a colony of white settlement. But first they had to clear the land of its African occupants. 800 000 hectares of land was thus set aside as 'reserves' for the colony's African population of more than 100 000. This left the remaining eighty-five per cent of the land for a few thousand white settlers.

African administration Theophilus Shepstone, the son of a Wesleyan missionary, was put in charge of 'Native Affairs'. He organised the removal of Africans into their 'reserves'. At first he met with little open opposition. Africans of the region were probably anxious to settle down and cultivate the land and were not yet ready to test the strength of the new white authority. In any case, white settlement was slow to take effect and many were able to remain on 'white-owned' land. Within the 'reserves' Shepstone used African chiefs and headmen as unpaid local administrators. Where traditional chiefs were not available or were unco-operative, Shepstone made his own appointments. In doing so he considered himself a sort of 'paramount chief' over all the Africans of Natal. A tax, known as a 'hut-tax', was charged on every African house. This raised £10 000 a year for the Natal government. It was supposed to pay for administration and development within the reserves. In fact most of it went to central government.

Land and labour During 1849–51 five thousand British immigrants were brought in, but most of them refused to settle on the land and preferred to work as artisans or traders in the towns. Most of the 'white' land in Natal was therefore bought up by wealthy merchants who had no intention of farming it. As the 'reserves' became overcrowded more and more Africans moved onto this land and paid rent to the 'absentee landlords' who owned it. Between this and the 'reserves' Africans had enough land to live on and most of them refused to work for white farmers. As a result the few white settlers who tried cotton and sheep farming constantly complained of the shortage of cheap black labour. In the 1860s the government imported six thousand contract labourers from India to work the sugar plantations of the coastal region. A quarter of these were women. At the end of their 5–10 year contracts most of the Indian immigrants chose to stay in Natal. Many remained in the servant class but some moved into shopkeeping and other self-employment in the towns.

By 1870 the black population of Natal had risen to 250 000, partly due to natural increase and partly due to immigration as a result of further warfare in Zululand. They still produced most of their own food and only worked for wages when they wanted to buy something specific like a gun for hunting. Nearly all the land, however, was owned by whites whose population by 1870 had risen to 18 000, of whom more than half lived in the towns.

The Zulu kingdom in the reign of Mpande (1840–72)

Historians have usually looked upon the reign of Mpande as an uneventful period of peace and recovery. Mpande is often portrayed as a lazy ruler, not interested in military exploits or expanding his kingdom. This picture is not entirely true, but it perhaps stems from the fact that Mpande had no major clashes with whites.

Mpande's reign was indeed a period of recovery from the wars of 1838–40, but it certainly was not entirely peaceful or uneventful. Mpande retained the military system of his brothers though he did not keep the men in regimental service for over-long periods of time. They were thus freer to marry and set up their own homesteads. Unlike his brothers Mpande himself married and produced a number of sons and potential heirs.

When the British took over Natal in 1843 they recognised Mpande as an independent ruler. Nevertheless, Mpande always remained anxious about the potential power of his southern neighbours. He therefore followed Dingane's final policy of trying to expand towards the north. In 1842 he attacked a number of minor chiefdoms forcing some to flee as refugees into Natal, among them a chief called Langalibalele (see below, Chapter 10, pp 93–95).

Mpande's long-term aim was to take over Swaziland, but on his first raid in 1847 the Swazi retreated to the mountains with their cattle. In 1851 Mpande's army raided the Pedi and this was followed the next

8.1 A Portrait of Mpande drawn by a European artist.

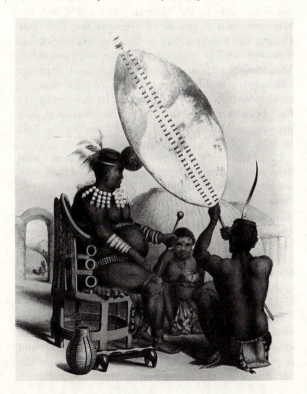

year by a major invasion of Swaziland. The Swazi were badly defeated and huge numbers of cattle were captured. But Mpande was unable to follow up his victory. His sons Cetshwayo and Mbulazi had risen to prominence during the Swazi war. For the next four years the Zulu kingdom was split by the rivalry of the two brothers struggling for position as Mpande's heir. The conflict culminated in the battle of Ndondakusaka in 1856 from which Cetshwayo and his Usuthu faction emerged victorious. Cetshwayo was henceforth recognised as Mpande's heir and succeeded as king on Mpande's death in 1872.

By any measures Mpande's was a successful reign. He had ruled longer than any previous Zulu king. He had expanded his kingdom to the north and scored a major victory over the Swazi. He left to his son a powerful and united kingdom which had recovered from the ravages of Dingane's unsuccessful wars. On Mpande's death the Zulu kingdom was the most feared in Southern Africa.

The Boer republics of the Transvaal, 1852–70

By the mid-1850s M. W. Pretorius had succeeded his father as head of the main Boer settlement of Potchefstroom which now called itself the 'South African Republic'. Other Boer 'republics' were at Lydenburg in the east and Soutpansberg in the north. There were attempts at political union but great personal rivalry between the leaders of the three groups led to armed conflict in 1858. Though they were united under the name 'South African Republic' in 1860, civil war continued until 1864 as rival factions struggled for control. Pretorius meanwhile had become president of the Orange Free State (1859–64), but he returned to the Transvaal to become its president in 1864. His military commander was Paul Kruger.

Land and labour policies The Afrikaners of the South African Republic (Transvaal) remained essentially trekboers. They owned huge stretches of land and lived off their livestock and hunting. Landdrosts controlled the registration of land claims and they and other government officials accumulated large numbers of farms. Field-cornets were locally elected officials whose main job was to see that each white farmer had enough black labour.

The Voortrekkers had brought to the Transvaal the same attitude towards Africans as they had tried to impose in Natal. Africans were not allowed to own guns or horses and had to carry a pass signed by a government official or employer. No more than five African families were allowed to live on each

8.2 A portrait of M. W. Pretorius.

farm. These were 'labour tenants' who were to provide the owners with a regular source of labour. They were allowed to own some livestock and grow their own food but they had to provide labour for the landowner by way of rent. All other Africans were to be pushed into small reserves or 'locations'. These were to pay taxes in cattle and to provide labour when needed. Tax collections and demands for labour were often more like raids conducted by the field-cornets.

To avoid these impositions large numbers of Africans attached themselves to neighbouring chiefs who attempted to remain independent from Boer control. The most successful African attempts to retain independence were by the Venda in the north and the Pedi in the east.

The Venda of the Soutpansberg

The ancient Venda chiefdoms formed the principal population of the Soutpansberg region. But they lacked unity and so offered little opposition to the Voortrekkers when they first arrived in the 1840s. The Venda worked as huntsmen for the Boers in exchange for guns and ammunition. But the whites of the Soutpansberg were particularly disorderly and clashes frequently occurred between them and the local Venda.

In an attempt to bring more direct control over the local African population the Boer leader, S. Schoeman, appointed a Portuguese trader, Albasini, as 'superintendant of native trives'. But Albasini only made matters worse. He was a slave-trader who captured Tsonga refugees from the Gaza empire and sold them to the Portuguese at Delagoa Bay. He built up a large African army and used it to raid Venda villages.

In the late 1860s the Venda and northern Sotho rose in rebellion. They burnt the village of Schoemansdal and drove out the whites from the whole of the Soutpansberg region. By 1867 there were no white settlers left between the Olifants and the Limpopo.

The rise of the Pedi

Following the early Ndebele raid of 1821–2 the Pedi withdrew to the Leolu mountains between the Crocodile and Steelpoort rivers. They had lost large herds of cattle to the Ndebele. The 1830s and 40s, however, was a period of recovery for the Pedi. Placing his headquarters in the mountains Sekwati followed similar principles to the southern king, Moshoeshoe. He used *mafisa* cattle and marriage alliances to build up and turn a confederation of chiefdoms into the Pedi kingdom. In due course the Pedi became a powerful rival to the Swazi and their growing wealth in cattle attracted a raid by the Zulu in 1851.

Like Moshoeshoe's Sotho, the Pedi too soon learnt the value of guns as defensive weapons of mountain warfare. In the 1850s and 60s increasing numbers of Pedi were sent to the Cape Colony to work for wages with which to buy guns and ammunition. This was prohibited by the whites of the Transvaal so they travelled at night in groups of several hundred to protect themselves from attacks by other blacks as well as whites. Passing through Moshoeshoe's Sotho kingdom they took care to pay him tribute on the way.

In 1861 Sekwati was succeeded by his son Sekhukhuni who continued to strengthen the Pedi kingdom. Under his rule it became an important and popular attraction for Africans wanting to escape the harsh labour laws of the South African Republic.

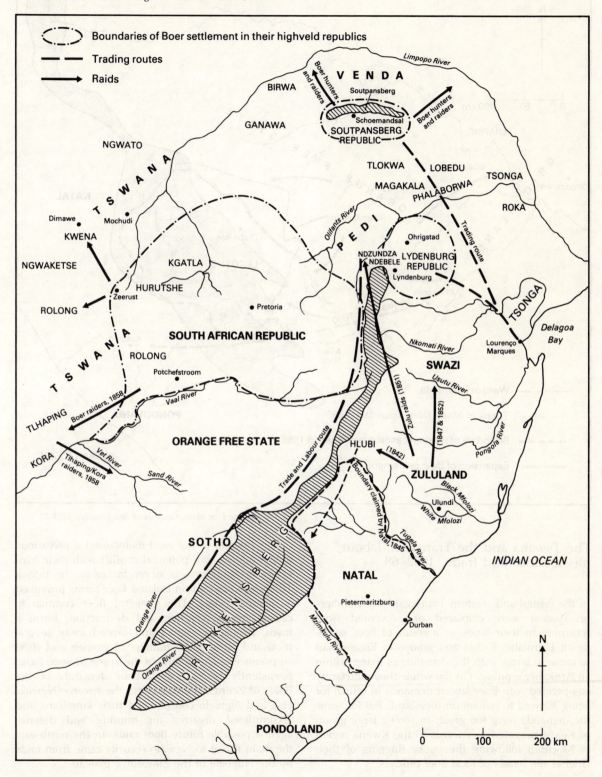

Boundaries of Boer settlement in their highveld republics

Trading routes

Raids

Limpopo River

VENDA

BIRWA

Boer hunters and raiders

Soutpansberg

Schoemandsal

SOUTPANSBERG REPUBLIC

Boer hunters and raiders

GANAWA

NGWATO

TLOKWA

LOBEDU

TSONGA

MAGAKALA

PHALABORWA

ROKA

Trading route

Olifants River

PEDI

Ohrigstad

NDZUNDZA NDEBELE

LYDENBURG REPUBLIC

Lyndenburg

T S W A N A

Dimawe

Mochudi

KWENA

KGATLA

NGWAKETSE

HURUTSHE

Zeerust

ROLONG

Pretoria

SOUTH AFRICAN REPUBLIC

Nkomati River

SWAZI

Usutu River

TSONGA

Delagoa Bay

Lourenço Marques

T S W A N A

ROLONG

Potchefstroom

Vaal River

Boer raiders, 1858

TLHAPING

KORA

Tlhaping/Kora raiders, 1858

Vet River

Sand River

ORANGE FREE STATE

Trade and Labour route

Boundary claimed by Natal, 1845

HLUBI

(1842)

Zulu raids (1851)

(1847 & 1852)

Pongola River

ZULULAND

Black Mfolozi

Ulundi

White Mfolozi

SOTHO

D R A K E N S B E R G

Orange River

NATAL

Pietermaritzburg

Mzimkulu River

Tugela River

Durban

INDIAN OCEAN

N

Orange River

PONDOLAND

0   100   200 km

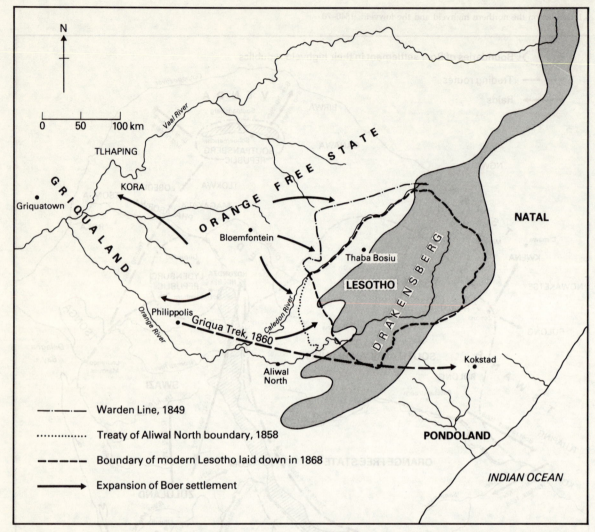

Map legend:

— - — Warden Line, 1849

.... Treaty of Aliwal North boundary, 1858

- - - - Boundary of modern Lesotho laid down in 1868

⟶ Expansion of Boer settlement

The Tswana and the Transvaal: labour, missionaries and trade, 1852–68

In the central and western Transvaal large numbers of Tswana were displaced or prevented from returning to their lands as a result of Boer settlement. Hurutshe, Kgatla and groups of Rolong had to come to terms with the demands of living within an Afrikaner republic. On the whole they reluctantly co-operated with Boer labour demands in return for being allowed to remain on their land. But for some the demands were too great. In 1869 a large group of Kgatla migrated westwards to the Kwena region of Mochudi following the public flogging of their chief at the hands of local Boer officials.

The Tswana to the west maintained a precarious independence, but potential conflict with their Afrikaner neighbours was never far away. In 1858 a Tlhaping/Kora raid on isolated Boer farms provoked a major reprisal. The vengeful Boer commando caused much slaughter and destruction, burnt a town, beheaded a chief and carried away several thousand cattle and a number of women and child 'apprentices'. The Rolong of the upper Molopo basin persistently resisted the labour demands of the Boers of Zeerust. Further north the Kwena, Ngwaketse and Ngwato consolidated their kingdoms and accumulated firearms for hunting and defence against possible future Boer raids. In the north-east the main threat to Ngwato security came from raids by the Ndebele of the Zimbabwe plateau.

The British LMS and Wesleyan missionaries made a few important converts among the Tswana chiefs, such as Molema of the Rolong, Sechele of the Kwena and Khama of the Ngwato. The missionaries welcomed British traders from the Cape and helped promote trade along the northern route through the western Tswana kingdoms. Despite the ban on the gun-trade imposed by the Sand River Convention, Cape traders evaded the law and supplied the Tswana with guns in exchange for ivory and ostrich feathers.

There is no doubt that the hunting trade and purchase of guns helped strengthen the ability of the western Tswana kingdoms to resist further Boer encroachment from the east. It was the constant ambition of the Transvaal Boers to cut this northern trade route. Meanwhile the Tswana came to see the British missionaries and traders as their allies against the Boers.

The Griqua and the Orange Free State

Trekboers from the Cape had been moving into Griqua territory between the Vaal and Orange since the 1820s. Following the Boer Trek more and more Boers began renting and buying farms from the Griqua of Philipolis. The Griqua chief, Adam Kok III, tried to prevent his people from selling their land. He feared he would soon become a ruler of a landless state. But the 1850s was a period of drought and cattle disease and many Griqua defied his ban and sold out to Free State Boers. Kok therefore decided to sell up all Griqua titles and move elsewhere while his people still had land to sell. Thus in 1860 Kok's entire Griqua community packed up their possessions and trekked eastwards across the Caledon and the Drakensberg. After a two-year trek they eventually settled on the eastern slopes of the Drakensberg in an underpopulated territory inland from the Mpondo. There they founded the town of Kokstad and the state of Griqualand East. Meanwhile the Griqua of Griquatown still laid claim to land south of the Vaal as well as north of it. Their chief, Waterboer, hired a legal agent from the Cape, David Arnot, to protect their interests against Free State claims.

The Orange Free State and Sotho, 1854–70

The British withdrawal from the southern highveld in 1854 had left the boundary between the Boer republic and the Sotho kingdom still unsettled. The Sotho assumed that British withdrawal meant the

end of the Warden Line and a return to the much more favourable boundary of the Napier Treaty of 1843. By the mid-1850s Moshoeshoe in practice controlled most of the territory listed in the Napier Treaty and a Sotho population of 100 000. The Boers on the other hand had a population of only 12 000. But they were determined not to give up a single hectare of the Sotho land they had gained during the period of British rule. Cattle-raiding between the two continued and war became inevitable.

The First Free State/Sotho War, 1858 In 1858 a Free State commando attacked Thaba Bosiu, but they were badly beaten and driven back. The Sotho retaliated by raiding unprotected Boer farms. Unable to defeat the Sotho, the Boer president, Boshof, appealed to the Cape Governor to help them make peace with Moshoeshoe. At the treaty of Aliwal North Moshoeshoe agreed to accept the Warden Line in the north and a compromise boundary in the south.

After 1858 the white settlers felt that their position was more secure. The white population of the Free State increased with more immigration from the Cape Colony. Sheep farming expanded and wool became an export. At the same time restrictions on the sale of guns to Africans enabled the Boers to build up their stocks of modern guns faster than the Sotho.

As the position of the Boers in the Free State strengthened, the personal strength of the ageing Moshoeshoe declined. He had lost his valuable French missionary adviser, Casalis, who had retired from Lesotho in 1854. He now also had difficulty controlling the independent actions of his sons and other subordinate chiefs. Cattle-raids between Boer and Sotho continued.

The Second Free State/Sotho War, 1865–8 In 1864 the Boers elected a new president, J. H. Brand, a recent immigrant from the Cape Colony. He provided the Boers with vigorous new leadership and was determined to defeat the Sotho kingdom once and for all. In 1865 Brand launched an attack on Thaba Bosiu. This was driven back and the Boers settled down to besiege the mountain stronghold. As the war dragged on into 1866 the Boers turned to a 'scorched earth' policy, burning Sotho crops and villages and rounding up their livestock. Brand then managed to force separate treaties on Moshoeshoe's son Molapo in the north and the Phuthi chief Moorosi in the south. Both of these ceded land to the Free State.

Moshoeshoe, however, was determined not to surrender though he knew he could not win.

Desperately he appealed to the British for protection. Believing he would do better under the British than Boers, he offered up his kingdom for British annexation.

British annexation, 1868 The British Government hesitated, but the war was disrupting trade and the defeat of the Sotho would send destitute refugees pouring into Natal and the eastern Cape. In 1868, therefore, the Cape Governor, Wodehouse, was authorised to intervene. Wodehouse brought the war to an end by stopping the supply of arms to the Free State. He then annexed Lesotho as the British colony of 'Basutoland'. In 1870 Moshoeshoe died, the remnants of his former kingdom now secure.

Moshoeshoe's achievement

Moshoeshoe was undoubtably one of the most remarkable leaders that Southern Africa has produced. He led his people out of the chaos of the Difaqane and from its remnants built up one of the most powerful kingdoms of the region. He was both a man of peace and a master of warfare. He knew when to make peace with those more powerful than himself. He paid tribute to the Zulu and sent cattle to the Ndebele. He tried to avoid war with the Boers and always sought peace with the British whom he recognised as the strongest military power of the region.

8.3 Moshoeshoe and his counsellors in the 1860s.

Moshoeshoe also adapted to changes and learnt much from the French missionaries whom he had welcomed to his kingdom. He was a great military tactician. He modernised his regiments with guns and horses and made full use of the mountains for defence. Just as he knew when to seek peace, he also knew when to make war, crushing Sekonyela's Tlokwa when he most needed unity.

As an individual Moshoeshoe was a man of great dignity who inspired trust and respect in all who met him. But he was not always mild. He was noted for his fierce temper and dealt firmly with those Sotho who opposed him. Above all, Moshoeshoe was a realist. Though he finally surrendered his kingdom to the British, in doing so he saved the Sotho nation from complete annihilation.

The Xhosa and the Eastern Cape frontier, 1836–66

As we saw in Chapter 6, following the end of the sixth Cape/Xhosa war the annexed land between the Keiskama and the Kei (present-day Ciskei) was handed back to the Xhosa. During 1836–46 the Cape government relied on a system of treaties with Xhosa chiefs for keeping the peace along the colonial border. The system worked reasonably well until the drought of 1842. Then Sandile began to lose control over his people who were by then buying guns and raiding into the colony. Meanwhile in the eastern Cape colonists were urging the government to take firm action against the Xhosa and seize back the land of Ciskei. Colonists wanted extra land for wool farming which was prospering. In 1844 a new Governor, Maitland, sympathised with the colonists and built a line of forts along the Keiskama including one in Xhosa territory east of the river.

The Seventh Cape/Xhosa War, the 'War of the Axe', 1846–7 In 1846 a Xhosa was arrested in Fort Beaufort for stealing an axe. His friends rescued him by killing a 'coloured' policeman. Maitland used this incident as an excuse for declaring war on the Xhosa. However, his large, slow invasion column was quickly overrun by the Xhosa, who were now well-armed with guns. For a while the various Xhosa factions united. All colonial soldiers were driven west of the Keiskama and some guerilla groups took the war deep into the colony. During 1847 the colonists regathered their forces and pursued a 'scorched earth' policy, burning Xhosa crops and huts and capturing their cattle. By the end of the year Sandile was captured and the western Xhosa were forced into surrender.

'British Kaffraria' Sir Harry Smith, who became Cape Governor in December 1847, had formerly been the military commander who had invaded and annexed the Ciskei territory as 'Queen Adelaide Province' in 1835 (see above, pp 59–60). Now he annexed it again, this time as the separate British colony of 'British Kaffraria'. He humiliated the Xhosa chiefs by forcing them to kiss his feet and divided up the land into white farms and African reserves. Smith's heavy-handed action merely provoked further Xhosa resistance. The Xhosa turned in despair to witchcraft and religious prophecy. The war doctor, Mlanjeni, urged them to

attack the whites, prophesying that their bullets would turn to water. In 1850 Smith dismissed Sandile as chief and the Xhosa rose in rebellion.

The Eighth Cape/Xhosa War, 1850–3 The eighth war was mostly a war of guerilla tactics, and Smith was unable to achieve a decisive victory. In 1851 the Xhosa were joined by dissatisfied Khoikhoi and 'coloured' peasants from the Kat River Settlement (see above pp 57–9). Fighting on the other side were the Mfengu whom Governor D'Urban had settled on former Xhosa territory between the Keiskama and the Fish in 1835. The Xhosa considered the Mfengu

8.3 The Xhosa and the eastern Cape frontier, 1836–66

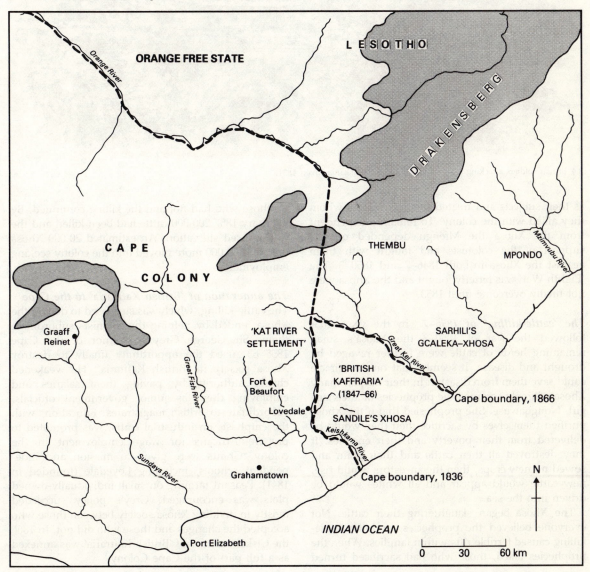

8.4 British soldiers attacking a Xhosa village on the Keiskama River, 1851.

as their subjects and treated them as traitors whom they allied with the colony. To remain independent from the Xhosa the Mfengu depended on the support of the colonists and fought with them against the Xhosa in both 1846–7 and 1850–3. The 'Eighth War' was bitterly fought and the Xhosa were not finally overcome until 1853.

The 'cattle-killing' of 1856–7 In the years that followed the war of 1850–3 the Xhosa's small remaining herds of cattle were further ravaged by drought and disease. It seemed that only a miracle could save them from disaster. In their despair many Xhosa willingly accepted the prophecies of a teenage girl, Nongqawuse. She prophesied that if the Xhosa purified themselves by sacrifice then they would be delivered from their poverty and their enemies. If they destroyed all their cattle and their grain and sowed no new crops, then the ancestors would rise, new cattle would appear and all whites would be driven into the sea.

The Xhosa began slaughtering their cattle. Not everyone believed the prophecies, and the cattle-killing caused terrible rifts within families. When the prophecies failed, those who had sacrificed turned on those who had not and the killing continued. By February 1857 200 000 cattle had been killed and the Xhosa faced starvation. An estimated 20 000 Xhosa died and 30 000 more moved into the colony seeking employment.

The annexation of 'British Kaffraria' to the Cape
The cattle-killing, which was supposed to deliver the Xhosa, ended by helping the colonists subordinate them. Sir George Grey, Governor of the Cape 1855–63, used the opportunity finally to destroy Xhosa society in 'British Kaffraria'. He weakened chiefly authority by paying them salaries and employing them as junior government officials, subordinate to British magistrates. Education, with the emphasis on industrial crafts, was promoted to prepare Africans for wage employment in the colony. Grants were given to mission and independent schools, including Lovedale (founded in 1841). Peasant farming on small individually-owned plots was encouraged. Grey's policy succeeded mostly in dividing Xhosa society between those who accepted the changes and those who did not. In 1866 the Ciskei territory of 'British Kaffraria' was annexed as a full part of the Cape Colony.

The Cape Colony

Government As the British Government withdrew from the highveld in the early 1850s they prepared to grant a greater level of self-government to the colonists of the Cape. In 1853 the Cape was granted *representative government*. This meant there was an elected House of Assembly which proposed new laws, though the Governor and his council of advisers were still in full charge of the executive. Full *responsible government*, with Cabinet and Prime Minister chosen from the·elected House of Assembly, did not come until 1872.

The franchise As in Britain at the time the vote was restricted to men who owned property or were in regular employment. The colonists would have liked the franchise to have been further restricted to whites only. The British government, however, insisted on a non-racial franchise qualification. They felt that this would encourage 'coloureds' and blacks to earn money and buy property and so become loyal members of colonial society.

In order to vote in 1853 a man had to own property worth at least £25 and to have an income of £50 a year. This gave the vote to most whites but very few 'coloureds' or blacks. The latter, however, were at least in theory entitled to vote if they met the necessary qualification. In this respect the constitution of the Cape was very different from that of the Afrikaner republics where only white citizens had any political rights.

In due course increasing numbers of mission-educated 'coloureds' and blacks qualified to vote, especially in the newly annexed territories of the eastern Cape. When that happened, however, the whites of the colony sought to maintain their monopoly of power by imposing further restrictions on the franchise.

The economy During the 1850s the economy of the Cape was based mostly on exports of wool and wine to Europe. Nearly all manufactured goods were imported from industrial Britain. In the 1860s the world market for wool went into decline. As the merchants of Port Elizabeth and Cape Town looked round for other goods to export, they turned to the hunting trade. To stimulate this trade they exported to African hunters of the interior hundreds of cheap muzzle-loading guns that were being cast off by the modernising armies of Europe. Thus by the late 1860s ivory and ostrich feathers from the northern interior had become major exports of the Cape Colony.

Conclusion: Southern Africa on the eve of the mineral revolution

The economy In the late 1860s the majority of people in the kingdoms, colonies and republics of Southern Africa lived on a mixture of self-sufficient pastoralism, hunting and small-scale crop cultivation. Products of the hunt (skins, furs, ivory and ostrich feathers) were the main trading items of the interior. They were used to purchase guns, ammunition, wagons, clothing and other manufactured goods. Hunting was most important in the northern, eastern and western fringes·of the region where the more valuable products, ivory and ostrich feathers, were still available.

Commercial capitalist farming, that is the use of wage labour on privately-owned land to produce cash crops for sale, was not yet widespread. It was restricted largely to the white-owned wine and wheat farms of the south-western Cape and the sugar plantations of Natal. The sheep farms of the eastern Cape employed a fair amount of seasonal labour at the annual wool-shearing. On most white-owned farms Africans were able to keep livestock and grow their own food. They paid for the use of their land by performing low-paid or unpaid labour services for the white landowner. Where landowners were absentees, as in Natal, rent was paid in cash, livestock or crops.

Outside Cape Town the urban areas of Southern Africa were very small. There was thus no large urban market to stimulate commercial food production in the interior. Food for sale in the towns was mostly locally-produced by small-scale African peasant farmers. These included the Sotho of the Caledon valley, the Nguni of Natal and the former Mfecane refugees of the Wittebergen district of the north-eastern Cape. The latter were particularly important during the Free State/Sotho war of 1865–8 when Sotho food production was disrupted.

The balance of power Politically, in the interior, a certain balance between black and white had been established. The days of the rapid white expansion of the Boer Trek period were over. White settlement had been permanently established on the highveld and in Natal, but African kingdoms had now recovered from the ravages of the Mfecane/Difaqane. Furthermore, they emerged militarily stronger than before, now arming themselves with guns and more able to challenge any further white expansion into independent African territory. The domination of white settlement over the whole of modern South Africa was at this stage by no means certain or inevitable.

Further white expansion would require a major military effort such as only Britain could provide. Britain, however, had as yet no great economic or political motive to intervene in the interior. As we shall see in the following chapter, this situation was about to change.

Exercises

A. Think, discuss, understand and write

1 With reference to Natal and the Voortrekker republics north of the Vaal, discuss the similarities and differences between British and Afrikaner attitudes to Africans living within their republic or colony.

2 Compare and account for the successes and failures of the first three Zulu kings: Shaka, Dingane and Mpande.

3 Why did the Orange Free State go to war with the Sotho in 1858 and 1865? To what extent did they achieve their objectives?

4 With reference to Chapters 5, 7 and 8, describe the work and assess the achievement of Moshoeshoe of the Sotho.

5 Describe and explain Cape/Xhosa relations between 1836 and 1853. Why did the Xhosa kill their cattle in 1856-7 and what was the result of this action?

B. Imaginative writing

Imagine you are a Pedi in 1860. You have just arrived in the Cape Colony where you have been sent by your father to work for wages in order to buy a gun. Write a letter home to your father describing your journey through the Transvaal, down the Caledon valley and into the Cape Colony. Describe where you are in the Cape Colony, the job you have got, the conditions of work and how soon you hope to return. Assume that your father to whom you are writing has never been outside the Pedi kingdom so concentrate on those things which are different from life at home.

C. Group-work and class discussion

Project: a time-chart. Using the information in Chapters 4, 5, 6, 7 and 8, draw up a time-chart of Southern African history for the period 1800–1870. Divide the work and the time-chart into five sections : (1) Cape Colony, (2) Africans on the highveld, (3) Boers and British on the highveld, (4) Xhosa and the eastern Cape, and (5) Zulu, Swazi and Natal. Assemble the information onto one large sheet of paper with seventy horizontal lines, each representing one year (if necessary use more than one sheet). Divide the time-chart into five perpendicular columns, one for each of the five sections listed above.

A time-chart is a useful aid for understanding and for revision. Use it, *not* for memorising dates, but for getting the *chronology* right and *comparing* events in one region with those of another in the same period. Study your time-chart carefully, looking both down the individual columns and across the columns. Can you see any way in which the events of one region may have been influenced by those of another?

CHAPTER 9

The Southern Africa mineral revolution, Stage I, 1870–85

Gold and diamonds were found in certain parts of Southern Africa during the last third of the nineteenth century. Many people from all over Southern Africa, and from Europe, America and Australia rushed to the sites in order to find these valuable minerals. They hoped to become wealthy or to find work. The discovery and mining of minerals brought enormous social, economic and political changes to the region. These changes were so great that they are sometimes referred to as the Southern African 'mineral revolution'. The present chapter follows the story of the first stage of this revolution.

Gold at Tati

Valuable metals, such as gold and copper, had been mined by Africans for many centuries, especially in the Zimbabwe region north of the Limpopo. By the middle of the nineteenth century most of these early mines were no longer being used. But white colonists from the Cape, Natal and the Boer republics had heard of the abandoned mines and wondered if they might still contain some gold.

In 1867 a trader named Hartley went north of the Limpopo with a German geologist, Carl Mauch. When they returned south at the end of the year, Mauch declared that there was still gold to be found in the old African mines of the Tati river area and the Zimbabwe plateau (see Map 9.1). During the following year a number of white prospectors rushed north, and by mid-1868 there were about sixty of them camped at the Tati 'goldfields'. But they experienced the same problem as the African miners who had worked there before. The gold was buried deep in the rock and it was very difficult to crush the ore and extract the metal.

When white prospectors first arrived in 1868, Mzilikazi had refused to give them permission to search for gold on the Zimbabwe plateau. The Tati region, however, lay within the disputed territory between the powerful kingdoms of the Ngwato (Tswana) in the west and the Ndebele in the east. So white prospectors simply set up camp in the Tati valley and started digging for gold. Most of them paid some sort of rent or licence fee to both Ndebele and Ngwato kings. That year, however, the old founder of the Ndebele kingdom, Mzilikazi, died; and the Boer government of the Transvaal decided to take advantage of the situation. They tried to persuade both Ndebele and Ngwato governments to grant them the sole right to search for gold in the 'disputed territory' of the Tati goldfields. When that did not work, they tried proclaiming that the whole of the territory west of the Limpopo as far as Lake Ngami belonged to the Transvaal.

This worried the British traders and missionaries who lived at the Ngwato capital, Shoshong. They persuaded the Ngwato King, Macheng, to write to the British Governor at the Cape asking for a British treaty of friendship and 'protection'. They argued that this was the safest way to control the whites at Tati and to stop the Boers from taking over the region. But the British government feared the expense of becoming directly involved and preferred to order President Pretorius to withdraw his proclamation. Shortly afterwards a British company, the London and Limpopo Mining and Exploration Company, persuaded the new Ndebele King, Lobengula, to grant them a gold-mining concession for the Tati region. By the middle of 1870 this company had managed to persuade most of the white diggers in the Tati valley to sell them their claims and leave the area.

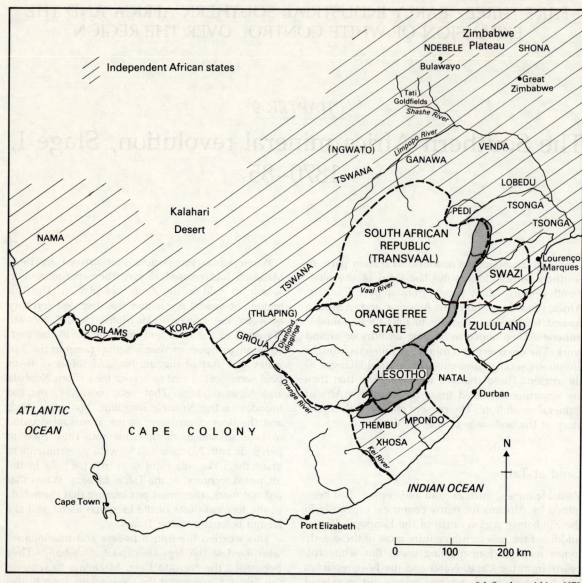

9.1 Southern Africa, 1870

Map labels:

Independent African states

Zimbabwe Plateau
NDEBELE
SHONA
Bulawayo
Tati Goldfields
Shashe River
Great Zimbabwe
VENDA
NGWATO
TSWANA
GANAWA
Limpopo River
LOBEDU
TSONGA
PEDI
TSONGA
SOUTH AFRICAN REPUBLIC (TRANSVAAL)
Kalahari Desert
NAMA
SWAZI
Lourenço Marques
TSWANA
Vaal River
ORANGE FREE STATE
ZULULAND
OORLAMS
KORA
THLAPING
GRIQUA
Diamond diggings
LESOTHO
NATAL
Durban
ATLANTIC OCEAN
Orange River
AFRICAN
C A P E   C O L O N Y
THEMBU
MPONDO
XHOSA
Kei River
N
Cape Town
Port Elizabeth
INDIAN OCEAN
0   100   200 km

The scramble for the diamond fields

In 1867, at about the same time as Hartley and Mauch were investigating the Zimbabwe plateau, a diamond was discovered in the region near where the Vaal river flows into the Orange (see Map 9.2). Over the next two years more diamonds were found in the valley of the lower Vaal. They were mostly picked up by local Griqua, Kora and Tswana and sold to white traders from the Cape Colony in exchange for wagons, horses, guns, clothing, brandy and cash.

Early mining at 'river diggings' and 'dry diggings'

In March 1869 a huge diamond, later called the 'Star of South Africa', was discovered by a Griqua herdsman and sold to a Boer for a horse, ten oxen and 500 sheep. By the end of 1869 fortune-seeking colonists from Natal, Cape Colony and the Afrikaner republics began to converge on the area. In the early months of 1870 white prospectors found a source of diamonds at Klipdrift (Barkly West) and across the river at Pniel. By July 800 whites had gathered in the area. Those at Klipdrift formed themselves into a diggers' committee under the leadership of a Cape brandy trader, Stafford Parker. The committee main-

9.1 Early diamond diggings. White claim holders seated at the sorting table surrounded by their diggers.

tained order among the whites and tried to keep out local black competitors who were already mining diamonds all along the 'river diggings' of the lower Vaal.

Meanwhile far richer deposits of diamonds were found on a group of farms 40 kilometres to the south-west. The farms were owned by Boers from the Orange Free State and they were quickly bought by a group of Cape merchants. Towards the end of 1870 diggers, black and white, rushed to the region, then known as the 'dry diggings'.

The territorial dispute The diamond-fields lay to the north of the Cape Colony and disputes soon arose over who the territory belonged to. Reference to Map 9.2 will show just how complicated this was. The Griqua chief, Waterboer, claimed the whole of the region, north and south of the Vaal. He employed a Cape lawyer, Arnot, to try and prove his claims. The Tlhaping (Tswana) of Jantjie Mothibi of Dikgatlhong and Mahura* and Mankurwane of Taung had moved to the area from Kuruman in the 1830s. Chief Moroka of Thaba 'Nchu put forward Rolong (Tswana) claims to the region, as the territory of their forefathers since the eighteenth century. Jan Bloem claimed authority over settlements of Kora in the valley of the Vaal. The Orange Free State claimed all land between the Orange and Vaal rivers. They also claimed to have bought the Griqua district of Campbell to the north of the Vaal. The Boers of the Transvaal claimed all land north of the

* Mahura died in November 1869 and was succeeded by his nephew Mankurwane.

Vaal, right across to the Kalahari desert, though they had not yet settled further west than Bloemhof. They had already tried to take over the Tati gold-fields in this way and in 1870 their president, Pretorius, tried to do the same with the diamond fields. Meanwhile the white diggers at the river diggings did not really mind who was in control so long as no-one stopped them mining diamonds.

There was one other group who wanted control of the region, but had no claim to it. This was the British of the Cape Colony. They wanted to prevent the Boers from taking over the valuable trade route to the interior (see previous chapter). They also thought that control of the diamond-fields would help make the Cape Colony rich and self-supporting.

British annexation of the diamond-fields, 1871

In November 1870 the presidents of the Boer republics agreed to divide the whole region between the Transvaal and the Orange Free State along the line of the Vaal. But the new British Governor at the Cape, Sir Henry Barkly, proposed that the dispute over the diamond fields should be decided by a special legal court. Thus in 1871 evidence was taken at Bloemhof and Keate, the Lieutenant-Governor of Natal, was asked to judge the case. As a British colonial official, Keate strongly favoured British interests. Firstly, in order to keep the Boers well away from the trade route to the north, he recognised Tswana claims against the Transvaal. Secondly, Keate accepted all Griqua claims to the diamond-

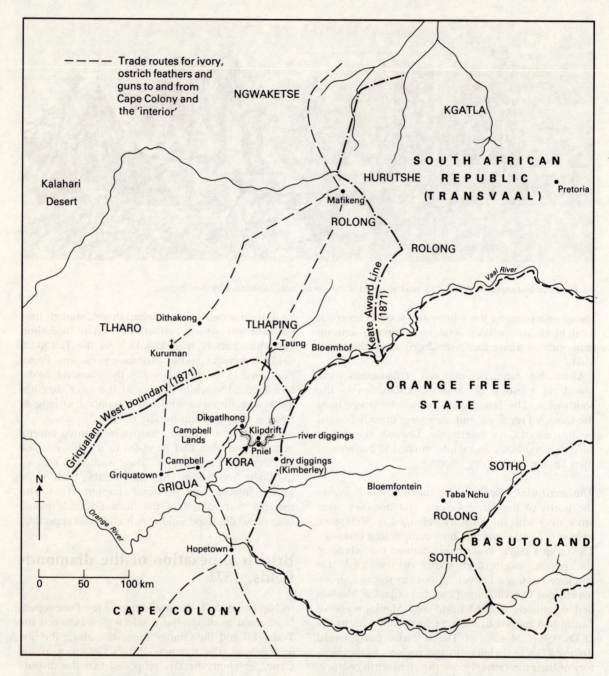

- - - - Trade routes for ivory, ostrich feathers and guns to and from Cape Colony and the 'interior'

NGWAKETSE

KGATLA

Kalahari Desert

SOUTH AFRICAN REPUBLIC (TRANSVAAL)

HURUTSHE

Mafikeng

ROLONG

Pretoria

ROLONG

Vaal River

Dithakong

TLHARO

Kuruman

TLHAPING

Taung

Bloemhof

Keate Award Line (1871)

ORANGE FREE STATE

Griqualand West boundary (1871)

Dikgatlhong

Campbell Lands

Klipdrift

Pniel

river diggings

Campbell

Griquatown

KORA

dry diggings (Kimberley)

GRIQUA

Bloemfontein

Taba'Nchu

ROLONG

SOTHO

N

Orange River

BASUTOLAND

SOTHO

Hopetown

0   50   100 km

CAPE COLONY

9.2 The Diamond-fields dispute, 1870–71

fields. Waterboer was persuaded to ask for British protection against the Boers and on the basis of this request Barkly declared the diamond fields to be British territory. Thus, though Britain had started the year with no legal claim to the region at all, by the end of 1871 the diamond-fields had become the British colony of Griqualand West.

The development of mining at Kimberley, 1871–89

By 1872 a township of some 30 000 people had sprung up around the four principal mines of the dry diggings. A third of these were whites, not only from the nearby colonies and republics, but also from as far away as Britain, America and Australia.

The remaining two-thirds were blacks from all over Southern Africa, Shangane, Pedi, Transvaal Ndebele, Natal Nguni, Mfengu, Xhosa, Sotho, Tswana, Griqua and Kora. The largest mine and the township itself were both called Kimberley, after the British colonial minister at the time. Another mine was named after the previous owners of the farm, the De Beer brothers.

The ownership of mining claims
Each prospector who rushed to a newly discovered site marked out a claim with wooden pegs and string. A claim was usually a square, nine metres across. Claim-owners were entitled to dig down as deep as they liked within the bounds of their own square. Claims were bought and sold as property and were subdivided into fractions which were sold or rented to other prospectors. By the mid-1870s there were over 1,000 working claims in Kimberley mine. Claim-holders, who were mostly white, were called 'diggers' though they employed black labourers to do most of the actual digging. Diggers' committees drew up rules and regulations to govern the mines and settle disputes.

Whites at the diamond fields used the diggers' committees to try and monopolise the ownership of claims. They feared competition from the far larger number of blacks who also came to the diamond-fields. Whites successfully dominated the larger and richer mines of Kimberley and De Beers. But blacks owned, shared or rented many claims in the smaller mines of Dutoitspan and Bultfontein.

The techniques of mining
Kimberley mine was so huge that the diggers had to agree to leave roadways between their claims so that those working the middle ones could reach them without falling into the holes made by others (see Fig. 9.2). As earth and gravel was dug from claims, small carts were used to haul it along the narrow roadways to dumping grounds surrounding the mine. The soil and gravel was separated by washing and the fine gravel was spread out on sorting tables where it was carefully sifted for diamonds. All this required picks, shovels, buckets, ropes, barrows, carts and lots of labour.

Living conditions
Dust, smell, flies, the hum of human labour swarming over the huge pits like bees round an open hive; terrific heat in summer and bitterly cold nights in winter: these were the things which struck visitors to the diamond-fields in the 1870s. There was no proper sanitation, no running water. In the early years even the better-off whites lived in tents or temporary tin and mud-brick shacks. Many African labourers slept in the open,

9.2 Kimberley mine, 1872 showing the 'roadways' across the mine.

or in crude temporary shelters, often erected near the tent or hut of their employers. The whole make-shift city was something like a huge shanty-town.

Financial problems: rates of profit and the price of diamonds Most of the diggers who rushed to the diamond-fields in the early 1870s hoped for quick and easy fortunes. Undoubtedly many fortunes were made, but on the whole, making a lot of money out of diamond-mining was neither quick nor easy. By 1873 many diggers were going bankrupt. The amount of diamonds found per tonne of earth was often disappointingly small. Sometimes by the time even a fairly large diamond was found the claim-holder had got into so much debt that there was little, if any, profit.

To make matters worse, the price of diamonds began to fall. Diamonds are the hardest natural material in the world and are used to provide sharp cutting edges in industrial tools. They also reflect light in a beautiful way and larger diamonds are among the world's most highly valued precious stones in personal jewellery. Diamonds had previously been very rare in the world. This had helped to keep their value extremely high. But once regular mines had been opened up in Southern Africa, diamonds were no longer so rare. Then

people in Europe, where most diamonds were sold, were not prepared to pay such high prices for them. They were still not cheap, but even a slight fall in price had a major effect on the miners of Kimberley.

White claim-holders blamed their losses on their black labourers whom they accused of theft. Whites believed their workers were finding diamonds at the bottom of the mine and secretly selling them at night to illegal buyers. There certainly was plenty of illegal diamond trade going on, and many blacks and whites did very well out of it. But that was only one of the reasons why diggers were going bankrupt. Employers also complained that wages were far too high. But when they tried cutting wages from £4 to £1 a month in 1873, workers left the diamond-fields in their thousands. At this stage the employers lacked unity, and wages were soon raised again as high as ever in order to attract enough workers back to the mines.

Problems of deep-level mining As the mines got deeper, problems increased. The roadways across the mines collapsed, filling in many claims and killing numbers of workers. As the claims were cleared of falling debris, they acted like huge wells and began to fill with water. By the mid-1870s it was no longer possible for individual diggers to employ

9.3 Kimberley mine, 1875 showing the network of steel rope stretching down to various claims.

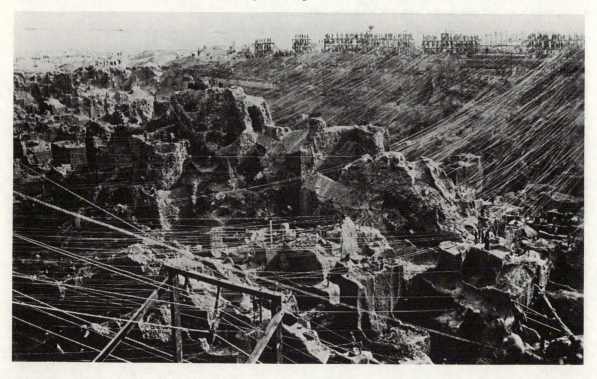

a handful of labourers to work a claim with any real hope of profit. More and more capital was needed. Huge wooden hoists were erected around the Kimberley mine, with wire ropes running down to the claims at the bottom. Thus hundreds of wire ropes stretched down into the open mine like a giant spider's web connecting each working claim to the surface (see Fig. 9.3). Buckets hauled up earth and ferried workers up and down. At first horses were used for turning the wheels which worked the hoists, but in the late 1870s, as the mines got deeper, steam engines were introduced.

The growth of mining companies With the rising costs of working deep in the mine and flood waters spreading across adjoining claims, it was clearly more efficient if mines were joined together (amalgamated) and worked as larger units. This began to happen with the formation of mining companies in the late 1870s. Claim-owners without enough capital sold their claims to those who owned or could borrow enough capital to form a company. One such company-owner was Cecil Rhodes. He had made a lot of money out of running a pumping company which got plenty of work pumping water out of other people's mining claims.

Rhodes, De Beers and the monopoly of diamond mining

In 1880 Rhodes formed the De Beers Mining Company. In a few years he and his partners had bought up all the claims in De Beers mine and began buying claims and companies in the bigger Kimberley mine. This one company soon swallowed up all the others. By 1889 the De Beers Consolidated Mining Company owned and controlled all the mining in Kimberley: it thus had a monopoly of diamond mining. It was now possible for the capitalist owners to introduce many changes in the way mining was organised.

The result of the mining monopoly

Labour Firstly, the larger company employers made production more efficient and profitable by establishing stricter control over their labour force. Thus mine workers lost their previous freedom to come and go or change employers more or less as they wished. The only way for a man to get a job in the mines now was to sign a three or six-month contract. He would then have to spend the whole

of the contract period – eating, sleeping, working – confined within the company compound. Contracts could not be broken and workers were forced to accept lower wages for working long and regular hours. They slept in bare, male-only dormitories. They could have no direct contact with family or friends outside the compounds. Workers were also stripped and searched before finally leaving the compound (see Fig. 9.4) and so there was little or no chance of making extra money from illegal diamond trading.

Control of production Secondly, the larger companies now had the money to develop deep-level, underground mining. All this increased efficiency meant greater profits for the owners of the companies. And once a monopoly was established, De Beers Consolidated was able to ensure even greater profits by cutting production. A cut in production meant that diamonds were once more very rare in the world. People could then be forced to pay higher prices for them.

Ever since then De Beers has tried to maintain its monopoly by buying up or controlling nearly every other diamond mine that has been discovered. The company has maintained a careful balance between producing and selling enough diamonds to make a profit from the business. At the same time it does not sell too many so that prices remain high and profits are very great.

The results of the early mineral revolution

The results of the development of diamond mining at Kimberley were felt all over Southern Africa. As the previous chapter has shown, before 1870 most Southern African peoples lived in self-sufficient, rural communities, supported by herding, hunting or agriculture.

The development of agriculture

Now suddenly, in the 1870s, there grew up around the diamond mines of Kimberley a large urban population. At 30 000 it may seem small by today's standards, but it rivalled Cape Town as the largest city in Southern Africa. And this great new influx of population had to be fed. Thus the growth of Kimberley provided a market for the development of agriculture in the 'interior' of Southern Africa.

Response to the new opportunities was rapid.

9.4 Miners being searched on leaving mining compound.

Local Tswana sold fresh milk, reeds for thatching and hay for animal fodder. They invested in wagons and ploughs and cultivated maize, sorghum and wheat for sale at the Kimberley market. Response was similar among other African groups, especially the Basotho. Wagon-loads of produce were marketed each day and most of the proceeds were spent on guns, horses, clothing and cheap Cape brandy.

Boers of the Orange Free State and Transvaal were also determined to reap the benefits of the new urban market. Most of the Boer farms were occupied by small communities of African farmers. Instead of demanding rent from his 'tenants', the Boer owner expected them to work for him, unpaid, whenever he needed them. Before 1870 these labour demands were often not too great. The 'labour tenants', as they were called, were able to work for themselves and their families as well as work for the landowner. But from the 1870s onwards the Boer landowners wanted to sell more and more crops and so they made heavier and heavier demands upon their

'labour tenants'. Another practice which was soon to become common on white-owned farms was 'sharecropping'. Instead of working directly for the landowner, tenants were expected to grow crops on their own. But when harvest time came a large proportion of the crop (usually half) had to be given to the landowner.

Over much of Southern Africa the 1870s brought greater competition for control of the best agricultural land. Tension and violence increased, among independent African producers, and on the farms and borderlands of the republics and colonies.

Industrial fuel and transport: firewood, coal and railways

Another cause of increasing conflict in Griqualand West and southern Bechuanaland was competition for firewood. As steam machinery was introduced into the mines, the demand for fuel became very high. The hardwood of local thorn trees was found

90

to be a better fuel than low-grade coal from the Orange Free State. So in the late 1870s and early 1880s black and white wagon-owners competed in stripping the surrounding countryside of its trees. Wagon-loads of firewood even came from as far away as Basutoland.

Mine-owners, who had to pay £15 per wagon-load of firewood in the early 1880s, were determined to find an alternative, cheaper source of fuel. In 1880 the British Government had handed over control of Griqualand West to the Cape Colony. Cecil Rhodes quickly moved into politics and became a member of parliament for the new province in 1881. He and other big mine-owners were then able to put pressure on the Cape Government, persuading them to agree to extend their railway system as far as Kimberley. Once this was completed in November 1885 it was possible to import cheap, high-grade coal from Britain. This meant the end of profitable wood-riding for hundreds of wagon-owners in southern Bechuanaland. The railway also brought cheaper bulk food imports. This helped the mining community, but not the local food producers.

Migrant Labour and the gun trade

By 1880 there were 9 000 blacks settled at Kimberley on a fairly permanent basis. Besides working as miners and domestic servants, many of these were self-employed as brick-makers, water-carriers and traders. But the bulk of mine labourers were migrants, drawn from all over Southern Africa. It has been estimated that during the 1870s an average of 50 000 Africans came to Kimberley each year for a few months temporary employment. They came on foot, often travelling many hundreds of kilometres. They came from independent African states as far north as the Zambezi as well as from the reserves and farms of the colonised territories. Wages, at £2 to £4 a month, were higher than elsewhere in Southern Africa. But workers were mainly attracted by their desire to buy guns. In the early 1870s traders in Kimberley sold 100 000 guns a year, mostly to migrant labourers, at about £4 each. African chiefs from as far away as Basutoland, Natal, southern Mozambique and the Pedi kingdom of the eastern Transvaal often deliberately sent their young men to Kimberley to buy guns for the defence of their land.

Boers of the Transvaal and Orange Free State resented the large number of migrant labourers passing through their territory armed with guns. Local officials arrested migrants, confiscated their guns and other goods and forced them to work for at least a month on white farms.

The colonial government in Kimberley knew that they had to allow the free sale of guns in order to attract enough labour to the mines. So despite Boer

9.5 Ox-waggons arriving at Kimberley market in about 1880. Note the large quantity of firewood being brought to the market.

efforts, blacks still arrived at the diamond-fields in their thousands. But other British authorities in Natal, Basutoland and the eastern Cape saw the sale of guns as strengthening African resistance. So in 1877 the sale of guns to blacks in Kimberley was finally stopped. By then, however, it was too late, as the next chapter will show.

The end of the African Iron Age Besides guns and often brandy, labour migrants bought many other things, such as clothing, cooking pots, knives, axes. These cheap manufactured goods, mass-produced in the industrial cities of Britain, had a major impact on hitherto self-sufficient African communities. African craftsmen, especially iron-smelters and metal-workers, had already been weakened by earlier colonial trading contact. Now they were no longer able to compete. In most Southern African communities, the mineral revolution dealt the final death-blow to the African Iron Age.

Exercises

A. Think, discuss, understand and write

1 Re-read the first paragraph of this chapter. In the light of what you have now learned, explain the use and meaning of the word 'revolution'.
2 Who were the various peoples or parties interested in the Tati goldfields between 1868 and 1870? Compare the 'goldfields dispute' in the Tati region with the 'scramble for the diamond fields' further south. Why did one turn out so differently from the other?
3 What social, economic and political changes took place as a result of the development of mining at Kimberley? When you have read the next chapter ('Revival of colonialism and African resistance'), you may want to come back to this question and expand your answer further.
4 Outline the different stages in the development of diamond mining at Kimberley. Start with the early trading of diamonds found on the surface before 1870 and end with the amalgamation of claims in 1889. Try to explain *why* each stage developed. Reference to illustrations in this chapter may help you to understand some of these developments. Before writing, think about

and discuss the different features shown in these illustrations.
5 Who benefitted, and in what way, from the mineral revolution which started at Kimberley in the 1870s?
6 The period 1870–85 was one of widespread violence and warfare in Southern Africa. What reasons can you find in this chapter which might partly account for this? Where do you think violence and warfare would be most likely to occur, between whom, why and with what result? When you have read the next two chapters, compare what you have read with your answer to this question.

B. Imaginative writing

Imagine that you are a migrant labourer working at Kimberley in the early 1870s. Write a letter home to your family describing your journey to and arrival at the diamond fields. Make it clear where you have come from and why. Describe also your work, wages, housing and general living conditions. Date your letter, show what you feel about your experience and keep everything as true to life as possible. Reference to illustrations 9.2 and 9.3 should help to stimulate your imagination.

Now write a similar letter from somebody working in the mining compounds of Kimberley in the late 1880s. See illustration 9.4.

Compare and discuss the differences between the two letters.

C. Mapwork, group-work and class discussion

'The Diamond-fields Dispute of 1871' Trace or otherwise copy Map 9.2, leaving out political boundaries. Enter the names of places, peoples and states on your map. Divide into groups, each group representing one of the contestants for the diamond-fields in 1871: Griqua, Tlhaping, Rolong, Kora, white diggers, Transvaal, Orange Free State and British.

By referring to this chapter (and previous chapters if necessary) make the case for your group and enter on your map the political boundaries which would suit your case.

Select someone as Governor Keate to arbitrate and let each group argue its case. See if it is possible to come to some just agreement. Compare your result, if any, with Governor Keate's actual award of 1871.

CHAPTER 10

Revival of colonialism and African resistance

We saw at the end of Chapter 8 that some degree of balance had been reached between black and white in Southern Africa by 1870. Further colonial conquest would require major military support from Britain and would be very costly. Before 1870 there was no great economic incentive for Britain to agree to this. The British Government was prepared to leave things as they were. The mineral revolution of the 1870s changed all that.

The development of the diamond-fields was an opportunity for white states (British colonies and Boer republics) to gain some level of prosperity. As we saw in the previous chapter, this meant wider use of land and greater control over labour. For some blacks within the white-controlled territories these developments brought greater oppression. For others they provided opportunities for greater prosperity through the sale of cash crops or the sale of labour for higher wages. Any prosperity like this was, however, resented by whites who wanted to keep Africans in the position of poor, low-paid workers.

Meanwhile in the independent kingdoms Africans bought guns to strengthen resistance to further white conquest. White colonists saw this as a threat to their own security. They were determined to convert the African soldiers and peasants of the independent territories into labourers on white-owned farms, mines, roads and railways.

1871–85 was thus a period of great conflict between black and white in Southern Africa. Whites attempted to extend control over Africans within their territory and beyond it. Africans resisted this control and were strengthened in resistance by the purchase of guns from Kimberley. This chapter examines the major resistance movements of the period.

The crushing of resistance in Natal, the Langalibalele affair, 1873–4

As we saw in Chapter 8 the Hlubi of Chief Langalibalele were attacked by Mpande's regiments and fled as refugees to Natal in 1848. They settled around the headwaters of the Bushmans River in the foothills of the Drakensberg, but they soon came into conflict with the Natal authorities. The Natal Secretary for Native Affairs, Theophilus Shepstone, used force to move them to a nearby 'reserve' in 1849. He seized half their cattle when they tried to resist the move. Thereafter Langalibalele and the Hlubi were criticised by local magistrates for their defiant and independent manner. During the 1860s the Hlubi settled down to become successful farmers. This was resented by local white colonists who wanted both their land and their labour. In the early 1870s the Hlubi began to buy guns from Kimberley.

Disarmament Alarmed at the spread of firearms in the colony Shepstone decided that all Africans in Natal should register their guns. When in 1873 Langalibalele failed to co-operate, he was summoned to the capital, Pietermaritzberg. The Hlubi remembered that in 1858 Shepstone's brother, pretending to be unarmed, had used a concealed gun to try and arrest Chief Matshana of the Sithole. On that occasion Matshana escaped but thirty of his people had been killed. Langalibalele, therefore, did not trust Shepstone and refused to go to Pietermaritzberg.

The crushing of the Hlubi By the 1870s blacks in Natal outnumbered whites by fifteen to one. The security of the whites depended on the success of

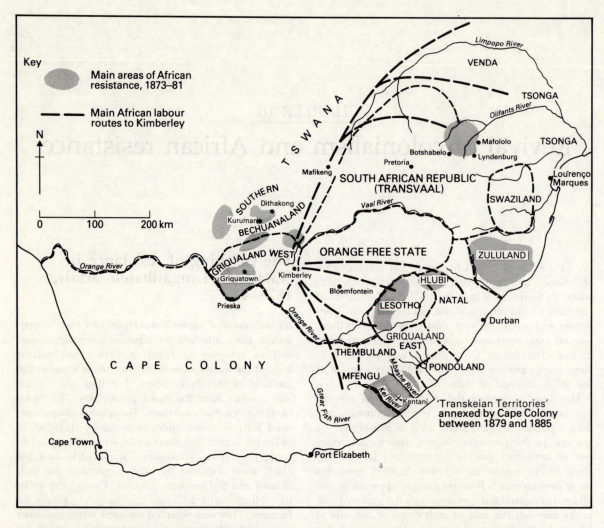

Key

Main areas of African resistance, 1873–81

Main African labour routes to Kimberley

N

0   100   200 km

Limpopo River

VENDA

TSONGA

Olifants River

TSONGA

T S W A N A

Mafololo

Botshabelo • Lyndenburg

Pretoria

Mafikeng

SOUTH AFRICAN REPUBLIC (TRANSVAAL)

Lourénço Marques

SWAZILAND

SOUTHERN BECHUANALAND

Dithakong

Kuruman

Vaal River

ORANGE FREE STATE

ZULULAND

GRIQUALAND WEST

Griquatown

Kimberley

HLUBI

NATAL

Bloemfontein

Prieska

Orange River

LESOTHO

Orange River

Durban

GRIQUALAND EAST

THEMBULAND

PONDOLAND

CAPE COLONY

MFENGU

Mbashe River

Great Fish River

Kei River

Kentani

'Transkeian Territories' annexed by Cape Colony between 1879 and 1885

Cape Town

Port Elizabeth

10.1 African resistance and labour routes, 1873–81

Shepstone's system of 'African Administration'. With only a small police force to back him up Shepstone depended on the co-operation of the blacks in the 'reserves', especially their chiefs whom he used as local administrators. In order to ensure that other chiefs did not follow Langalibalele's defiance, Shepstone decided that strong action should be taken against the Hlubi. The new Governor, Sir Benjamin Pine, ordered a large force up the Bushmans valley. It consisted of 200 regular British soldiers, 200 local white volunteers and 5000 blacks supplied on demand by 'loyal' African chiefs. The Hlubi men retreated with their cattle into Basutoland leaving their women, children and elderly hiding in caves. A Government scouting party clashed with the retreating Hlubi and three whites and a Mosotho were killed. Pine used this incident as an excuse to

bring terrible vengeance on the Hlubi. He ordered the 'reserve' to be 'broken up'. Women and children were slaughtered, houses burned, property taken or destroyed and the land seized for white farms.

The trial of Langalibele In December Langalibele and his followers were captured by the Sotho chief Molapo and handed over to the British. In January 1874 Langalibalele was tried for treason in Natal. He was allowed no defence and was assumed to be guilty even before the trial began. The trial was in effect merely an attempt to justify the terrible punishment which had already been inflicted on the Hlubi. Langalibalele was banished for life and sent to Robben Island. Two hundred of his followers were gaoled.

The Anglican bishop of Natal, Colenso, was

shocked at the injustice of the trial and protested vigorously to the British Government in London. It was a clear case of Natal officials denying a black man the basic rights of a fair trial and 'equality before the law'. The British Government was embarrassed by the obvious injustices committed by their colonial officials. Pine was replaced as Governor of Natal, but little else was done to rectify the injustice. Shepstone was left in control of 'Native Affairs'. Langalibalele was allowed to leave Robben Island, but was confined to a farm in the western Cape. The Hlubi never got back their land.

The 'Langalibalele affair' was a clear case of whites overreacting through fear in the face of defiance by a small section of the overwhelming African majority.

10.1 Portrait of Langalibalele taken while in prison.

The Transvaal/Pedi war of 1876

In the late 1860s the main threat to the security of Sekhukhuni's Pedi kingdom had come from the Swazi and their allies the Lydenburg Boers. In 1869 the Swazi launched a major attack on the Pedi kingdom with the support of Mampuru, a rival claimant to the Pedi throne. But the Swazi were unable to penetrate the mountains and suffered a severe defeat from the Pedi's guns. Without their Swazi allies the Lydenburg Boers were no longer a serious threat to Pedi security. It was now easier for Pedi to move out from the mountains and onto the fertile land of the surrounding district.

Origins of the war The early 1870s saw a growing conflict over the land and labour resources of the region. It was a long way from the diamond-fields of Griqualand West, but in 1872 white prospectors opened up small-scale gold mining in the Lydenburg district. This provided a local market for agricultural produce. Boers increased their exploitation of the African labour on their farms as they tried to produce more grain for the market. Africans fled to the protection of the Pedi to begin cultivating on their own account.

Increasing numbers of Pedi were now living on land previously claimed by the Boer republic. They were rejecting Boer authority and turning to Sekhukhuni for support. One of the most outspoken of these was Sekhukhuni's Christian brother Dinkwanyane. He had left the mission station of Botshabelo in 1873 because of high rents and taxes. He settled at Mafolofolo on the eastern edge of the Pedi kingdom. He was joined by several hundred Christians from the mission stations of Botshabelo and Lydenburg. Dinkwanyane openly defied Boer tax-collectors and claimed allegiance to Sekhukhune.

The Boers of Lydenburg feared the growing strength of the Pedi kingdom. If the Pedi were not crushed quickly, they might ally with the Zulu and drive the Boers from the whole region. (The Venda and northern Sotho had done just this in the Soutpansberg in 1867). White prospectors at the Lydenburg goldfields also pressed the Boer authorities for action against the Pedi. Some of them had bought the titles to Boer 'farms' which lay within the Pedi kingdom. They believed the land might contain gold or even diamonds but they could not occupy it until the Pedi were removed.

In 1875 Boer officials at Lydenburg began preparing for war and negotiating with the Swazi and with Mampuru for assistance. They were supported by the president of the Boer republic,

Burgers, who feared that the Pedi might soon take over the whole of the eastern Transvaal, including the goldfields. Following further acts of defiance by Dinkwanyane, Burgers declared war on the Pedi in 1876.

The war of 1876 To conquer the Pedi Burgers gathered the largest army the South African Republic (Transvaal) had ever assembled. It consisted of 2000 Boers, 2400 Swazi and 600 Africans from the farms of the Republic. But the war, which began in July 1876, lasted only a few weeks and ended in Boer defeat and withdrawal. The reason for the Pedi victory lay partly in the strength and tactics of the Pedi and partly in the weaknesses of the Boer commando system.

Many of the Boers came from the central and western Transvaal. They resented being so far from home when they should have been moving their livestock to winter pastures. They refused to stay in the field for more than a very short time. The Pedi on the other hand denied the Boers a quick victory by avoiding an open battle. Instead they kept to the mountains from where they attacked isolated and unguarded farms. This left the Boers with the choice of an open attack on the mountains which was highly dangerous. They persuaded the Swazi to attack Mafolofolo which they did successfully, killing Dinkwanyane. But the Boers had given them no support. The Swazi, who had lost heavily in the battle, gave up in disgust and withdrew from the war.

A Boer attack on Sekhukhuni's capital was repulsed and the Boers refused to fight anymore. Burgers was forced to withdraw his army. He ordered the building of two forts in the region and employed white mercenaries to raid Pedi villages and burn their crops. By early 1877 Burgers' Government was running out of money and the Pedi were suffering from a shortage of food. In February a peace treaty was signed but it only provided a lull in the fighting. Neither side recognised the authority of the other.

For the Boers the lesson of the war was that the Pedi could not be conquered without a large, well-equipped standing army. The Boer republic had neither the men nor the money to provide such an army. And yet without this there could be no security for the goldfields or for white settlement in the eastern Transvaal. It was at this point that the British stepped in and offered a solution to the problem.

Federation and the annexation of the Transvaal

Southern African *federation* (that is, the joining of separate states to form one large unified state) was an idea first tried by Cape Governor Sir George Grey in the 1850s. He thought it would strengthen white security and end minor wars with neighbouring African states. But he could not get the co-operation of white settlers and the British Government ordered him to drop the idea.

The issue was raised again in 1874 by Lord Carnarvon, the new British colonial minister. Carnarvon had recently succeeded in federating the states of Canada and he thought the time was now right to apply the same principles to Southern Africa.

The aims of federation The diamond-fields had shown that the region had potential for economic development. If Southern Africa became a single, large, prosperous, self-governing British colony, it could protect British trade and shipping in the region. At the same time it could pay for its own government and defence. Thus British interests would be secured at no extra cost to the British Government. But none of this future white prosperity could possibly be achieved while there still existed the danger of wars with powerful independent African states. An essential part of the scheme, therefore, was that Africans should be disarmed. (Langalibalele's defiance had shown the importance of this). And if independent African states were brought into federation, their former soldiers would provide useful wage labour. At the same time more land could be taken for white settlement.

Opposition to federation In Southern Africa itself, however, the Boer republics and Cape Colony were opposed to federation. The Cape had only recently acquired parliamentary self-government (1872) and their first Prime Minister, Molteno, refused to agree to the scheme. Molteno feared that the Cape would lose some of its new-found independence and would be expected to pay the expenses of the other, poorer states in the region. The Orange Free State refused to co-operate because the British had cheated them out of the diamond-fields in 1871 (see previous chapter). In 1875 the British Government paid them £90 000 as compensation for their loss of the diamond-fields. But still the Free State would not agree to federation under British domination. Meanwhile the Boers of the Transvaal were known to be fiercely independent of all British interference. The independent African states of the region were as usual not consulted.

The case of Natal The only positive response to Carnarvon's plans came from Theophilus Shepstone who went to London to argue Natal's case in favour of federation. Shepstone argued that the future of Natal depended on its ability to expand northwards through Zululand and the Transvaal. The 'surplus' African population of Natal could then be cleared off white-owned land and moved northwards into new 'reserves'. British expansion northwards would also give access to the fabulous mineral wealth of the Transvaal and Zimbabwe plateau where there would be plenty of Africans to provide taxation and labour.

At the same time arguments were building up against continued Transvaal independence. In 1875 an international European court had confirmed Portuguese possession of Delagoa Bay. President Burgers of the Transvaal had already begun plans to build a railway to the coast at Delagoa Bay. If that happened Britain would lose control of the Transvaal's trade, especially that of the Lydenburg gold-fields, and Natal's port of Durban would be the first to suffer. In 1874–5 there were complaints from Griqualand West that Transvaal officials were stopping black migrant workers from going to the diamond-fields and forcing them to work on Boer farms.

Annexation of the Transvaal By 1876 Carnarvon had decided that federation should begin with Britain's annexation of the Transvaal. He believed that once that proved a success, the other states would be eager to join in. The Transvaal's defeat by the Pedi in 1876 gave Carnarvon the chance he needed to take over the Boer republic. The Transvaal was bankrupt: bankers in the Cape who had lent them money were demanding repayment but the government was unable to pay its debts. Burgers was forced to levy taxes on the Boers and his government became increasingly unpopular. In addition he appeared to be in danger of losing the goldfields and the whole of the eastern Transvaal to Pedi domination.

In December 1876 Sir Bartle Frere was appointed new Cape Governor and High Commissioner for Southern Africa with instructions from Carnarvon to bring about federation. Shepstone was sent back to Natal with instructions to take over the Government of the Transvaal, if possible with the agreement of its citizens and the *volksraad*.

In January 1877 Shepstone entered the Transvaal

with a small force of police and a handful of officials. He was welcomed by the largely British gold miners of Lydenburg and the bankers and shopkeepers of Pretoria. Burgers resigned and the vice-president, Paul Kruger, retired to his farm. In April 1877 Shepstone raised the British flag and declared the Transvaal a British colony. The Boers had not been in a strong enough position to oppose annexation, but they greatly resented their loss of independence.

The ninth and final Cape/Xhosa War, 1877–8

If he was to achieve his objectives of Southern African federation, the first independent African states Frere would have to confront were those of the southern Nguni, east of the Kei. As we saw in Chapter 8, the western or Ngqika-Xhosa of Chief Sandile had been incorporated into the Cape in 1866. 'Reserves' had been set aside for them and large stretches of their land were given out for white settlement. Chiefs were brought under the authority of local white magistrates. Across the Kei the Gcaleka-Xhosa of Chief Sarhili were still politically independent of the Cape. While trying to avoid direct conflict with the Cape, the Gcaleka-Xhosa greatly resented the Cape's settlement of Mfengu to the east of the Kei (see Map 10.1).

Outbreak of war In August 1877 a fight at a Mfengu wedding party quickly led to war between Mfengu and Gcaleka-Xhosa. The Cape Government intervened on the side of their Mfengu allies and suffered some defeats. The final Cape/Xhosa war had begun.

Frere took personal control of the campaign and decided that firm action must be taken to safeguard the colony and bring a final end to Xhosa independence beyond the Kei. While assembling his imperial army, Frere began disarming all Africans on the Cape side of the border. This provoked Sandile and the Ngqika-Xhosa into rebellion. In December 1877 they crossed the Kei and joined the Gcaleka-Xhosa.

The defeat of the Xhosa The turning point of the war came on 7 February 1878 when an alliance of 5000 Xhosa attacked the main colonial force at Kentani. The muzzle-loading guns of the Xhosa could not compete with the nine-pounder cannons and new breech-loading rifles of the colonial army. The Xhosa attack was finally beaten off by the arrival of colonial reinforcements. They retreated leaving

10.2 A contemporary engraving of Sandile

400 dead on the field. After the battle of Kentani Sarhili escaped east of the Mbashe where he was eventually captured in 1881. Ngqika resistance continued in the colony until Sandile was shot by a patrol at the end of May 1878. Sandile's 'reserve' was seized for white settlement and the remnants of Xhosa resistance finally collapsed.

The 'Transkeian' territories of Thembu, Xhosa, Mfengu and Griqualand East were brought under the rule of Cape magistrates. Immediate annexation to the Cape was delayed while the British prepared for war with the Zulu. Formal annexation took place between 1879 and 1885. By then the strength of African resistance here and elsewhere in Southern Africa had shocked the British. It was therefore decided that it would be wise to allow very little white settlement on African land east of the Kei. Xhosa independence, however, had finally been destroyed.

Griqualand West and Southern Bechuanaland, 1878–9

Rumours of anti–colonial conspiracy In the early months of 1878, while the Cape/Xhosa war was still in progress, rebellion erupted in Griqualand West. Added to this were fears of a Zulu invasion of the Transvaal or Natal. Colonists became convinced there was a conspiracy for a general anti-white rising throughout Southern Africa.

News of African resistance in one area undoubtedly encouraged resisters in another. But there is no evidence of any co-ordinated plan of black resistance or anti-white conspiracy. Throughout the region blacks were now better armed and more determined to resist. At the same time whites were putting more pressure on them for their land and labour. In the circumstances widespread conflict between black and white was almost inevitable.

Rebellion in Griqualand West The rebellion began with a group of 200 Ngqika-Xhosa who had been settled in the Prieska region just south of the Orange River for two generations. They had been gradually squeezed off their land by the expansion of white settlement in the northern Cape Colony. In the early

10.3 A portrait of Sarhili.

months of 1878 they crossed the Orange River and together with local Kora and San they raided white farms in the southern districts of Griqualand West. They were soon joined by Griqua and Tlhaping and rebellion became widespread in the region.

The main Griqua and Tlhaping grievance was loss of land to white settlement and their leaders' loss of authority over their own people. The rebellion consisted mostly of isolated attacks on white farms, traders and police posts. It took a couple of months for British colonial troops and local white volunteers to organise their response. Then Government attacks drove most of the western rebels into the mountains of the southern Langeberg. Meanwhile north of the colony the mission and trading station of Kuruman came under threat from local Tlhaping and Tlharo. And in the east of the colony white farmers and traders were attacked by Tlhaping from across the border.

The rebels of Griqualand West put up determined resistance and achieved a number of minor military successes. They were mostly experienced hunters and were well armed with muzzle-loading guns. But in the end they were no match for the colonial army, well equipped as it was with modern breech-loading rifles and heavy cannon. In July 1878 the colonial forces crossed north of the border and inflicted a major defeat on the Tlhaping at Dithakong. Resistance in the Langeberg was finally crushed by heavy colonial cannon-fire in October.

The occupation of southern Bechuanaland, 1878–9
The colonial commander, Warren, then brought southern Tswana territory north of the colony under military occupation. In the closing months of the year Warren toured the region with his army. He persuaded the main southern Tswana chiefs to submit to British rule and deposed those that resisted him. The British High Commissioner, Frere, planned that southern Bechuanaland should be joined to Griqualand West or the Transvaal as part of his overall plan for Southern African federation. But all these plans were halted by the disaster which befell the British invasion of Zululand in January 1879.

The Anglo-Zulu War, 1879

Origins of the war When Cetshwayo became king in 1872 the main outside threat to Zulu security seemed to come from the Boers of the Transvaal. To

try and keep the Boers in check Cetshwayo sought an alliance with the British in Natal. He therefore invited the Natal Secretary for Native Affairs, Theophilus Shepstone, to his coronation at Ulundi in 1873.

The north-western border of Zululand had long been in dispute with the Boers. Their claims to territory east of Blood (Ncome) River went back to the time of their victory over Dingane in 1838. Shepstone supported Zulu claims against the Transvaal. He wanted to prevent the Boers from cutting off British access to the northern interior. He also believed that if the territory was kept out of Boer hands it could be used for the 'surplus' African population of Natal.

When Shepstone annexed the Transvaal and became its administrator in 1877, however, his attitude towards the Zulu and the 'disputed territory' changed. Since the Transvaal was now a British territory, he supported Transvaal claims against those of the Zulu. Shepstone and the newspapers of Natal began an active propaganda campaign against the Zulu. They claimed the Zulu military system was a threat to white security. In 1878, with war in the eastern Cape and Griqualand West, colonists were easily persuaded that Cetshwayo and the Zulu were the promoters of a general anti-white conspiracy.

Cetshwayo, in an attempt to avoid war, asked for the claims to the 'disputed Blood River territory' to be put before a special court. A commission was set up which, after careful investigation, recognised the claims of the Zulu against those of the Transvaal. But the British High Commissioner, Frere, was determined to have his war with the Zulu. He therefore suppressed the report of the commission until it was too late to avoid a war.

Frere saw the powerful and independent Zulu kingdom as a major obstacle to his plans for Southern African federation. He arrived in Natal in September 1878 and soon began preparations for war. British troops were gathered in Natal and Frere devised an ultimatum which would give him the excuse he needed to order the invasion of Zululand. In December 1878, on the same day as he released the report of the land commission in favour of Zulu claims, Frere issued the following ultimatum to the Zulu. Frere accused the Zulu of raiding across the border into Natal. They were therefore to accept a British Resident in Zululand and their entire military system was to be completely disbanded within thirty days. Frere knew very well that Cetshwayo could never agree to such an ultimatum and on 11 January 1879 the British army invaded Zululand.

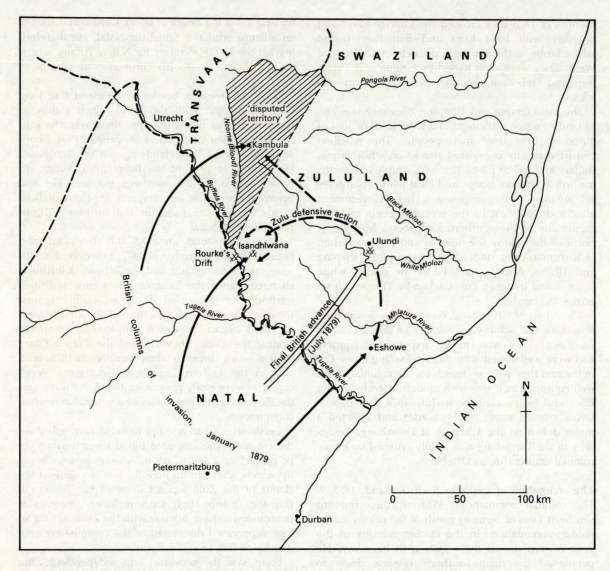

10.2 The Anglo-Zulu War, 1879

Isandhlwana The British army entered Zululand in three columns, north, centre and south, intending to converge on Ulundi. The Zulu army, however, took them by surprise. On 22 January 1879 they attacked the central column and overran the British headquarters camp at Isandhlwana. The Zulu adopted the traditional 'cow-horn' formation, smashing into the British defences with the 'chest' and encircling and cutting off their retreat with the 'horns'. Even the British use of modern rifles was no defence against the massive onslaught of the Zulu regiments. Altogether some 1500 British troops were killed. Only a handful managed to escape to carry news of their defeat back to Frere and the

frightened colonists of Natal. The other British columns dug in at Kambula in the north and Eshowe in the south and managed to beat off further Zulu attacks. But the invasion had now ground to a halt and had to await major reinforcements from abroad.

The end of federation The Zulu's successful defence of their kingdom ended British plans for the federation of Southern African states. Instead of bringing added security for white settlement, Frere's invasion of Zululand had done the opposite. The colonies of Natal and the Transvaal were now in even greater danger of Zulu attack and the long campaign which followed Isandhlwana cost the

10.4 The battle of Ulundi, July 1879. On this occasion the Zulu Army was unable to break through the British defences.

British Government enormous sums of money. Eventually, however, a huge British army, 5000 strong, defeated the Zulu at Ulundi in July 1879.

The end of the war Having at last achieved a major victory over the Zulu the British Government ordered General Wolseley to arrange a peace settlement and withdraw the British army. Cetshwayo's army was by no means entirely defeated, but the Zulu, too, badly needed peace. The war had cost the Zulu dear. They had lost several thousand men in the two major battles of the war. Homes had been burned, cattle captured and most of an agricultural season disrupted. The Zulu were desperately short of food and needed to get back to their homes before the next planting season in the spring. It became increasingly difficult for Cetshwayo to keep his army in the field. When Cetshwayo himself was captured at the end of August, he ordered his people to lay down their arms.

The British division of Zululand, 1879–80 The British Government now wanted to withdraw from the expense and problems of the military occupation of Zululand. But they feared to leave a united

kingdom under the continued rule of their king. Cetshwayo was therefore exiled to Cape Town and the Zulu kingdom was divided up into thirteen separate chiefdoms. These were supposed to represent the northern Nguni chiefdoms before the rise of Shaka. But in practice they were artificial divisions drawn up by the British. Several of the appointed chiefs had little if any real 'traditional' authority over the people or area they ruled. They were chosen according to their supposed 'loyalty' towards the British. One of the 'Zulu chiefs' was a white trader long settled in the area. The settlement was greatly resented by many of the Zulu, especially by the supporters of the exiled king. The Zulu civil war which followed will be discussed in the following chapter.

The Conquest of the Pedi, 1877–79

The British and the Pedi, 1877 When the British took over the Transvaal in 1877 a renewal of the war with the Pedi became inevitable. The conflict over land and political authority which had led to war in 1876 still remained. In addition, the Pedi's successful challenge to Transvaal authority conflicted with British federation plans which required the conquest of powerful independent African kingdoms. Shepstone issued demands for the collection of a 'hut-tax' from Africans to pay for the administration of the colony. He supported all the land claims of the former Boer republics and even expected payment of the 2000 cattle which the Boers had demanded from the Pedi in the treaty of February 1877.

The renewal of war, 1878–79 As the Pedi defied Shepstone's tax-collectors and refused to pay the cattle-fine, events moved towards a renewal of the war. Fighting began in 1878 as white mercenaries raided Pedi cattle and crops. In August a direct assault on the Pedi capital was repulsed. The British then awaited the defeat of the Zulu which Shepstone hoped would frighten the Pedi into submission. But as we have already seen, conquest of the Zulu was more difficult than expected.

Meanwhile, however, the Pedi's strength was gradually being worn down. The lengthy war had led to a severe shortage of food within the kingdom. Political unity began to weaken as groups of people decided to move away to more peaceful regions.

Conquest of the Pedi, November 1879 Following the capture of Cetshwayo, Wolseley arrived in the Transvaal at the end of September 1879. He demanded the complete surrender of the Pedi and the payment of 2500 cattle. Sekhukhuni called a *pitso* to discuss their course of action. Sekhukhuni himself argued for peace and the payment of the cattle, but

he was shouted down. The Pedi were determined not to submit without a fight. Wolseley, however, was equally determined. He feared that other Africans would refuse to pay taxes if Pedi defiance was allowed to continue. He also felt it was important to give a display of British military strength as this would help quieten rumblings of Boer discontent within the Transvaal.

The British in 1870 were able to provide the two things the Boers had lacked in 1876: a large standing army and the money to keep it in the field as long as necessary. Wolseley realised that conquest of the Pedi required a direct frontal attack. This would involve heavy casualties so Wolseley turned to African allies to bear the brunt of the assault. In this he followed the tactics of the Boers and looked to the Swazi for assistance. The Swazi, relieved at the recent defeat of the Zulu, eagerly joined the attack on their old enemy.

While Wolseley advanced up the valley towards the Pedi capital, the Swazi swept over the mountains and descended on the Pedi from the rear. A British officer later admitted: 'No white men could have swept over that hill as the Swazi did'.* As Wolseley planned, the Swazi bore the brunt of government casualties. They lost over 500 killed and an equal number wounded before the Pedi were overcome. Total white casualties were thirteen killed and thirty-five wounded.

Independent Pedi power was finally smashed.

* Quoted in P. Bonner *Kings, Commoners and Concessionnaires*, Cambridge, 1983, p. 155

10.5 A reproduction of part of the front cover of 'The Graphic', a popular British magazine, January 1880. The picture shows the captured Sekhukhuni being carried on a litter, November 1879.

More than a thousand Pedi had been killed in the final assault, among them three of Sekhukhuni's brothers and nine of his children. Sekhukhuni himself was captured and imprisoned in Pretoria while the Swazi followed up their victory with ten days of raiding in the surrounding districts. Mampuru established himself as chief in the Pedi heartland and when Sekhukhuni was released from prison in 1881, Mampuru had him murdered.

Basutoland and the Cape

The British Government handed over control of 'Basutoland' to the Cape Colony in 1871. During the 1870s the Sotho made a remarkable recovery from the poverty and destitution of the wars of the late 1860s. Their recovery was helped by migrant labour to the diamond-fields and the development of plough-cultivation for growing grain to sell in Kimberley and Bloemfontein.

The Cape appointed magistrates to take over many of the duties of the chiefs. Moshoeshoe's eldest son, Letsie, who succeeded to the Sotho paramountcy, followed a policy of co-operation with the colonial authorities. He seems to have felt that his authority over his brothers and other chiefs depended on the support of the colonial government. His nephew, Jonathan Molapo had also co-operated in handing over Langalibalele in 1873. Many Sotho, however, refused to accept the loss of their former independence. Much of the Sotho opposition centred around Masopha, Letsie's defiant younger brother. Masopha had gained a great reputation and personal following for his action in the wars of 1852 and 1858 and as Moshoeshoe's closest military adviser in the final war of 1865–68. On Moshoeshoe's death Masopha became a focus of Sotho power rivalling that of the paramount Letsie. He established his village at Taba Bosiu and refused to pay taxes or accept a Cape magistrate.

In 1878 the Cape introduced its 'Disarmament Act' as part of the general British policy of subordinating the African peoples of Southern Africa. As we have seen, this policy was applied with varying degrees of success to the Hlubi, Xhosa, Griqua, Tswana, Zulu and Pedi. Basutoland by then had become one of the most heavily armed African territories in the region. The Phuthi of Moorosi defied the authority of the local Cape magistrate, attacked the magistrate's camp and freed some Phuthi prisoners. It took colonial troops six months to conquer Moorosi's mountain stronghold, killing Moorosi and large numbers of Phuthi in November 1879.

The 'Gun War', 1880–81 The Cape Prime Minister, Sprigg, then announced to the Sotho that taxes would be raised and they would be disarmed. The Sotho were shocked. Opposition was immediate and widespread. Letsie tried to avoid war by appealing to the Cape parliament, but his son Lerotholi joined Masopha in leading the opposition. A minority of Sotho followed Letsie's recommendation and co-operated with the Government. They handed in their guns to the magistrates only to be branded 'traitors' and attacked by the followers of Lerotholi and Masopha. In September 1880 magistrates were forced to abandon their posts and retire to Maseru. A colonial army was sent up from the Cape but it was unable to confront the Sotho in open battle. The war dragged on into 1881 and cost the Cape government more than £3 million.

Results of the war: the end of Cape rule and British re-annexation

Finally in April 1881 the new British High Commissioner, Robinson, brought the war to an end by accepting that the Sotho would not be forcibly disarmed. Lerotholi, anxious to secure his position as heir to the Sotho paramountcy, now co-operated with the Government against the continued resistance of Mashopa. What amounted to a minor civil war ensued and the Cape was unable to bring the territory under its control. In desperation the Cape handed back direct control of Basutoland to the British government in March 1884.

By their resistance to Cape rule the Sotho had won an important victory. They were now a British colony, separate from the other white-controlled states of Southern Africa. This gave them protection from any further Free State encroachment onto their

10.6 Scene from the 'Gun War', 1880.

land. The British government agreed that no Sotho land would be taken for white settlement. The magistrates' powers were reduced and the Sotho chiefs were left with most of their authority over their own people.

Document 10.1 *Following Cetshwayo's surrender to the British in 1879 the Zulu king was imprisoned in Cape Town. While there he was interviewed by a number of white people. As a result of some of these interviews Cetshwayo's version of Zulu history and the origins of war in 1879 were recorded. This was published under the title 'Cetshwayo's Story' in the February 1880 edition of* Macmillan's Magazine. *The following is an extract:*

After the annexation of the Transvaal by the English, Mr Shepstone met the Zulus at Conference Hill, to hear the boundary dispute. Every Zulu chief of any note came. It was a great gathering of chiefs. Only a few Boers were present. The chiefs asked Mr Shepstone to let them argue the question out then and there, before him, with the Boers. Shepstone told them he had come to see the disputed boundary, and to hear what they had to say about it; he then asked them to tell him what they considered was their boundary. They replied that they claimed the Buffalo River, as the original and proper Zulu boundary. Mr Shepstone replied, 'Oh, that is too hard. You have allowed the Boers to settle around and about Utrecht so long, you cannot expect to turn them out of so much country now.' But the Zulus would not give in. Mr Shepstone then said, 'If I were called upon to point out what I consider a fair boundary, I should say the Blood River and the old hunting road, which runs close by Kambula, to the Pongola, or the Zulu side of Luneburg,' but the Zulu chiefs would not agree to this, and said they had never given up the Luneburg district at all, and had allowed the Boers to settle at Utrecht only on the condition that they came no further; that the Boers had broken their agreement, and therefore forfeited their rights to remain on the Zulu side of the Buffalo.

The chiefs then complained to Mr Shepstone, saying, 'Why do *you* talk? Why do you not sit and listen, as the representative of the Queen? The Boers now belong to the Queen of England, and we consider the

Queen our mother, since she sent her representative to crown Cetshwayo. Let the Boers argue it out before you, and when you have heard both sides, then decide between us.'

Shepstone replied that he was not then making a decision, but was only talking over the question with the Zulu chiefs, and that a commission would by and by decide the question. The chiefs went away, much dissatisfied, as they said Mr Shepstone had come to a judgement without hearing the question argued out. The Boers had not spoken.

(Extract from a reprint in *A Zulu King Speaks, statements by Cetshwayo ka Mpande on the history and customs of his people* (ed. by C. de B. Webb and J. B. Wright), Pietermaritzburg & Durban, 1978)

Exercises

A. Think, discuss, understand and write

1 Why did the British try to form a federation of states in Southern Africa during the 1870s? Who supported this and why? Who opposed it and why?
2 What were the reasons for the British annexation of the Transvaal in 1877? Why was annexation so easily achieved?
3 Describe the causes and results of the Transvaal/Pedi wars of 1876 and 1879. How and why did the British succeed where the Boers had failed?
4 Why did the British invade Zululand in 1879? What were the immediate results of the war?
   OR
   Why did the Cape government and the Basotho go to war in 1880? What were the immediate results of the war?
5 Select two of the wars of African resistance described in this chapter. Describe and account for African successes or failures in these wars.
6 Why was there such widespread conflict between black and white in Southern Africa between 1873 and 1881? Compare your answer with that for Question 6 at the end of the previous chapter (p. 92).

B. Imaginative writing

Imagine you are Cetshwayo on the day after the battle of Isandhlwana. You hope now to get the British to call off their invasion and make peace with the Zulu. Write a letter to High Commissioner Frere explaining your view of the current situation. In your letter try and persuade him to withdraw the rest of his army and make peace.

C. Mapwork, group-work and class discussion

Draw a map of Southern Africa and indicate on it the main areas of African resistance during this period. Discuss the different African tactics used in these wars. Why did some Africans fight on the side of the whites? *If* there *had* been a general anti-white conspiracy, might these wars of resistance have turned out differently? If so, how and why?

Document study   Read Document 10.1 and discuss the answers to the following questions:

1 Why had the British annexed the Transvaal in 1877?
2 Who had been the British representative at Cetshwayo's coronation?
3 What had been Shepstone's attitude to the 'disputed territory' at the time of Cetshwayo's coronation? In what way had Shepstone now changed his attitude? Why had he done this?
4 Why, in your view, had the Boers not spoken at the meeting?
5 What was the decision of the boundary commission which sat after this meeting? What happened to its report and why?

CHAPTER 11

The 'scramble' for white domination of Southern Africa

The First Anglo-Boer War, 1880–81, causes and results

Origins of the war When the British annexed the Transvaal in 1877, the Government of President Burgers had been too weak to offer effective resistance. Burgers' Government was bankrupt and unpopular after the failure of its war against the Pedi. From the start, however, their loss of independence to the British was greatly resented by the Boers. Former vice-president Paul Kruger led delegations of protest to Britain in 1877 and 1878. When these protests were ignored a number of mass meetings were held in the Transvaal during 1879. In December that year plans were laid for passive resistance, that is, refusing to co-operate with government officials. Meanwhile the Boers were encouraged by political events in Britain. In a British general election campaign the leader of the Liberal Party, Gladstone, attacked the Conservative Government's South African policy, especially their annexation of the Transvaal. The Boer leaders had great hopes that if the Liberal Party won the election, the new Government would listen sympathetically to their demands for independence. But they were soon disappointed.

The Liberal victory in April 1880 brought no immediate change in South African policy. This was largely because the Transvaal Administrator, Lanyon, assured the British Government that all was well in the Transvaal. Lanyon, however, was out of touch with the true nature and strength of Boer feelings. Boer resentment continued to rise during 1880 and the first shots of rebellion were fired before the end of the year.

The main grievance of the Boers was their loss of political independence. This meant they no longer ruled themselves. The British ruled through their own appointed officials. There was no elected *volksraad* or Boer say in government. The aspect of British rule the Boers resented most was the regular collection of taxes. The Boers were used to the informality and inefficiency of republican government. They were not used to the regular payment of taxes. Finally, the British had removed the main threat to the security of the former republic, namely, the powerful African kingdoms of the Zulu and the Pedi. Wolseley's defeat of the Pedi in 1879 meant that the Boers no longer needed the protection of the British and their army. Wolseley's clear contempt for the Boers merely raised their resentment further.

The First Anglo-Boer War, 1880–81 The Boers' passive resistance campaign turned into open defiance in a clash with tax collectors at Potchefstroom in November 1880. News spread rapidly and Boers all over the Transvaal rose in rebellion. At a mass meeting on 16 December an independent republic was proclaimed, the flag of the former 'South African Republic' was raised and Kruger, M. W. Pretorius and Piet Joubert were appointed to run the new government.

The small British forces in the Transvaal were quickly tied down in the towns. The Boers laid siege to these and so prevented the British from taking effective military action against them. Meanwhile the Boer commandos inflicted a number of humiliating defeats on the British forces that tried to relieve the towns. A force of 250 marched into a Boer ambush at Bronkhorstspruit on 20 December. Fifty-six were killed, a hundred wounded and the rest captured. General Colley, the British High Commissioner, then tried moving up colonial forces from Natal. But his way was blocked by Boer

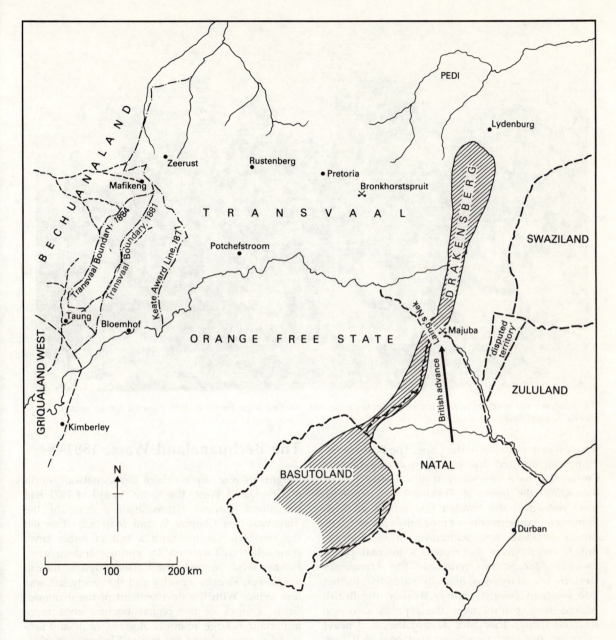

11.1 The First Anglo-Boer War, 1880–81

commandos at the narrow Drakensberg pass of Laing's Nek. The final British defeat came at Majuba Hill on 27 February 1881. In that battle the British lost 200 killed or wounded. Among those killed was General Colley himself.

The Pretoria Convention, 1881 After Majuba the British agreed to negotiate their withdrawal from the Transvaal. At the Pretoria Convention of 1881 internal self-government was restored to the Boers. But the British would not agree to their total independence. The British retained control over all foreign relations and a British Resident was appointed to Pretoria. He was supposed to protect the interests of Africans in the Transvaal and ensure that adequate reserves of land were set aside for them.

Result of the war As we shall see in Chapter 13, the extent of Boer success in 1881 gave a great boost to the new movement for Afrikaner nationalism

11.1 British sick and wounded soldiers retreating from the battle front, the First Anglo-Boer War, 1881. Note the African women offering food and drink.

which was developing in the Cape. The Boers of the Transvaal regarded the restrictions of the Pretoria Convention as a temporary feature. After further discussion, the terms of Transvaal independence were revised at the London Convention of 1884. Republican government was now fully restored. The British Resident was withdrawn from Pretoria. British control over the republic's internal policy towards Africans was removed The Transvaal's western boundary was officially extended further into southern Tswana territory. Finally, the British relaxed their control over the republic's foreign relations though they later claimed they had never given up the right to reassert that control if they chose to do so.

The Transvaal Government which the Boers regained control of in the Conventions of 1881 and 1884 was much stronger than it had been in 1877. Efficient British tax collection had brought its debts under control. The Zulu and the Pedi had been defeated. And victories over the British had boosted Boer military strength and confidence. The period following British withdrawal in 1881 was thus one of renewed Boer assaults on the land and labour of Africans in and around the Transvaal.

The Bechuanaland Wars, 1881–84

Origins of war   In 'southern Bechuanaland', north of Griqualand West, the Keate Award of 1871 had recognised Tswana claims against those of the Transvaal (see Chapter 9, and Map 9.2). This left the southern Tswana with a belt of fertile land, reasonably well-watered by springs and streams. Further west, towards the Kalahari desert, rainfall was lower, streams ran dry and the sandy soil was less fertile. With the development of the diamond-fields, control of the region became even more important as large amounts of grain, cattle and firewood were produced for sale at Kimberley market. This led to increasing competition for the best land between different groups of Rolong, Tlhaping and Kora. But the situation was made worse by pressure from the Transvaal.

For years Boers of the western Transvaal had laid claim to some of the best land around the Molopo basin. They refused to recognise the Keate Award boundary and throughout the 1870s they continued to push their settlements westwards. They too sought to control the best land and use the Kimberley market for selling grain, cattle and firewood.

The outbreak of war, 1881–2 Towards the end of 1881 conflict between Rolong in the north and Tlhaping and Kora in the south developed into full-scale war. Boers of the Transvaal, who had recently regained their independence from the British, seized this opportunity to expand once more into African territory to the west. In the Molopo basin Boers hired themselves as mercenaries to Chief Moswete of the Rapulana Rolong and joined in attacking the Tshidi Rolong of Chief Montshiwa at Mafikeng. Meanwhile in the Harts valley Boers sided with Mossweu's Kora in attacking Mankurwane's Tlhaping at Taung. In both regions the Boers demanded payment in land, to be taken from the conquered territory of the Rolong and Tlhaping. Though in theory fighting as the 'volunteers' of Moswete and Mossweu, the Boers themselves soon assumed complete control of the war. For most of 1882 the Tshidi Rolong and Tlhaping were besieged in Mafikeng and Taung while white mercenaries raided cattle and cut firewood for sale to Kimberley.

Stellaland and Goshen, 1882–3 By the end of 1882 the Boer mercenaries had forced the surrender of both besieged towns, Taung and Mafikeng. They then proclaimed the 'republics' of 'Stellaland' and 'Goshen' in the lands which they had conquered. But Tlhaping and Rolong resistance continued during 1883 and prevented Boers from settling on most of the farms which they claimed. Both Mankurwane and Montshiwa consequently appealed to the British for protection from the Boer invaders of their land.

British and Cape interests in the 'road to the north' The British Government came under pressure from three main groups arguing in favour of British intervention. For most of 1883 the LMS missionary John Mackenzie campaigned in Britain on behalf of the southern Tswana. He appealed to the British to protect the Tswana from losing their land to the Boers. Mackenzie was joined in his appeal by the merchants of Kimberley and the Cape Colony. They feared that the Boer republics of Stellaland and Goshen would cut off the Cape's trade route to and from the northern interior. Finally, Cecil Rhodes and the mine-owners of Kimberley also opposed the formation of Stellaland and Goshen. However, Rhodes was not interested in protecting African land rights. He wanted Cape control of the region so that Boers from the Transvaal could not cut off the flow of migrant labour to the mines. In addition, he wanted to keep the 'road to the north' open for possible future British expansion into the northern interior.

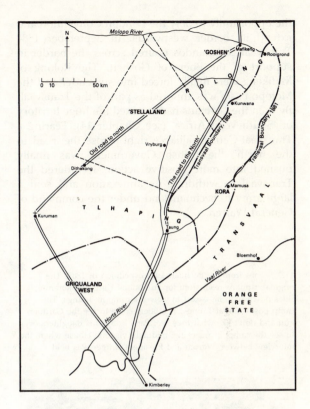

11.2 The Bechuanaland Wars, 1881–84

British intervention in southern Bechuanaland, 1884 At the London Convention of February 1884 the Transvaal got British agreement to the extension of its western boundary. This took over much of the territory of the Rapulana Rolong and the Kora whom the Boers had supported in the recent war, but it stopped just short of the 'road to the north'. Southern Tswana territory west of the Transvaal was brought under British 'protection' and Mackenzie was appointed as its Deputy Commissioner. But Mackenzie was unable to bring peace to the region because he refused to recognise all the land claims of the whites. Mackenzie was replaced by Rhodes. He agreed to recognise all Stellaland land claims, without enquiry, on condition they agreed to Cape annexation. But Rhodes failed to get agreement from the men of Goshen and fighting continued in the Molopo region.

British annexation and division of Bechuanaland, 1884–5

British protection of the Tswana had so far been weak and ineffective. The Transvaal therefore seized the opportunity to defy the London Convention and extend its border westwards. In September 1884 Transvaal commandos poured across the border in support of the Boers of Goshen. The Rolong of Mafikeng were finally forced into surrender and the Molopo basin was annexed as part of the Transvaal. By then the Germans had annexed the huge territory of 'South West Africa' (see Chapter 14). Fearing a Transvaal-German alliance right across the 'road to the north' the British Government was finally pushed into more positive action. It ordered the Transvaal to withdraw its annexation and sent a large army to Bechuanaland under the command of General Warren.

11.2 Scenes from the Bechuanaland expedition of 1885. The original captions read, from top to bottom: King Mankoranne rides down with his escort to view the camp at Taungs; The camp post-office at Taungs; The Boers come to see the Gardner gun and don't like what they see; Papa brings his daughters over to see the camp; Bivouacking: midnight visitors; House where the interview between Warren and President Kruger was held.

The Warren expedition Warren's army occupied southern Bechuanaland in the early months of 1885 and the Boers of Goshen quickly withdrew into the Transvaal. But there remained the danger of German or Boer expansion north of the Molopo. Warren was therefore ordered north to proclaim a British 'protectorate' over the rest of Bechuanaland as far as latitude 22 degrees south.

British 'protection' and the northern Tswana
Warren went first to Shoshong, the capital of the Ngwato, the largest of the northern Tswana kingdoms. The Ngwato were ruled by Khama III (also known as 'Khama the Great'). Khama was a devout Christian who had long favoured some kind of defensive alliance with the British. He had asked for British protection from the Boers in 1876, but his request had been turned down. Since then Khama had extended his control over surrounding peoples and had come into conflict with the Ndebele in the north-east. An alliance with the British would provide useful further protection from the Ndebele. Khama therefore welcomed Warren's offer of British protection. In order to induce the British to make their protection effective Khama offered a large stretch of country for British settlement. This lay along the Limpopo border of the Transvaal and in the Kalanga territory disputed with the Ndebele. Neither of these regions were at the time under the direct control of Khama's Ngwato. So Khama's 'generous' grant of land was no real loss to the Tswana themselves.

Further south Gaseitsiwe of the Ngwaketse followed Khama's example. He accepted British protection on similar terms and offered land for British settlement that was in reality mostly desert. The Kwena of Sechele, however, were less enthusiastic about Warren's uninvited British 'protection'. But after protest they too accepted British protection and offered land for British settlement bordering their kingdom.

Following Khama's lead all three Tswana kings consulted laid down terms for the agreement. The Tswana were to retain complete control over their own land and their laws. The rule of the chiefs was not to be interfered with in any way. And Khama's ban on alcohol was to be maintained.

The division of Bechuanaland To the northern Tswana kings 'protection' meant an active British presence on their borders. But the British Government turned down their 'magnificent offer' of land for British settlement. Britain was determined to avoid the expense of taking an active part in the ruling of so vast a territory.

South of the Molopo, however, the situation was different. Here a number of white settlers were already established. It was therefore decided to set aside land for African 'reserves' and to make the bulk of the land available for sale to white settlers. It was hoped this would persuade the Cape Colony to take the region over in due course. In the meantime it came under direct British rule. Thus by British proclamation in September 1885 Bechuanaland was divided along the line of the Molopo. The north, brought under nominal authority, became the Bechuanaland Protectorate (present-day Botswana).

The south came under direct British rule as the 'crown colony' of British Bechuanaland.

Consolidation of Boer authority in the Transvaal

Following Britain's withdrawal from the Transvaal in 1881, Paul Kruger became the country's president in 1883. Piet Joubert was appointed Commandant-General. Under Joubert's leadership the South African Republic pursued an aggressive policy in bringing Africans within the republic under Boer control.

11.3 War of conquest in the Transvaal, 1883–98

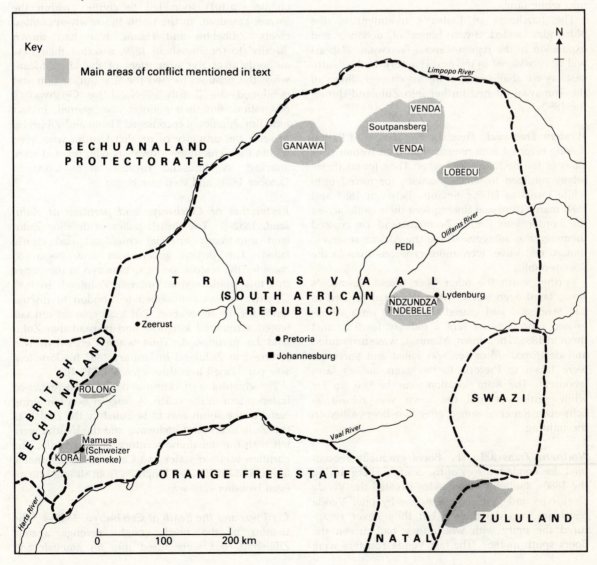

111

Eastern Transvaal The republic's newfound strength and determination was most clearly displayed in its handling of the Ndzundza Ndebele. They were a mixed Nguni/Sotho chiefdom of the eastern Transvaal, located in the Lydenburg area between the Pedi and the Swazi (see Map 11.3). Former rivals to Pedi power, the Ndzundza Ndebele defied Boer tax collectors in the early 1880s. In 1883 Joubert launched a massive assault on the mountain stronghold of the Ndzundza. In contrast to the Boer compaign against the Pedi in 1876, Joubert was now able to keep a force of 2000 Boers campaigning in the field for eight months. The Ndzundza were finally starved and blasted out of their mountain caves with dynamite. The survivors were given out as 'apprentice' labourers to local Boers and their land divided into white farms.

The harshness of Joubert's treatment of the Ndzundza ended Swazi hopes of defiance and expansion in the region. (Swazi-Transvaal relations will be considered in the next chapter). In the southeast, as we shall see later in this chapter, Boers of the Transvaal pushed further into Zululand during the 1880s.

Western Transvaal Here the Rapulana and Ratlou Rolong received little reward from their former Boer allies of the Bechuanaland wars. They found themselves confined to small 'locations' or forced onto white farms as labour tenants. Between 1885 and 1888 many Transvaal Rolong sent their cattle across the border into British Bechuanaland or crossed themselves as refugees. There the African reserves, though restrictive, were more generous than in the Boer republic.

Further south the other Boer allies, Mossweu's Kora, fared even worse. After they had refused to pay taxes and had grazed their cattle on a white-owned farm, Joubert sent a military force against them in 1886. Their town, Mamusa, was surrounded and destroyed. Mossweu was killed and survivors were taken to Pretoria to be given out as farm labourers. The Kora 'location' was broken up for white settlement and the town was rebuilt as Schweizer-Reneke, named after two Boers killed in the fighting.

Northern Transvaal The Boers gradually reoccupied the Venda territory of the Soutpansberg during the 1880s. Joubert's commandos isolated the Venda chiefdoms and defeated them one by one. Venda resistance was determined but they never recaptured the unity with which they had driven the Boers south in 1867. The last Venda resisters were finally defeated and driven across the Limpopo by a huge force of Boers in 1898. Further African resistance by the Gananwa and Lobedu was similarly crushed in the 1890s.

In all it had taken the Boers of the South African Republic more than sixty years to make good their claims to all the Transvaal highveld south of the Limpopo.

Civil war and the division of Zululand

Origins of civil war, 1880–81 Wolseley's division of Zululand into thirteen chiefdoms (see previous chapter, p 101) soon led to conflict within the former kingdom. In the north the newly-appointed chiefs, Zibhebhu and Hamu, who had shown 'loyalty' to the British in 1879, asserted their new authority over the supporters of the king. Meanwhile the royalists formed the 'Usuthu' faction and petitioned the British in Natal for Cetshwayo's restoration. But their petition was ignored. In fact local British officials encouraged Hamu and Zibhebhu to seize the property of royalist Usuthu who lived within their chiefdoms. Royalists who resisted were attacked. A thousand royalists were killed in October 1881, and civil war began.

Restoration of Cetshwayo and partition of Zululand, 1882–3 The British policy of dividing Zululand into many artificial chiefdoms had clearly failed. The British government now began to consider the restoration of Cetshwayo in the hopes that this would restore order in Zululand. In 1882 Cetshwayo was summoned to London to discuss terms for his restoration. But local colonial officials feared a reunited kingdom and insisted that Zululand be partitioned. Thus when Cetshwayo was returned to Zululand in January 1883 his kingdom was partitioned into three (see Map 11.4).

The chiefdoms of Hamu and Zibhebhu remained independent in the north. A huge region bordering Natal in the south was to be ruled by the British as the 'Zulu Reserve'. Cetshwayo and the Usuthu were left with the remaining territory in the middle. The partition was a disaster and Cetshwayo was unable to prevent his divided kingdom from sliding into an even bloodier civil war.

Civil war and the death of Cetshwayo, 1883–4 The Usuthu of the north sought revenge against Zibhebhu, but were lured into an ambush and

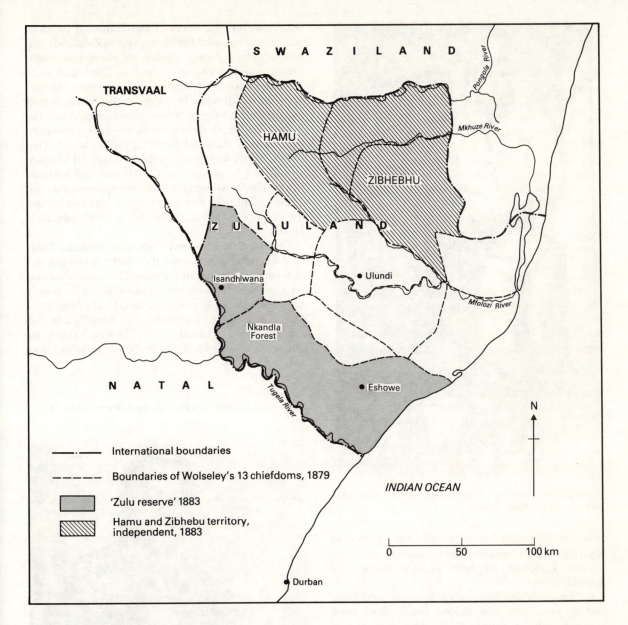

11.4 The partition of Zululand, 1879–83

heavily defeated. Zibhebhu's victorious Mandlakazi invaded Usuthu territory and sacked Cetshwayo's capital Ulundi in July 1883. The Usuthu were surprised by the swiftness of the attack. Thousands were massacred including most of the great *izinduna* of the old Zulu kingdom. Cetshwayo himself escaped to the Nkandla forest and most of the surviving Usuthu fled south into the 'Reserve'. When Cetshwayo died in 1884, it was rumoured he was poisoned.

Boer intervention and the 'New Republic', 1884–5
The Usuthu refugees moving into the 'Reserve' received no sympathy from the British. Local colonial officials felt this was the chance to make the Zulu become low-paid wage-labourers in Natal. But the Usuthu were determined to recover their land and cattle. Their situation, however, was desperate. The followers of Zibhebhu and Hamu raided freely over the whole of central Zululand. Many of the Usuthu, hiding in forests and caves, were weak from starvation. If they were to survive they needed

11.3 John Dunn, the white trader who worked for Cetshwayo, and who adopted Zulu customs.

to regain their land before the next spring rains in September. As a last resort they turned to the Boers of the Transvaal for help against Hamu and Zibhebhu.

Cetshwayo's son Dinuzulu was proclaimed king, and in June 1884 a combined Usuthu/Boer force invaded northern Zululand. Zibhebhu's Mandlakazi retreated to the Lebombo mountains where they were defeated at the battle of Etshaneni. As Mandlakazi refugees retreated southwards to the 'Reserve', the worst fears of the Usuthu leaders were confirmed. Their Boer allies treated the conquered territory as their own. Despite Usuthu protests the Boers marked out farms and in 1885 they proclaimed a 'New Republic' over five-sixths of Zululand from the Transvaal to the sea.

British annexation of Zululand, 1886–7 By extending the boundaries of their 'New Republic' as far as the

sea, however, the Boers of the Transvaal unintentionally reawakened British interest in Zululand. The Germans had already shown an interest in establishing a protectorate over the area. The British were therefore anxious to separate the Boers from the sea. As with the Tswana in the west the British feared an anti-British alliance between the Germans and the Boers. The British therefore extended their authority over eastern Zululand north of the 'Reserve'. This left the Boers with much of the best upland territory around the headwaters of the Mfolozi and Mkhuze rivers. The 'New Republic' was incorporated into the Transvaal and the remaining region was proclaimed the colony of 'British Zululand' in 1887 (see Map 11.5).

Zibhebhu was allowed back into northern Zululand and once more drove the northern Usuthu out of their homesteads. In response Dinuzulu launched an Usuthu attack on the Mandlakazi. The British seized this as an opportunity to get rid of the Zulu king. Dinuzulu was arrested and banished to the remote Atlantic island of St. Helena. There he remained until 1897, the year British Zululand was joined to Natal.

11.4 Portrait of Cetshwayo taken during a visit to London in 1882.

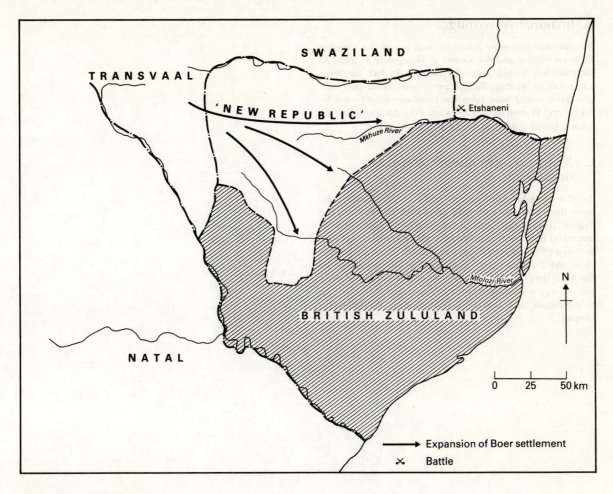

11.5 Partition of Zululand, 1887

The end of Zulu independence Within British Zululand the chiefs were brought under strict colonial control. They were forced to co-operate in the collection of a 'hut-tax' imposed on all married men. This, combined with drought in the late 1880s, finally drove the Zulu onto the Southern African labour market. The old Zulu economic independence had finally been broken. From now on Zulu men went out regularly to work for cash wages. They soon became one of the major sources of labour on the new gold mines of the Witwatersrand in the Transvaal.

Exercises

A. Think, discuss, understand and write

1 Discuss the causes and results of the First Anglo-Boer War (1880–81). Explain why, since annexation had been so easily achieved in 1877, the British were so easily ejected from the Transvaal in 1881.
2 Discuss the origins of the Bechuanaland wars of 1881–84. Who wanted British intervention and why? Do you think the various people concerned were satisfied with the way the British did eventually intervene?
3 How and why did the British take control of Bechuanaland in 1884–85? Why was Bechuanaland divided into 'crown colony' and 'protectorate' in 1885?
4 Why was Zululand torn by civil war between 1881 and 1884? In the long term, to what extent did the civil war suit the overall aims of British policy in the region?

B. Imaginative writing

Imagine that you were acting as secretary at the meeting between Warren and the Kwena at Molepolole in 1885. At that meeting Sechele's son Sebele was in fact the most outspoken in rejecting British 'protection'. Write out what you think would have been the main arguments used by Sebele and Warren at that meeting. Why do you think the Kwena finally agreed to accept British protection?

C. Mapwork, groupwork and class discussion

'In all it had taken the Boers of the South African Republic more than sixty years to make good their claims to all the Transvaal highveld south of the Limpopo.' Refer back to maps and text concerning Boer expansion north of the Vaal between 1836 and 1898 (Chapters 7 to 10). Draw up a time-chart and discuss why the Boers took so long to occupy all the land they claimed between Vaal and Limpopo. Why was African resistance eventually overcome? You may like to refer back to this exercise after reading the following chapter.

CHAPTER 12

The Southern African mineral revolution, stage II, 1886–99

The Witwatersrand gold rush and the founding of Johannesburg

Ever since the gold rushes of California (1849) and Australia (1851) European prospectors had wondered whether the rocky outcrops of the Southern African highveld might also contain gold. The Tati gold discoveries of 1867–8 had heightened expectations. In 1873 alluvial gold workings were discovered at Pilgrim's Rest near Lydenburg in the eastern Transvaal. But the Lydenburg goldfields were small-scale workings and European prospectors from America, Australia and Southern Africa itself scoured the region for richer deposits. 'Rushes' at De Kaap and Barberton in the eastern Transvaal in 1884–5 raised the hopes of financial speculators. But the Barberton

12.1 Gold-mining on the Witwatersrand reef with early Johannesburg visible on the horizon.

reefs did not last long and the search for gold continued elsewhere.

During the first half of 1886 prospectors began turning up finds of gold-bearing rock along the Witwatersrand ('white water's ridge') sixty kilometres south of Pretoria. By the middle of the year it was realised they had stumbled on a major gold-bearing reef. Here at last was gold in sufficient quantity for profitable large-scale mining. J. B. Robinson led the rush of mining capitalists from Kimberley who began buying up claims in the area in July. Robinson was followed by other more cautious Kimberley capitalists, including Rhodes. In September 1886 the Transvaal government officially proclaimed the Witwatersrand a 'public diggings' and ordered surveyors to lay out a village on the site. Within little more than a decade that 'village', named Johannesburg (after the government surveyor Johannes Rissik), had become the largest city in Africa south of the Sahara.

The importance of gold and the 'gold standard'
Gold is a rare and beautiful metal which does not deteriorate no matter what its age. Pure gold is relatively soft with a low melting point and so throughout the ages it has been highly valued for making jewellery, ornaments and other works of art. In the monied economies of Europe valuable metals such as gold, silver and copper had long been used as coins. With the industrialisation of Europe and North America in the nineteenth century world trade expanded and there was great demand for a universal world currency. Gold was most commonly chosen partly because of its beauty and quality but also because of its rarity and therefore high value.

Countries accepting gold as their standard form of currency were said to be on the 'gold standard'.

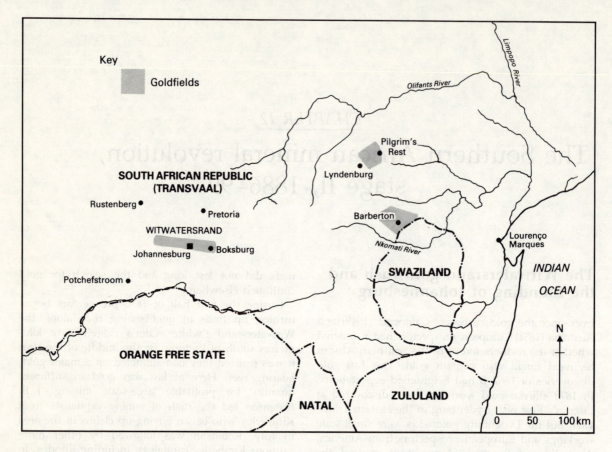

Goldfields

SOUTH AFRICAN REPUBLIC
(TRANSVAAL)

Rustenberg ●

● Pretoria

WITWATERSRAND

Johannesburg ■ ● Boksburg

Potchefstroom ●

ORANGE FREE STATE

NATAL

Limpopo River

Olifants River

Pilgrim's
Rest

Lyndenburg

Barberton

Nkomati River

SWAZILAND

Lourenço
Marques

INDIAN

OCEAN

ZULULAND

N

0   50   100 km

12.1 Goldfields of the Transvaal, 1873–86

The values of their currencies were fixed in relation to a standard universal price for gold. When dealing with large sums of money banks found it more convenient to issue special paper notes *representing* that amount of gold. The banks issuing the notes, however, had to *own* the gold their notes represented. The notes were only a *substitute* for the real thing. The notes were signed by the governor of the bank who stated on the note that he promised to 'pay the bearer on demand' that amount of gold. Many notes today still carry this phrase even though gold is no longer generally used as a standard of currency.

The rapid expansion of world trade in the late nineteenth century demanded ever greater quantities of gold. The supply from America and Australia, though rich at times, was irregular and unreliable. The discovery at the Witwatersrand of the largest single source of gold in the world thus came at a very important time. It provided bankers and governments with a large-scale, long-term, reliable supply of gold for the further expansion of

business and world trade. To Britain, striving to maintain her position as the dominant industrial and trading nation in the world, it was particularly significant that the goldfields fell within Southern Africa. Though technically in an independent Boer republic, the Witwatersrand lay within what Britain considered was her 'sphere of influence'. As we shall see, Britain was to go to extreme lengths to preserve her interests in the region.

The development of mining capitalism on the Rand

Learning from the experience of Kimberley, mining capitalists were quick to form companies on the goldfields of the Witwatersrand, often referred to simply as 'the Rand'. They raised capital by selling shares in their companies. In 1887 the Johannesburg Stock Exchange was founded. This was a place where new companies were registered and where people bought and sold shares in the companies.

Investors and speculators Bankers and capitalists from Europe as well as Southern Africa were eager to buy gold shares. They were so impressed by the extent of the gold reefs that they believed huge profits could be made out of mining on the Rand. As demand for shares rose, sellers charged higher prices for them and still the investors bought more. Many had no direct connection with mining at all. They were speculators. For them the buying and selling of shares was a business in itself. They bought shares in certain companies, waited until the share prices rose and then sold the shares and kept the profit. Because of the activities of speculators, share prices rose higher and higher until they bore no relationship to the actual amount of gold being *produced* by the companies.

Financial difficulties In 1889 the mining companies ran into difficulties. The richer surface deposits were largely worked out and deep under the ground the ore was of poorer quality. Profits after all would be neither quick nor easy and banks began to withdraw their loans. The speculators panicked. Suddenly everybody was selling gold shares and nobody wanted to buy. Prices of shares tumbled to a fifth of what they had been a few weeks earlier. Speculators lost fortunes and some mining companies went out of business altogether. This was Johannesburg's first stock market 'crash' but by no means its last.

Deep-level mining The big companies survived the crash and managed to persuade banks to lend them money again. It was known that the Rand contained huge reefs of gold but it was mostly in low quality ore found hundreds of metres below the surface. It would take time to extract and needed huge investment in machinery, explosives and labour. But this was where the long-term future lay. Only the biggest companies could afford the investment for deep-level mining. Scientists developed a new chemical process for extracting the tiny grains of metal from the low-grade ore. This used cyanide and was able to extract nearly twice as many grammes per tonne of ore as the earlier chemical process using mercury. The deep-level mines began producing gold in 1892. By then the goldfields were dominated by eight large companies, the largest being the Wernher-Beit Company and Rhodes's Consolidated Goldfields.

Social and economic effects of the Witwatersrand's mineral revolution

The social and economic effects of Kimberley's early mineral revolution (see Chapter 9) were repeated on the Rand, but on a far larger scale.

Labour Wage labour was recruited from all over the region, but this time right from the start

12.2 Johannesburg in 1888.

unskilled African workers were carefully controlled and housed in compounds. Strenuous efforts were made to keep down wages. At the insistence of the mine-owners pass laws were introduced on the goldfields in 1896. All Africans had to carry passes issued by a government official or by an employer. This prevented Africans from moving about in search of a different employer or better-paid work. The Witwatersrand Native Labour Association (WNLA, known as 'Wenela') recruited cheap contract labour from as far afield as Mozambique and the Zambezi. These contract workers were used for the dangerous underground work that the more experienced local workers were not prepared to do. By the end of the century there were an estimated 100 000 blacks working on the Rand and some 14 000 whites. The whole economic centre of Southern Africa had shifted to the Rand. It was a transformation that was to dominate the future course of Southern African history.

Fuel Huge machines were needed for crushing the ore and for operating the winches up and down the mines. These were powered by steam engines. But the fuel was not such a problem as it had been for Kimberley. There was coal nearby and a small local railway was soon built to the coalfields of Boksburg thirty kilometres east of Johannesburg.

Transport The development of the Witwatersrand was a huge stimulus to the agriculture and trade of the whole of Southern Africa. As the city of Johannesburg grew in size, it imported ever larger quantities of machinery, building materials, food, clothing and luxuries. The harbours of Natal and the Cape Colony thrived on the customs duties charged on imports. Harbours were expanded and the two British colonies competed in building railways to the Rand. They each hoped to benefit from a monopoly of the traffic. The Cape railway through the Orange Free State was the first to reach the Rand in 1892.

Agriculture The growth of a huge labour force on the Rand provided a thriving new market for agricultural producers, black and white, throughout the region. In some favourable agricultural areas, such as the eastern Cape where Africans still had access to land, peasant farmers prospered. As new opportunities opened for blacks, on the other hand, white farmers experienced a severe shortage of labour. Wages on the mines and on the rail and harbour construction works were much higher than those offered by white farmers who were used to using

labour tenants. Africans who had to find cash to pay taxes or buy goods, and who no longer had free access to good agricultural land, were thus attracted away from the rural areas. And yet with the expansion of agriculture white farmers needed even more labour than before. Throughout the British colonies and Boer republics, therefore, it was a period of new restrictive laws to force Africans to work on farms as well as on the mines and railways.

Boer participation The Boers of the Transvaal were greatly affected by the development of the Witwatersrand. Though they took little part in the early development of the mines, they profited from Johannesburg as a market for their agricultural produce. By the late 1880s a hundred ox-wagons a day were bringing the agricultural produce of black and white farmers of the Transvaal to Johannesburg market. The mines themselves were owned and run almost exclusively by European outsiders, especially from Britain. The mining industry, however, gave a great boost to the finances of the state. Taxation on the mines and markets of the Rand raised huge amounts of revenue for the republican government. In the twelve years from 1883 to 1895 government revenue was multiplied twenty-five times. This newly strengthened state was able to raise a loan in Europe for building its own rail link with the Portuguese port of Lourenço Marques (present-day Maputo) at Delagoa Bay. In 1894 the Netherlands-South African Railway Company opened its line from Lourenço Marques to Pretoria and Johannesburg. The Boer republic was now at last in a position to break loose from British domination. The consequences of this will be discussed in the following chapter.

Further colonial expansion

The opening of the Witwatersrand goldfields stimulated further colonial expansion all over Southern Africa. In little more than a decade the remaining independent African states were brought under colonial control. Mining capitalists and colonial farmers sought further African land and labour while speculators bought land for its mineral wealth and sought mining concessions from independent African rulers.

The colonisation of Zimbabwe

The existence of ancient African gold workings on the Zimbabwe plateau was well known in colonial

12.2 Transport and labour to the Rand in the 1890s.

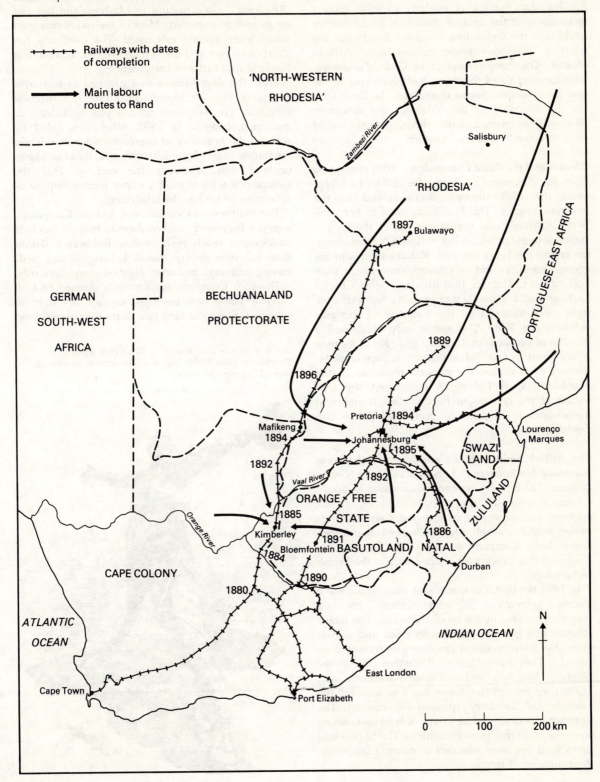

South Africa. It was believed by some, especially Rhodes, that the use of modern scientific mining techniques on the ancient goldfields of Zimbabwe could turn the region into a 'second Rand'. But the territory was still under independent African control. The former empires of Great Zimbabwe, Munhumutapa and the Rozvi had given way in the east to numerous Shona chiefdoms. To their west lay the kingdom of the Ndebele, the dominant power of the plateau, with whom colonists would have to come to terms or conquer.

Rhodes and the Rudd Concession

With prompting from Rhodes, among others, the British had kept open the road through Bechuanaland to the northern interior. The British, anxious to keep the Boers, Germans and Portuguese out of the region, signed a treaty of friendship with the Ndebele king, Lobengula, in February 1888. Rhodes then sent his agents north to get a mineral concession from Lobengula. In October 1888 Rhodes's agent Charles Rudd tricked Lobengula into granting him exclusive right over minerals in the kingdom. Lobengula believed the Rudd Concession only concerned a handful of prospectors. In fact it gave Rhodes's men a free hand to take 'whatever action they consider necessary' to exploit the mineral resources of the kingdom. When Lobengula discovered the true nature of the concession he cancelled it and sent messengers to England to protest to the British Government.

The British South Africa Company and the occupation of Mashonaland

Lobengula's protests were ignored. The British Government favoured Rhodes's scheme of colonisation by private company. It was a cheap and easy way of bringing Central Africa under British control. Rhodes formed the British South Africa Company which in 1889 was granted a royal charter (document of approval) by the British Government.

In 1890 the BSA Company sent into Zimbabwe a 'pioneer column' of 200 white settlers with their wagons protected by 200 mounted police. The whole column was heavily armed with rifles and maxim guns (the latest model of machine-gun mounted on wheels). They skirted the south-eastern edge of the Ndebele kingdom and occupied 'Mashonaland'. There they hoisted the British flag and founded the township of 'Salisbury' (present-day Harare). The Company handed out free grants of land and mining concessions to the 'pioneer' settlers. The Shona sold them food but were reluctant to provide labour for their mines and farms.

The invasion of 'Matabeleland' and founding of 'Rhodesia'

Gold mining in Mashonaland did not do as well as expected. Most of the old Shona gold mines were already exhausted. The Company ran short of money and the settlers looked with envy at the land and cattle of the Ndebele.

From the start Rhodes had planned to take over the whole of the region, including the Ndebele kingdom. He had even tried a plot to kidnap or murder Lobengula in 1890. When this failed he realised the best way to overcome Ndebele military resistance would be to establish a foothold in Mashonaland first. Towards the end of 1893 the Company's settlers used a minor border dispute as an excuse to invade 'Matabeleland'.

The swiftness of their invasion and the Company's superior firepower enabled them to beat off Ndebele attacks and reach their capital, Bulawayo. Rather than fall into enemy hands Lobengula had fled, leaving Bulawayo in flames. He died soon afterwards.

The BSA Company settlers then claimed that all Ndebele cattle now belonged to them by right of conquest. Over the next two years they seized land

12.3 A cartoon of Cecil Rhodes in 1892 which appeared in 'Punch', a popular British magazine. The cartoon suggests his imperial ambitions in Africa.

and cattle and pushed the Ndebele into 'reserves'. The Company now laid claim to the whole of modern Zimbabwe and began to call the territory 'Rhodesia', after the name of their founder, Rhodes.

Resistance and conquest, 1896–7   The Ndebele had not been properly defeated. They had kept their guns and in 1896 they rose in rebellion against the oppression of the white invaders. They were soon joined by the Shona who rebelled against the violent methods used by the Company to collect tax and forced labour. Many whites were killed in the first few days and the survivors were driven to form defensive laagers in the towns. The Africans of Zimbabwe might have succeeded in expelling the intruders had the 'Rhodesian' settlers not been able to call on the military support of the British empire in the form of a British relieving force which soon arrived from the Cape. Even so it was only after a long and fierce struggle that Ndebele and Shona resistance was finally overcome.

The consequences were bitter for the Africans of the region. They were disarmed, pushed into reserves, taxed and forced to labour on the mines and farms of the whites. Nevertheless their heroic resistance of 1896–7 was to become an inspiration for the freedom fighters of a later generation who ended the colonial occupation of Zimbabwe in 1980.

The Bechuanaland Protectorate and Tswana resistance to Company rule, 1885–99

The early Protectorate, 1885–91   When the British declared the Bechuanaland Protectorate in 1885, it extended north only as far as Latitude 22 degrees south. This cut off the northern claims of Khama's Ngwato kingdom and omitted altogether the region of Ngamiland which was dominated by the expanding Tswana state of the Tawana. For the first few years the only real British presence in the territory was the Bechuanaland Border Police who mostly patrolled the Transvaal border along the Limpopo. In 1890, in agreement with Germany, the British extended the boundary of the Protectorate as far as the Zambezi. This was done without consulting the Tawana of Ngamiland. In 1891 the British High Commissioner issued proclamations setting up administrative control over the Protectorate. Assistant commissioners were appointed to the police camp at Gaborone and to Khama's new capital, Palapye. It was a minimal adminstration and was intended to respect African law and custom, providing this did not conflict with British interests.

Rhodes's grasp for Ngamiland, 1893–4   Towards the end of 1893, while the BSA Company was busy attacking the Ndebele, Rhodes was scheming to extend his colony over the northern half of the Bechuanaland Protectorate. He sent his agent. Bosman, to the Tawana king, Sekgoma, to trick him into signing away his country. Bosman pretended he was an agent of the British Queen, there to sign a treaty of friendship with Sekgoma. In practice the English and Dutch versions of the 'treaty' which Sekgoma signed granted the land and minerals of Ngamiland to Bosman and the BSA Company.

There had been rumours for some time that Boers from the republics and Cape Colony intended to trek across the Kalahari to settle in this region. Rhodes was determined not to lose control of Ngamiland in the same way as he had nearly lost the 'road to the north' to the Boers of Stellaland and Goshen. He decided in fact to use a 'Boer trek' of his own to establish control of Ngamiland. Rhodes therefore advertised for Boers to join the 'Ngamiland trek' which he promised to finance.

Sekgoma immediately protested that he had given away no such rights to Bosman. J. S. Moffat, the assistant commissioner at Palapye, supported his protest. Moffat had been shocked by the brutality of the BSA Company's conquest of Matabeleland. He was also particularly anti-Boer in sentiment. To the protests of Sekgoma and Moffat were added those of the other major Tswana chiefs, Khama, Bathoen and Sebele. They refused to allow the Boers to pass through their territory.

The settlement of the Ghanzi farms, 1896–98   The British Government set up an enquiry into the Bosman concession. This found that it had been obtained by fraud so it was disallowed. The British Government meanwhile had decided that a small white settlement in the Ghanzi district would help establish a British presence in the region. In 1896 it persuaded Sekgoma to give away the Ghanzi district for white settlement in return for a guarantee that the rest of Ngamiland would remain a Tawana 'reserve'. In this way Sekgoma retained the bulk of his precolonial state intact. The British used a small party of Boers to settle the Ghanzi farms in 1898. Some of their descendants still live in the region today.

Tswana resistance to BSA Company rule   When the BSA Company had been granted its royal charter in 1889 the whole of Bechuanaland was included within its future territory. Early in 1895 the British Government agreed to the transfer of the Bechuanaland Protectorate to the Company's control. The southern colony of British Bechuanaland was to go to the Cape, of which Rhodes was Prime Minister (since 1890).

When news of the proposed transfers leaked out, the Tswana chiefs, north and south of the Molopo, vigorously protested. The protests of the southern Tswana were easily overruled and in November 1895

12.3 The Bechuanaland Protectorate in the 1890s

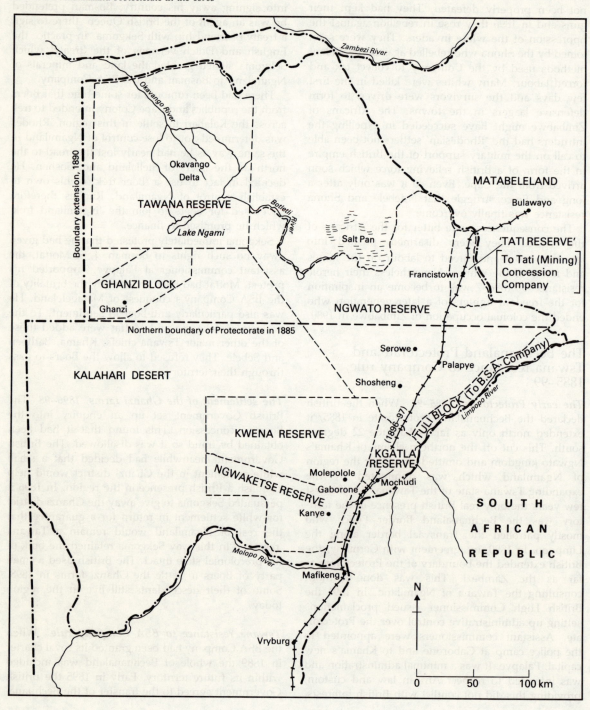

British Bechuanaland was joined to the Cape. The chiefs of the Protectorate, however, considered that they had consented merely to the protection of the British Queen. The British Government had no right to hand them over to a private company, especially not one with the reputation of the BSA Company. The Tswana did not trust Rhodes or any of his Company agents. They had seen the way he had tried to cheat Sekgoma in Ngamiland. Most important, they had seen the Company's brutal conquest of the Ndebele and the wholesale confiscation of Ndebele land and cattle. Khama, Bathoen and Sebele travelled to England and took their protests direct to the British Government.

When the colonial minister, Chamberlain, refused to discuss the matter, the Tswana chiefs appealed to the British public. Helped by a LMS missionary who acted as interpreter, Khama, Bathoen and Sebele staged a series of public protest meetings in several major British cities. They revealed the true nature of Rhodes's dealings and their own desire to continue under genuine British 'protection'. Their appeal worked. Faced with strong British opposition Chamberlain was forced to come to terms with the Tswana chiefs.

In November 1895 Chamberlain agreed to cancel the transfer of the Protectorate to the BSA Company. In return the chiefs agreed that a narrow strip of territory should be handed over to the Company for the construction of a railway from Mafikeng to Bulawayo. They also agreed to an annual hut-tax of ten shillings to pay for a British administration though the actual collection of the tax remained in the hands of the chiefs themselves.

The actions of Sekgoma in Ngamiland and Khama, Bathoen and Sebele in London were important displays of successful African diplomacy against the might of colonial South Africa and a major capitalist company. Their success was a great victory for the Tswana for it allowed their country to remain a 'Protectorate'. And in due course a later generation was able to lead that country to independence.

Swaziland: concessions and annexation, 1880–1902

During the minority of Mbandzeni (1874–81) the main danger to Swazi independence seemed to come from the Pedi and the Zulu. The Swazi regents

12.4 The Tswana chiefs in London, 1895, to petition the Queen against the handing over of the Bechuanaland Protectorate to Rhodes's British South Africa Company. Seated: (second from left) Bathoen, Khama, Sebele and General Warren (who had established the Protectorate in the first place ten years earlier). Standing in rear (far right)is Rev Willoughby, LMS missionary who acted as guide and interpreter to the chiefs during their visit.

cleverly used alliances with British and Boers to protect themselves from each of these. We have already seen how a Swazi alliance with the British had brought about the downfall of the Pedi in 1879. In the Anglo-Zulu war the Swazi claimed friendship with the British but avoided direct invasion of Zululand in case of future Zulu reprisals. As the Zulu kingdom disintegrated through civil war in the 1880s the Swazi were, for the first time ever, freed from the danger of Zulu attack. New and hitherto unsuspected dangers were, however, already taking hold of the kingdom.

Conquest by concession   For some time Boers from the Transvaal had been hiring grazing rights in Swaziland. The Swazi regents allowed this in return for payment on the understanding that it gave away no rights to the land itself. Then came the gold 'rushes' of Barberton and De Kaap in 1884–5 and the Witwatersrand in 1886. Concession-hunters poured into Swaziland seeking mineral concessions from the Swazi king Mbandzeni.

Concessions were paid for in cash, luxuries and alcohol. Mbandzeni appears to have given way to the temptation of these and granted enormous numbers of concessions. He soon began to lose track of the mass of conflicting titles. He appointed 'Offy' Shepstone (son of the better-known Theophilus Shepstone) to take charge of granting concessions. But this only made matters worse for Shepstone was not to be trusted and pocketed much of Mbandzeni's income for himself. By 1880 Mbandzeni, a sick man, gave up all effort to retain control. Referring to the luxuries he received he said: 'Why should I not eat before I die?' The scramble for further concessions quickened during 1889 as whites realised Mbandzeni was dying.

The majority of the concessions were for grazing rights, firewood and minerals. By 1890 whites controlled two-thirds of the land of the Swazi kingdom. Other concessions concerned the rights over many important affairs of government such as posts, telegraph, trade and customs dues as well as many manufacturing monopolies. Following Mbandzeni's death Shepstone took over effective control of government in conjunction with a special committee of whites from the South African Republic (Transvaal).

Annexation of Swaziland   The republican president, Paul Kruger, saw Swaziland as his opportunity to gain access to the sea across Tongaland to Kosi Bay (see Map 12.4). His citizens already controlled most of the land. But an official takeover of the Swazi kingdom needed the approval of the British Government who still demanded the right to approve or disapprove the republic's foreign relations. In a deal with the British, Kruger agreed to give up all claims north of the Limpopo in exchange for British acceptance of a republican takeover of Swaziland.

After a series of meetings, at which Shepstone acted as representative of the Swazi, the Third Swaziland Convention of 1894 officially approved the deal. Despite vigorous Swazi protests, including a delegation to London, Swaziland became a 'Protectorate' of the South African Republic in 1895.

Having forsaken the Swazi in order to gain freedom from Boer intervention north of the Limpopo, the British now cheated the Republic out of its access to the sea. No sooner had the Boers taken over Swaziland than the British annexed Tongaland, including Kosi Bay.

A British Protectorate   Republican control over Swaziland did not last long. During the South African War, 1899–1902 (see next chapter), Swaziland was abandoned by the Boers. After the war it officially became a British 'Protectorate'. The British decided to recognise the land concessions as full freehold ownership. That left the Swazi with only one-third of the land. In this respect the colonisation of Swaziland was very different from that of Bechuanaland or Basutoland.

The colonisation of Bechuanaland, Basutoland and Swaziland

The land of Bechuanaland was believed by whites to be mostly desert. Most of it therefore was not greatly coveted by potential white farmers. The small-scale gold mines of the Tati region suggested there might be valuable mineral deposits elsewhere in the territory. But in such a vast and sparsely populated country they would be hard to find. The territory's value to the British therefore was mostly strategic. In addition the Tswana of the Protectorate had long experience of British missionaries and merchants. They had learnt to distrust British concession-hunters as much as they distrusted Boers and they were very wary about what rights they gave away.

Basutoland was mostly mountain. The Sotho had already lost much of their valuable agricultural land in wars with the Boers. And they had demonstrated their determination and ability to use force to defend what remained.

Swaziland by contrast was fertile, well-watered

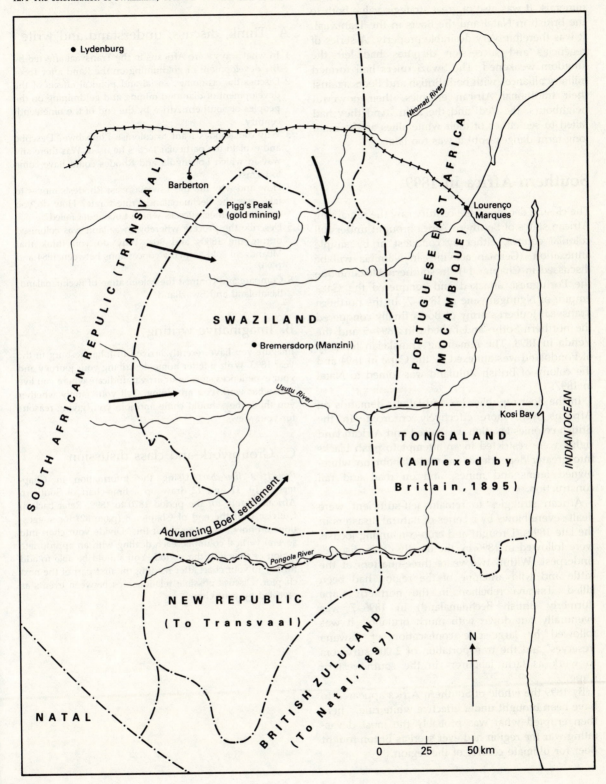

- Lydenburg

SOUTH AFRICAN REPUBLIC (TRANSVAAL)

- Barberton

- Pigg's Peak
  (gold mining)

SWAZILAND

- Bremersdorp (Manzini)

Usutu River

Nkomati River

PORTUGUESE EAST AFRICA
(MOCAMBIQUE)

- Lourenço
  Marques

Kosi Bay

TONGALAND

(Annexed by
Britain, 1895)

INDIAN OCEAN

Advancing Boer settlement

Pongola River

NEW REPUBLIC

(To Transvaal)

NATAL

BRITISH ZULULAND
(To Natal, 1897)

N

0   25   50 km

and productive and was believed to be rich in minerals. It was also of great strategic value both to the British in Natal and the Boers in the Transvaal. It was therefore very desirable property. A series of regencies and succession disputes had left the kingdom weakened. The Swazi rulers had formed military alliances with both British and Boers against their traditional African enemies, their powerful neighbours, the Pedi and the Zulu. And they had failed to see either of their white allies as the main long-term danger until it was too late.

Southern Africa in 1899

The closing decade of the century saw the remaining African states of Southern Africa brought under full colonial control, either by conquest or by simple annexation. (German activities in Namibia will be discussed in Chapter 14). In southern Mozambique the Portuguese attacked and conquered the Gaza empire of Ngungunyane in 1895–7. In the northern Transvaal Joubert's army of Boers finally conquered the northern Sotho and Lobedu in 1894–5 and the Venda in 1898. The remaining Transkeian territory of Pondoland was annexed by the Cape in 1894 and the colony of British Zululand was joined to Natal in 1897.

In the Boer republics tax and labour demands on Africans were more effectively enforced. In the British colonies taxation was raised and African land rights were restricted in an attempt to push blacks into greater dependence on wage labour on white-owned farms and mines, and on road and rail construction.

African struggles to remain self-sufficient were dealt severe blows by a series of natural disasters in the late 1890s. Drought and crop-consuming locusts were followed in 1896 by the deadly cattle disease, rinderpest. Within two years three-quarters of the cattle and wild antelope of the region had been killed. Tswana rebellion in the northern Cape (formerly British Bechuanaland) in 1896–7 was eventually put down with much brutality. It was followed by large-scale confiscation of Tswana 'reserves' and the transportation of 2 000 survivors to work as farm labourers in the south-western Cape.

By 1899 the whole of Southern Africa appeared to have been brought under effective white rule. There then erupted what was probably the most devastating war the region had ever seen as Briton fought Boer for ultimate control of the region.

Exercises

A. Think, discuss, understand and write

1 In what ways were Africans in the Transvaal affected by the development of goldmining on the Rand after 1886?
2 Discuss the economic, social and political effects of the development of diamond mining and goldmining on the peoples of Southern Africa by the end of the nineteenth century.
3 Why did Rhodes want to colonise Zimbabwe? Describe and explain the particular tactics he used. Was there any way in which Lobengula and Rhodes could have come to terms?
4 How and why did the Tswana resist Rhodes's moves to take over the Bechuanaland Protectorate? How do you account for their success where Lobengula failed?
5 Describe the process whereby Swaziland was colonised during the 1880s and 90s. Why do you think that Mbandzeni sold so many concessions between 1884 and 1890?
6 Compare and contrast the colonisation of Bechuanaland, Basutoland and Swaziland.

B. Imaginative writing

Imagine you have recently arrived in Johannesburg in the year 1890. Write a letter home describing your journey and your experiences since your arrival. Indicate where you live and what work you are doing. Tell your family whether you think they should come and join you, giving reasons for your views.

C. Groupwork and class disussion

Project: a time-chart Using the information in Chapters 9, 10, 11 and 12 draw up a time-chart of Southern African history for the period 1870 to 1899. Refer back to Exercise C at the end of Chapter 8 (page 82) for suggestions on how best to go about this. Divide your chart into several vertical columns, each dealing with an appropriate region or theme of the period. You should be able to add further to your chart after reading the first part of the next chapter. Discuss possible relationships between events as revealed by your chart.

CHAPTER 13

War and Union: triumph of imperialism, 1895–1910

Origins of Afrikaner nationalism

Until the 1870s most Dutch-speaking colonists of Southern Africa referred to themselves as *Boers* (farmers), *Burghers* (citizens) or simply *Volk* (people). Their language was influenced by various European and African usages. It had thus drifted from the original Dutch to form the distinctive South African dialect *Afrikaans*.

British movements for federation under British domination in the 1870s helped promote a reaction among 'Afrikaners'. The Afrikaners' language, pastoral culture and religion (the extreme protestant Christianity of the Dutch Reformed Church) were in danger of being swamped by English influences. Cultural movements to promote the Afrikaans language, culture and religion were started by Church ministers and teachers. In 1880 a political party, the *Afrikaner Bond*, was formed in the Cape Colony by S. J. du Toit, a minister of the Dutch Reformed Church. It was soon taken over and developed into a powerful Cape parliamentary party by Jan Hofmeyr, a wealthy farmer from the western Cape.

Afrikaner nationalism received a great boost from the success of the Transvaal's rebellion against the British in 1881. Use of the term 'Afrikaner' grew more widespread. Under Hofmeyr's direction the Afrikaner Bond became an important influence in Cape politics though it still believed in a close alliance with Britain for defence and protection of trade.

In the Transvaal, however, members of the Bond came into personal conflict with the recently elected President, Paul Kruger, so the movement made little headway in the newly independent republic. Kruger's Government remained strongly suspicious

of any kind of alliance with the British. He turned instead for support to the Netherlands and to Britain's main European rival, Germany. Kruger's nationalism was local, republican and anti-British rather than the wider Afrikaner nationalism of the Afrikaner Bond. But the nationalism of Kruger's republic cannot alone explain the developing conflict between the Boers and the British which finally erupted in war in 1899. The origins of that war are to be found in competition for control of the wealth of the Witwatersrand.

13.1 A cartoon which appeared in a popular French magazine in 1899. It shows Queen Victoria (representing Britain) crushing Paul Kruger, President of the Transvaal Republic. The original caption read 'England eternal champion of justice, protects the weak'. France as a competitor in the scramble for Africa was highly critical of British domination in Southern Africa at this time.

Origins of War

Kruger's Republic and the industrialisation of the Transvaal As we saw in the previous chapter, the development of gold mining on the Rand greatly increased the income of Kruger's Republic. Within ten years the Transvaal was transformed from a backward pastoral economy into the richest state in Southern Africa. But the source of this newfound wealth, the gold-mining industry, remained in the hands of *uitlanders* (European 'outsiders'). They had brought in the skills and capital needed to develop the Witwatersrand. Kruger, however, was determined that this increasing wealth should be turned to the benefit of the Afrikaner people of the Republic.

Kruger's Government placed heavy direct taxes on the mining industry's profits. It charged high customs duties on the huge imports of machinery and other manufactured goods essential for the development of the Rand. In order to keep the profits from other industries within the Transvaal, Kruger introduced monopoly concessions. Monopolies were granted for the manufacture of such things as dynamite and alcohol, the supply of water to Johannesburg and the construction of railways in the Republic. The point about a monopoly is that the concession-holder can charge as high a price as he wants without fear of competition from others charging less. The concession system therefore raised huge profits for the companies concerned and many important Afrikaners invested heavily in them. But, as we shall see below, the high prices charged by the concession companies added greatly to the cost of production in the gold-mining industry.

Finally there was Kruger's policy towards the *uitlanders* themselves. The *uitlanders* and their capital were largely British in origin. By the 1890s they were thought to outnumber the adult male Afrikaner population of the Republic. There was thus a real danger that if they were granted full citizenship and allowed to vote in elections, they would take over the government of the country. They could then lower import duties, abolish concessions and introduce other laws which would benefit the gold-mining industry rather than the rural Afrikaners. To prevent this happening Kruger raised the qualification for voting to fourteen years residence. This brought protests from the *uitlanders*: white mineworkers, shop-keepers, merchants, bankers and mine-owners. But the most dangerous opposition to Kruger's policies came from the people most affected by them, the small number of capitalist owners of the larger mining companies.

Mining magnates and Kruger's Republic We saw in the last chapter how owners of the larger mining companies invested huge sums of money in deep-level mining in the early 1800s. They were thus deeply committed to the long-term development of the Rand. In addition, the deep-level ores were of low grade, that is, each ton of ore yielded only a tiny amount of gold. In order to make a profit out of low-grade ores from so deep below the ground, it was essential that production costs were kept to a minimum.

The mining magnates, therefore, wanted Kruger's Government to introduce laws which would favour the mining industry rather than the rural Afrikaners. Taxes and customs duties were too high. The whole system of monopolies raised prices of essential manufactured goods like dynamite, so vital to deep-level mining. The Netherlands-South African Railway Company, which held the railway monopoly, charged very high transport rates for machinery and other essential imports. Finally there was the problem of labour. The mining magnates needed a large, regular supply of cheap, unskilled labour. But Kruger's Government was unable and unwilling to provide this. Its priority was to keep labour in the rural areas working on the Afrikaners' farms.

The Jameson Raid By 1895 several of the mining magnates began secretly plotting to remove Kruger's Government. Rhodes, who was Prime Minister of the Cape (since 1890), devised a plot to stage a *coup d'etat* (that is, to seize the Government by force). He secretly sent rifles into Johannesburg to encourage the *uitlanders* to rise in rebellion. He planned to support this rising with an invasion from across the border in Bechuanaland. This was why Rhodes particularly wanted the transfer of the Protectorate to his BSA Company before the end of 1895 (see previous chapter).

BSA Company Police were summoned down from 'Rhodesia' and stationed at Pitsani near the Transvaal border. They were commanded by Rhodes's friend, the administrator of Rhodesia, Dr Leander Star Jameson. But Rhodes's plan failed. The *uitlanders* in Johannesburg were disorganised and failed to rebel. Jameson meanwhile refused to be put off and launched his attack anyway in the final week of 1895. His band of 480 raiders was surrounded by Boer commandos and forced to surrender before it reached Johannesburg. Jameson, his troops and the leaders of the Johannesburg *uitlanders* were imprisoned in Pretoria gaol. As a gesture of goodwill Kruger soon released them after the payment of heavy fines.

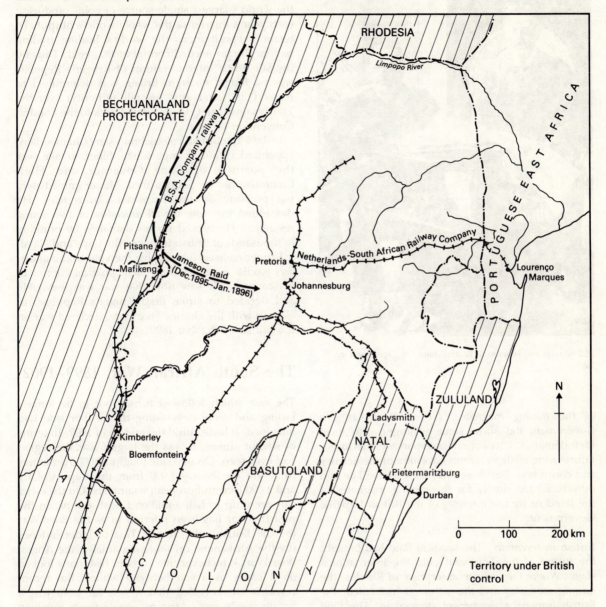

Results of the Raid The disaster of the Jameson Raid had a number of important results. As soon as it became known that Rhodes was behind the plot, he had to resign his position as Prime Minister of the Cape. The parliamentary alliance between British South Africans and the Afrikaner Bond, which Rhodes and Hofmeyr had so carefully built up, now lay in ruins. The Raid prompted an anti-British feeling among Afrikaners throughout Southern Africa. It brought additional support for Kruger who was elected by a huge majority for a further five-year

presidency in 1898. It also strengthened the alliance between the Transvaal and the Orange Free State.

The failure of the Raid even endangered the security of Rhodes's colony of Rhodesia. While Jameson and the colony's BSA Police were in Pretoria gaol, the Ndebele seized the opportunity and rose in rebellion in March 1896. As we saw in the previous chapter, they and the Shona very nearly succeeded in driving out their brutal white conquerors.

The Raid, of course, failed to solve the problems

131

13.2 Rhodes and Jameson at Rhodes' house in Cape Town in 1891.

international trade. The Witwatersrand had become the world's largest single source of gold, producing each year a quarter of the whole world's output. To retain its position as the world's leading trading nation, Britain needed control of that gold. Thus by the late 1890s internal reform of Kruger's Republic was no longer enough. Britain was determined to reassert its 'suzerainty' (overall authority) over the Transvaal which it claimed dated back to the London Convention of 1884.

In 1897 the British colonial minister, Chamberlain, appointed a staunch imperialist, Milner, to take over the position of Cape Governor and High Commissioner for South Africa. Milner immediately put pressure on the Transvaal Government. He demanded the vote for all *uitlanders* of five years' residence. He backed up his demands by bringing in thousands of British troops to the Cape and Natal.

Kruger realised that to give the vote to the *uitlanders* would mean handing them political control of his country. He saw now that war was inevitable and decided to strike first. Kruger's Republic, in alliance with the Orange Free State, declared war on the British in October 1899.

The South African War, 1899–1902

The war which followed turned out to be longer-lasting and more devastating than either side had imagined. It lasted until the middle of 1902. In terms of size of armies, it was the largest war the region had ever seen. On one side fought 73 000 Afrikaners from the republics, 13 000 from the Cape Colony and 2 000 foreign European volunteers. On the other side were up to half-a-million British troops. In the past the war has been referred to as the Boer War (by the British), the Second War of Independence (by the Afrikaners) or, more impartially, the Anglo-Boer War. Whichever title chosen, historians looked on it solely as a war between whites. But recent research has revealed that it was far from just a 'white man's war'. Africans were actively involved on a large scale, many in armed conflict, and, in one way or another, the war affected all the peoples of South Africa. It is therefore more appropriate to call it 'the South African War'. We shall look first at the three main stages of the war and then consider the role of Africans in it.

Stage one: Boer invasions, 1899–1900 The Boers aimed to achieve a number of quick early victories before the arrival of large-scale British reinforcements from overseas. They hoped that this,

of the mining magnates. Nevertheless Kruger's Government did show some willingness to meet their demands. Rates of rail transport were reduced. Efforts were made to reform government inefficiency and corruption. But these reforms were too late and introduced too slowly for the mining magnates of the Rand or for the interests of the British Imperial Government.

British intervention The Jameson Raid had brought the future of the Transvaal onto the international stage. Where the 'private enterprise' of Rhodes, the mining magnates and the *uitlanders* had failed, the British Imperial Government stepped in. The Raid had brought home to the British Government the danger and urgency of the situation in the Transvaal. When Jameson's raiders were captured, the German emperor had sent Kruger a telegram of congratulations. By the late 1890s the European rivalry which was eventually to lead to World War I in 1914 was already building up. A firm Transvaal/German alliance could threaten the whole future security of Britain's position in Southern Africa and, indeed, the world.

We have already seen the importance of gold to

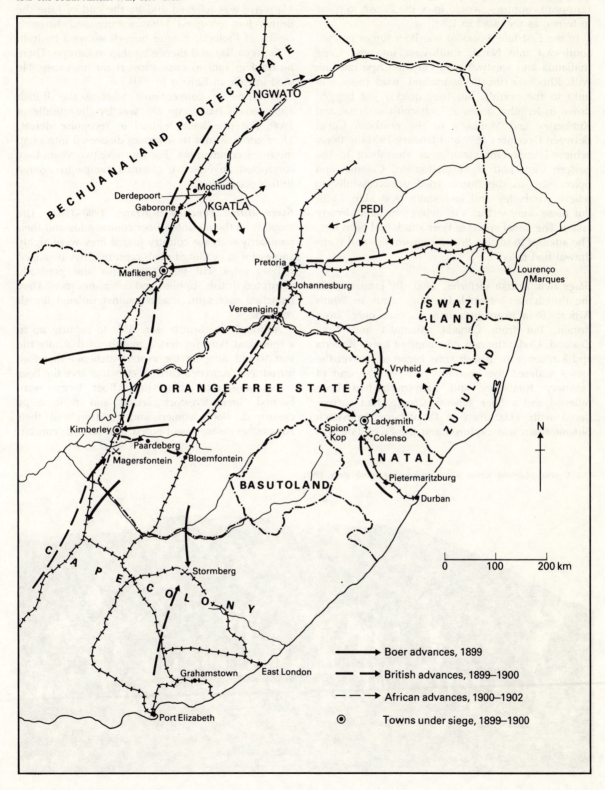

NGWATO

BECHUANALAND PROTECTORATE

Derdepoort
Gaborone
Mochudi

KGATLA

PEDI

Mafikeng

Pretoria

Johannesburg

Lourenço
Marques

Vereeniging

SWAZI-
LAND

ZULULAND

Vryheid

ORANGE FREE STATE

Kimberley

Paardeberg

Magersfontein Bloemfontein

BASUTOLAND

Spion
Kop

Ladysmith

Colenso

NATAL

Pietermaritzburg

Durban

N

CAPE COLONY

Stormberg

0   100   200 km

Grahamstown   East London

Port Elizabeth

→ Boer advances, 1899

⇢ British advances, 1899–1900

⇢ African advances, 1900–1902

◉ Towns under siege, 1899–1900

combined with diplomatic pressure from other European countries, would force the British to come to terms, as they had in 1881.

In the first few weeks of war Boer forces pushed south-east into Natal, south-west into the Cape midlands and westwards to cut the Cape rail link with Rhodesia (the Bechuanaland 'road (now rail-link) to the north'). But they quickly got bogged down in lengthy sieges at Ladysmith in Natal and Kimberley and Mafikeng in the northern Cape. Between December 1899 and January 1900 the Boers achieved important victories at Stormberg in the eastern Cape and at Magersfontein, Colenso and Spion Kop as the British tried unsuccessfully to relieve Kimberley and Ladysmith (see Map 13.2). But these were victories in defence of land already taken. The initial speed of Boer attack had been lost. The attempt to force a British compromise and withdrawal had failed.

Stage two: British victories, 1900 By January 1900 the British had assembled a huge army in South Africa. Reinforcements arrived, not only from Britain, but from Canada, Australia and New Zealand. Under the new command of Lords Roberts and Kitchener the British army began to recover the losses suffered the previous year. By the end of February Kimberley and Ladysmith had been relieved and a Boer general, Cronje, had surrendered with 4 000 men at Paardeberg. In March Bloemfontein was captured and the Free State was

annexed as the 'Orange River Colony'. In May Mafikeng was relieved and by the end of June the British had occupied Johannesburg and Kruger's capital of Pretoria. Kruger himself escaped by train to Delagoa Bay and thence by ship to Europe. There he tried in vain to raise support for his cause. He died in exile in Europe in 1904.

In terms of conventional warfare the British appeared to have won the war by the middle of 1900. But the Boers refused to recognise defeat. Their generals and their armies dispersed into small mounted commandos. For the next two years they conducted an effective guerrilla campaign against British occupation.

Stage three: guerrilla warfare, 1900–1902 The mobility of the mounted Boer commandos and their familiarity with the country meant they were highly successful in evading British capture. They damaged railway lines, cut telegraph wires and generally disrupted British supplies and communication. They launched successful attacks against isolated British columns.

Although the British were able to capture up to a thousand Boer fighters a month, at that rate the war would drag on for years. Kitchener therefore introduced 'scorched earth' tactics to starve the Boer commandos into submission. Boer farms were burned, their livestock seized and their crops destroyed. Boer women and children and their African servants were herded into fenced 'concen-

13.3 A group of armed African scouts working for British army, 1901.

tration camps'. There thousands died of disease in the filthy, crowded conditions. Some 27 000 whites, mostly children, and possibly as many blacks, died in the concentration camps between June 1901 and May 1902. The British erected thousands of kilometres of barbed-wire fencing to prevent the free movement of commandos across the highveld. Thousands of earth-and-iron blockhouses were erected to guard the fences and railways. Gradually the wire and blockhouse system was extended over most of the Transvaal and Orange Free State. More and more Boer resisters were shot or captured and eventually their commanders were forced into submission. The war ended with the peace treaty of Vereeniging in May 1902.

African participation in the South African War In the early stages of conflict Africans were widely used as unarmed labourers by both armies in the war. They worked as personal servants, dug trenches, drove wagons, grew crops and tended livestock. Mobile Boer commandos made heavy demands on rural Africans to provide them with livestock and food. The growing British army of occupation made increasing use of Africans in the final phase of the war, both as unarmed workers and wagon-drivers and as armed combatants.

Officially both sides declared it their policy not to involve Africans in the fighting of the war. It must be remembered that most of the larger African states had only recently been conquered by whites. To have armed them now, even as allies, might have provided them with guns for future rebellion. In practice, however, Africans were fairly extensively involved in the fighting, especially on the side of the British, either as allies or directly employed as scouts and soldiers.

Mfengu and Thembu were employed to defend the Transkei from Boer attack and 'Coloured' regiments were widely used in the western Cape. Once defeat of the Boers was fairly certain the Sotho of Basutoland became enthusiastic supporters of the British. They were widely used as labourers and became important suppliers of horses to the British army. Following the early Boer abandonment of Swaziland, the Swazi remained relatively uninvolved and effectively independent for the duration of the war.

The Rolong of Mafikeng who were caught in the siege took an active part in the defence of the town. But they received little recognition or thanks for their vital contribution. Deprived of equal access to food and ammunition, Africans suffered far greater hardships than whites during the siege and many died of starvation. In the Bechuanaland Protectorate the Ngwato of Chief Khama played an important role · in protecting the northern rail link with Rhodesia. The Kgatla of Mochudi fought the Boers

13.4 The inter-colonial conference, 1908. This group portrait includes three future prime ministers of the Union: General Botha (seated third from left), Jan Smuts (standing third from left) and J. B. Hertzog (standing fourth from left).

at Derdepoort. In the later stages of the war they invaded the Transvaal, drove the Boers from their farms and occupied much of former Kgatla territory. Chief Lentshwe hoped to join the western Transvaal with the Bechuanaland Protectorate to form a huge Kgatla 'reserve' after the war.

Africans, generally, in the Transvaal behaved similarly to the Kgatla in plundering Boer farms and reoccupying their land. The Pedi of Sekhukhuni II took the opportunity to expand their 'location' to something like the size of the heartland of the former Pedi kingdom. Sekhukhuni tried to get British recognition for Pedi independence under British 'protection', much as the Tswana of the Bechuanaland Protectorate had done. But the Pedi were disunited and after the war the British were quickly able to reassert authority and disarm them.

Meanwhile in the Vryheid ('New Republic') section of Zululand the Boers made heavy demands on the Zulu for labour, livestock and food. Towards the end of the war a Zulu regiment took its revenge and killed two-thirds of the Vryheid Boer commando.

The impact of the war on the African majority
To some extent Africans prospered from the war. The British army offered relatively high wages and many Africans refused to go back to lower wages after the war. In some areas peasant farmers benefitted from the high prices which the army paid for food. Africans, especially in the Transvaal, used the war as an opportunity to raid Boer farms and restock their cattle herds after the severe losses as a result of rinderpest.

On the other hand, blacks as well as whites suffered from the British 'scorched-earth' policy. In certain areas, especially the Orange River Colony, those living on Boer farms were crowded into concentration camps where their death rate per thousand was even higher than in the white camps.

Finally the war created rising expectations among Africans who expected to benefit from a British victory. They hoped for more land, better wages and working conditions, freedom of movement and generally a better opportunity to share more equally in the region's growing wealth. The better-educated looked for political gains. They hoped for an extension of the Cape's limited but non-racial franchise to Africans all over South Africa, thus giving them a real share in the government of the country. But the British domination and control of the region's growing industrial wealth had been the object of the war. Having lost 22 000 British lives and spent £200 million of British money to win the war, the British were not about to give it up to the African majority.

The reconstruction and unification of South Africa

The Peace of Vereeniging, May 1902 By the terms of the Peace of Vereeniging the Boer leaders agreed to recognise overall British authority. Their former republics became British colonies though they were promised internal self-government as soon as possible. The question of African voting rights was to be left up to the individual colonies to decide once they had control over their own affairs. Britain's first priority was to get Boer agreement to an end of the war and a recognition of British authority. To this end they were prepared to sacrifice the political rights of those Africans who had supported them during the war. Further British betrayals of their wartime black supporters were soon to follow.

Economic reconstruction In the period of economic reconstruction which followed the war, it soon became clear that white supremacy was to be restored and even strengthened. The first priority was the reconstruction of the mining industry. The dynamite and railway concessions were abolished and wages were cut to half their pre-war levels. Africans, however, refused to work at these rates and the mines suffered from a severe labour shortage. The problem was temporarily solved by the importation of 63 000 workers from northern China. They were brought in on five-year contracts at low fixed wages. By the time the Chinese were repatriated in 1908, the recruitment of African labour was well under way. WNLA was recruiting contract workers at low rates from as far away as Mozambique and Nyasaland (colonial Malawi).

Milner's post-war administration was determined to make agriculture more efficient in order to reduce food costs in the urban areas. (Lower food prices on the Rand would mean employers could pay lower wages.) The British government poured money into agricultural investment. Boers were restored to their farms and modern scientific techniques were encouraged. Moves were taken to promote white capitalist farming at the expense of African agricultural self-sufficiency. Labour-tenancy agreements began to be substituted by low-paid wage labour. Even with British loans, however, most white farmers lacked the skills and capital for the full development of capitalist farming. Sharecropping agreements between African farmers and white farm-owners remained widespread for years to come.

Africans of the former republics had hoped for greater economic freedom after the war. But they found that the British administration was even more efficient at enforcing 'pass laws' and collecting taxes. African occupation of former Boer farms was disallowed. The Kgatla failed to get their cross-border 'reserve'. The Pedi were reconfined to their former 'location'. Africans generally got no financial compensation for losses suffered during the war. African resentment at British post-war economic policies boiled over into open rebellion in Natal in 1906.

The Bambatha rebellion, 1906–8 When the Natal Government needed to raise extra money to pay off debts incurred during the war, they introduced a

poll tax of £1. This was to be paid by all adult men and was intended to get at those young unmarried African men not yet liable for payment of 'hut tax'. The Africans of Natal were already suffering from a severe shortage of land and well-paid employment. When the Government attempted to enforce this additional burden in 1906, they met with open African resistance.

In February 1906 two white tax-collectors were shot dead and the Government promptly imposed martial law. In an action reminiscent of the 'Langalibalele affair' (see pp 93–5), colonial troops rampaged through African 'reserves', burning crops and houses, seizing cattle and deposing chiefs.

13.3 The Union of South Africa, 1910

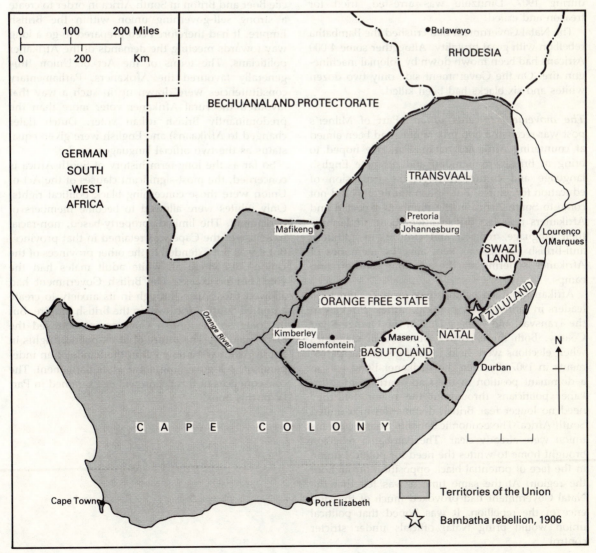

By April 1906 African resistance had become more organised. 'Rebels' gathered in the Nkandla forest under the leadership of a minor chief named Bambatha. There they held out for several months. The Natal Government called on the Cape for support, and Bambatha's resistance was eventually overcome by a large, combined colonial force in June 1906. At the battle of Mome gorge in the Nkandla forest Bambatha himself and hundreds of his followers were killed.

The Bambatha 'rebels' had used the royal name of Dinuzulu to try and unite the Zulu against the colonists. In fact Dinuzulu himself deliberately avoided open involvement in the rebellion. Nevertheless the Natal authorities turned on Dinuzulu as small-scale disturbances continued in Zululand during 1907. Dinuzulu was arrested, tried for treason and exiled.

The Natal Government had crushed the Bambatha rebellion with great brutality. Altogether some 4 000 Africans had been mown down by colonial machine-gun fire. On the Government side only two dozen whites and six blacks had been killed.

The movement towards union Part of Milner's post-war reconstruction programme had been aimed at countering Afrikaner nationalism. He hoped to bring in British immigration and promote English language and culture through the expansion of education for whites. But British immigrants did not come to South Africa in the numbers expected and Afrikaners resented British attempts to undermine their language, religion and culture. In addition, anti-British feeling was kept alive by memories of Afrikaner suffering in the wartime concentration camps.

Afrikaners rallied behind their former commando leaders in forming new political parties: *Het Volk* in the Transvaal and *Orangia Unie* in the Orange River Colony. Both these parties won overall majorities when elections were held for self-governing parliaments in 1907. By then the Afrikaner Bond was in a dominant position in the Cape parliament. Afrikaner politicians throughout the region felt they need no longer fear British domination in a united South Africa. The economic benefits from a customs union were already clear. The Bambatha rebellion brought home to whites the need for political union in the face of potential black opposition throughout the region. At the same time it was felt that the Natal Government had provoked much of the violence of the rebellion. It was hoped that political union would bring Natal officials under stricter control.

During 1908–9 the white politicians of the four colonies held a National Convention at Bloemfontein to discuss terms for political union. The Act of Union was passed by the British parliament in 1909 and came into effect in May 1910.

The Act of Union (1910) The Act of Union brought the Transvaal, Orange Free State, Natal and Cape under the authority of a single parliament based in Cape Town. Pretoria became the executive capital containing the central government civil service. The official head of state was a British-appointed Governor-General. The former Boer commando leaders Louis Botha and Jan Smuts became Prime Minister and Deputy respectively.

The British Government's main aim was to reconcile Boer and Briton in South Africa in order to create a strong self-governing union within the British Empire. It had therefore been prepared to go a long way towards meeting the demands of the Afrikaner politicians. The terms of the Act of Union thus generally favoured the Afrikaners. Parliamentary constituencies were drawn up in such a way that favoured the rural Afrikaner voter more than the predominantly British urban voter. Dutch (later changed to Afrikaans) and English were given equal status as the two official languages.

So far as the long-term history of South Africa is concerned, the most significant clauses of the Act of Union were those concerning black political rights. Only whites were allowed to become members of parliament. The limited, property-based, non-racial franchise of the Cape was retained in that province. But it was not extended to the other provinces of the Union. Elsewhere all white adult males had the vote, but no blacks. The British Government had allowed this clause through in its anxiety to create a unified South Africa within the British Empire. But in doing so the British Government betrayed the black majority. The future of black political rights in South Africa were now left in the hands of an independent, self-governing, local white parliament. The consequences of this action will be examined in Part IV of this book.

Exercises

A. Think, discuss, understand and write

1 To what extent do you think the discovery of diamonds at Kimberley and gold on the Rand affected relations between Britain and the Boer republics from 1870 to 1900?
2 Explain the mining magnates' grievances against Kruger's Republic in the 1890s; and explain the attitude of Kruger's Government to the industrial development of the Rand between 1886 and 1895.
3 Describe events leading to the outbreak of the South African War in 1899. Why was each side prepared to go to war?
4 Discuss the extent of African participation in the South African War. What did Africans hope to achieve as a result of participating in the war? Were their hopes fulfilled?
5 Explain British policy in South Africa between 1902 and 1910. What was the impact of this policy on Africans in the region? To what extent had British pre-war aims been fulfilled by 1910?
6 Discuss the main terms of the Union of South Africa in 1910. How did its terms affect the different peoples of South Africa ?

B. Imaginative writing

Imagine you are an African newspaper editor in 1910 commentating on the proposed Act of Union. Write your editorial in not more than 200 words.

C. Mapwork, groupwork and class discussion

Study Maps 13.1 and 13.2. Discuss the successes and failures of Boer and British tactics during the South African War. How significant was African participation in terms of helping either side to win?

Document study Read Document 13.1 and discuss the answers to the following questions:

1 What was the purpose of the South African National Convention to which the petitioners addressed their petition?
2 Did the petition succeed in its object?
3 Explain the terms of the Peace of Vereeniging which allowed the difference in policy between Transvaal and Cape Colony.
4 Discuss the terms of the Cape franchise which the petitioners wanted to have extended throughout South Africa. Do you consider it to have been a 'generous policy'? Explain your answer.

CHAPTER 14

German colonialism and African resistance in South West Africa

Namibia in the early nineteenth century

As we saw in Chapter 2, the early settlement and way of life of the people of Namibia was greatly influenced by the region's harsh, dry environment. Apart from the extreme north, settled by Ovambo mixed farmers, most of the region was suitable only for hunting, gathering and pastoralism. And huge areas of desert were too dry even for that. With the Namib desert along the west coast and the Kalahari to the south-east, the most suitable area for pastoralism was the central highveld region. Much of the country's nineteenth-century history was dominated by conflict between Nama and Herero pastoralists who struggled for control of the dry thornveld grasslands of the central Namibian plateau.

The Herero were organised in a variety of separate chiefdoms, with main centres at Otjimbingwe and Okahandja on the Swakop river. They grazed their huge herds of cattle southwards towards Rehoboth. The Nama were divided into many separate clans ranging in size from a few hundred people to several thousand. The main Nama clan with whom the Herero came into conflict were the Hoagana (also known as 'Red Nation' because of the ochre which they spread on their bodies). The Hoagana lived between Rehoboth and Oasip. Other important Nama clans were the Topnaars in the west and the Bondelswarts in the south (see Map 14.1).

Into this region in the early 1800s came the Oorlams from the Cape Colony, peoples of Khoikhoi and mixed European/Khoi ancestry (see Chapter 3). They were mainly traders and hunters but they also kept cattle. They arrived in small family groups and brought to the region horses, guns and the Dutch language. They soon achieved positions of domi-

nance among the various Nama clans and several assumed the role of leaders of the Nama themselves. They became so integrated that within a couple of generations they were generally considered Nama rather than Oorlam. Among the more important Oorlam/Nama families were the Amraals of Gobabis, the Witboois of Gibeon and the Afrikaners who started near the Bondelswarts just north of the Orange River.

The Afrikaners of Windhoek In the 1830s Jonker Afrikaner took his clan northwards to serve as mercenaries for the Hoagana Nama in their war with the Herero. In a series of battles in 1835 Jonker Afrikaner drove the Herero north of the Swakop river and occupied the central Windhoek district. There he set up his own chiefdom, with Bergdama, Nama and Herero clients to look after the huge herds of cattle he had captured from the Herero.

During the 1840s and 50s Jonker Afrikaner used violence to extend his authority over the surrounding Herero and Nama clans. He traded ivory, ostrich feathers and cattle southwards to the Cape Colony and westwards to Walvis Bay where European ships had begun calling. From both these sources he imported guns and ammunition. In 1858 Jonker led the first of several raids on the cattle of the Ovambo in the extreme north. During this time European traders and missionaries began venturing inland and settling at the Herero town of Otjimbingwe.

The First Nama-Herero War, 1863–70 Following the death of Jonker in 1861 the Herero decided to revolt against Afrikaner domination. War started in 1863 and continued on and off until 1870. The Herero were encouraged by European traders who hoped to clear a safe, overland trade-route through

14.1 Namibia in the nineteenth century

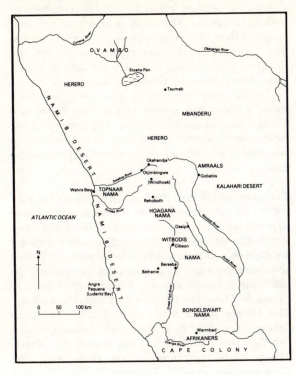

14.2 Namibia: German colonisation and African resistance, 1884–98

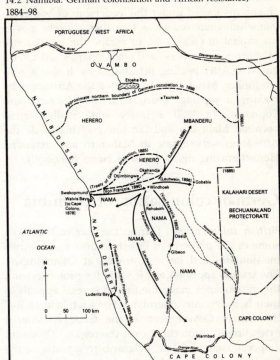

14.3 The Nama and Herero risings, 1904–07

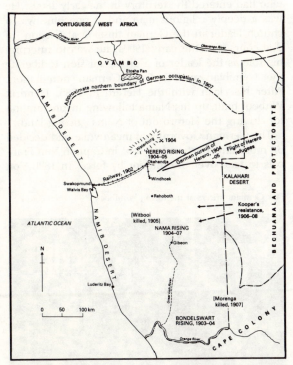

14.4 German South West Africa, 1908–15

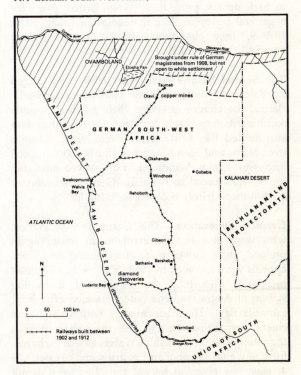

Nama country to the Cape Colony. Several Herero chiefdoms united under the leadership of Maherero (sometimes referred to as Kamaherero). He moved his capital to Okahandja to escape the interference of European traders and missionaries at Otjimbingwe. After beating off attacks by Jonker's son, Jan Jonker, Maherero then isolated the Afrikaners by making a separate peace with the Hoagana and Topnaars. In 1870 a treaty was finally signed between Maherero and Jan Jonker. This made the Afrikaners subordinate to Maherero and extended Herero grazing rights south as far as Rehoboth.

German colonisation of Namibia

British intervention During the war of the 1860s some of the property of British traders and German missionaries had been destroyed at Otjimbingwe. The traders appealed to the Cape for protection and the missionaries made the first of several appeals to their home country, Germany. For a while in 1876–7 the British Government at the Cape considered extending its 'protection' over the region. They sent a special commissioner, Palgrave, to investigate the territory. He offered Maherero protection from possible Boer Trekkers and from the Nama to the south. But it soon became clear that Palgrave had no force to back up his 'protection'. When British plans for a general Southern African federation collapsed in 1878–9, they abandoned the idea and merely annexed the port of Walvis Bay.

The Second Nama-Herero War, 1880 Encouraged by Palgrave's recognition of Maherero's territorial claims, the Herero extended their grazing grounds southwards into Nama territory. By 1880 they had surrounded the Afrikaners at Windhoek. Clashes over Nama and Herero grazing rights soon erupted into war again. Windhoek was sacked and Jan Jonker was forced to flee. The German missionary at Windhoek barely escaped with his life.

German annexation The German missionaries, who were also heavily involved in trade, again pressed their Government for protection. Their appeals were followed in 1883 by those of a German merchant, Lüderitz, who established a trading station at Angra Pequena (later renamed after him, Lüderitz Bay). He made treaties with local Nama chiefs, persuading them to 'sell' the coastland from the Orange River to north of Walvis Bay in exchange for a few guns, alcohol and paltry sums of cash. On at least one occasion he got the chief very drunk

before persuading him to sell. Lüderitz then demanded German 'protection' of his territory and trading interests. This was a much more solid proposal than the vague appeals of the missionaries. The German Government responded in 1884 by declaring a 'Protectorate' over the whole of 'South West Africa' from the Orange to the Cunene rivers.

The German annexation, however, had been made without the consent of the main Nama and Herero peoples further inland. The history of the next twenty years was one of persistent African resistance to the inland extension of German colonial rule.

Extension of German control The German Government was determined to use the minimum possible expense in colonising the country. They therefore decided to sign treaties of protection with individual local chiefs and then use private German companies to exploit the minerals and trade of the territory. In 1885 the German consul, Goering, managed to persuade Maherero to agree to a protection treaty. The Herero had recently clashed with the Nama followers of Hendrik Witbooi and Maherero hoped the Germans would help them against the Nama. When Maherero received no help from the Germans, he cancelled the treaty.

Hendrik Witbooi was the grandson of an Oorlam who had entered the territory in the early 1800s. He was a deeply religious man and at one time was a church leader in the German mission at Gibeon. In due course, in the early 1900s, he was to interpret his role as the leader of a divine mission to liberate the Namibian people from German domination. After his clash with the Herero in 1885, Hendrik Witbooi built up his Nama following in preparation for driving the Herero out of Nama grazing land.

The German Government meanwhile had decided on more direct action and sent in Captain Von Francois to take over the interior by force. In 1890 Von

14.1 German officers at the fort in Windhoek.

Francois set up his headquarters at Windhoek. This had recently been temporarily vacated following the death of Jan Jonker, killed in a clash with Hendrik Witbooi. Von Francois' first action was to end the gun trade between Walvis Bay and the Herero. He recognised that the two major powers in the region were the Herero of Maherero and the Nama of Witbooi. He decided to exploit the century-long rivalry between the two groups and to deal with Witbooi first. Von Francois hoped that a quick victory over the Nama would frighten the Herero into submission. He could then confine both Nama and Herero into small reserves and take the bulk of the land for white settlement.

The Nama When it was clear that Von Francois was going to attack the Nama, Maherero was persuaded to renew his treaty with the Germans (1890). Witbooi wrote to Maherero warning him against the action he had taken:

> You think you will retain your independent Chieftainship after I have been destroyed. . . but my dear Kaptein you will eternally regret your action in having handed over to the White man the right to govern your country. After all our war is not as serious as you think . . . . But this thing you have done, to surrender yourself to the Government of the White man, will be a burden that you will carry on your shoulders. You call yourself Supreme Chief, but when you are under another's control you are merely a subordinate Chief.*

In 1893 Von Francois launched an attack on Witbooi at Gibeon, but he had underestimated the strength and mobility of the Nama. Witbooi's people vacated Gibeon and conducted guerrilla raids on Von Francois' troops. Communications were cut with Walvis Bay and the Germans found themselves isolated at Windhoek.

Von Francois was replaced by Major Leutwein and German reinforcements were brought in. Leutwein started by isolating Witbooi's Nama. He attacked the Nama of Gobabis and captured and shot their leader Andries Lambert. In 1894 Leutwein attacked and defeated Witbooi, but he did not have the military strength to totally destroy the Nama. Witbooi agreed to a peace treaty whereby his people kept their arms and became allies of the Germans.

* *The Diary of Hendrik Witbooi,* Van Riebek Society, vol 9, 1929, p. 77

The Herero Meanwhile Maherero had died and the Herero were divided in a succession dispute. Leutwein took the side of Samuel Maherero and got him to agree to accept a German garrison at Okahandja and to grant the Germans a large tract of land around Windhoek. In 1896 the eastern Herero under Nicodemus and the Mbanderu (an eastern branch of the Herero) under Kahimemua rose in rebellion against the Germans. Leutwein was able to crush the rebellion with the aid of troops from Witbooi and Samuel Maherero. The rebels' land and cattle were seized by the Government and Nicodemus and Kahimemua were shot for treason. Surviving men, women and children were taken to Windhoek and given out as labourers to white settlers.

By the middle of 1896 the Germans were in control of most of the country apart from Ovamboland in the north. It had taken them ten years and they had only succeeded this far because they had been able to take advantage of ancient rivalries and divisions within Namibian society.

Origins of the Nama and Herero risings of 1904–07

Impact of German rule, 1896–1904 Between 1896 and 1904 significant numbers of German settlers began to pour into South West Africa. They bought land at cheap rates and on credit from the Government. The Government had taken large tracts of some of the best-watered grazing land as a result of wars and treaties with both Nama and Herero.

The colonists were helped by the spread in 1896–7 of the rinderpest epidemic which killed up to 90 per

14.2 Governor Leutwein (seated left) with Samuel Maherero (standing right).

cent of African cattle. With vast stretches of African grazing lands now vacant the Government was able to take over more land for white settlement. At the same time impoverished Africans were forced to accept low-paid wage labour on white-owned farms or on the new copper mines at Otavi. Africans became indebted to white traders who lent them money and then demanded payment, with interest, in their few remaining livestock. There were also no restrictions on white traders buying land cheaply from those Africans who found themselves in debt. In this way more and more African land and cattle passed into the hands of white colonists. Two unsuccessful Nama risings by Swartboois and Bondelswarts in 1898 gave the Government the chance to seize more land in the south and west.

By the early 1900s about a third of the land in the territory was in the hands of a small group of powerful private companies. These were largely speculative companies which for a long time refused to sell their land to white settlers. They were waiting for the price of land to rise which they hoped would come with an extension of white settlement and the building of railways. They also hoped that minerals such as diamonds or gold would be found on their land. It is not surprising to find, therefore, that a large part of the shares of the companies was owned by the De Beers mining company of Kimberley. The refusal of the companies to sell their land created an artificial shortage of land for white settlement. This increased the pressure among whites to buy or take land from blacks.

By 1902 the German Governor, Leutwein, was concerned about the speed with which Africans were losing their land and cattle through indebtedness to white traders. He was worried that their widespread loss of land and cattle might drive the Nama and Herero into revolt. He decided on two courses of action, both of which in fact made matters worse for Africans and drove them closer to rebellion. In 1903 Leutwein announced the allocation of 'reserves' for Nama and Herero. Though this guaranteed them a little land, it was a fraction of their former territory. Secondly he placed a ban on all future loans to Africans, but he allowed a year for the collection of outstanding debts. The result was widespread looting and violence as whites tried to extort as much as possible from Africans before the ban came into effect in July 1903.

Nama and Herero were driven to despair. Samuel Maherero wrote to Witbooi urging a united rising, but the letter was intercepted by the Government. When Maherero rose in rebellion in January 1904, the Herero were on their own.

The Nama and Herero risings of 1904–07

The Herero rising, 1904–05 The Herero rising started with the killing of over a hundred German colonists. Significantly, most of them were traders. Maherero had taken advantage of the absence of Leutwein and his troops in the south of the country, quelling a minor revolt among the Bondelswarts. White settlers immediately demanded the disarming of Witbooi and all the Nama. But Leutwein knew he needed the support of Witbooi if he was to overcome the Herero. In fact Witbooi lent him a small force of Nama troops to help him in action against the Herero. Despite this support Leutwein was unable to crush the Herero revolt.

For six months the Herero regained control of much of their former territory, driving the Germans off their farms. But in due course large German reinforcements arrived from overseas and Leutwein was replaced by General von Trotha. The Germans gradually pushed the Herero into the Waterberg where they hoped to force them to surrender. A prison camp was prepared to house up to 8 000 Herero captives; but after a major battle in August 1904 the bulk of the Herero broke out of German encirclement and escaped to the east. Frustrated in his attempt to capture the Herero *en masse*, von Trotha decided on a policy of extermination. He issued the following infamous proclamation on 2 October 1904:

> The Herero are no longer German subjects. They have murdered and plundered. . . . The Herero nation must leave the country. If it will not do so I shall compel it by force. . . . Inside German territory every Herero tribesman,

14.3 Hendrik Witbooi, second from the right and his officers, 1905.

armed or unarmed, with or without cattle, will be shot. No women and children will be allowed in the territory: they will be driven back to their people or fired on. These are the last words to the Herero nation from me, the great General of the mighty German Emperor.*

In the months that followed Herero were indiscriminately shot and driven ruthlessly into the eastern desert. There thousands died of thirst together with their cattle. No more than 2000 Herero escaped as refugees to Bechuanaland and South Africa. By the time the order was lifted in December 1905 a mere 16 000 Herero were left out of a former population of 80 000.

The Nama rising, 1904–07 Once Leutwein was replaced by von Trotha in July 1904 it was clear to Witbooi that Nama disarmament could not be far off. Within days of von Trotha's extermination proclamation the Nama rose in widespread rebellion. Under the inspiring leadership of Hendrik Witbooi they adopted the tactics of guerrilla raids and avoided open battles. They achieved remarkable success and paralysed much of the southern half of the colony until Witbooi was killed in October 1905. Then Nama unity began to fall apart and many surrendered during 1906. Nevertheless two Nama

* (H. Bley, *South West Africa*, London, 1971, 163–4.)

14.4 Starving Herero after the Herero rising, 1905.

14.5 Captured Herero women in front of German fort, 1905.

14.6 Nama prisoners taken during the war.

leaders, Morenga and Simon Kooper, continued the struggle, conducting guerrilla raids on German farms during 1907. Then in September 1907 Morenga was shot while crossing the border into the Cape Colony. With his death effective Nama resistance came to an end. For a few more months Kooper continued raiding from his place of exile in Bechuanaland. But in March 1908 he was persuaded to renounce the struggle and accepted a German pension.

The final years of German rule

The war had resulted in an appalling loss of life. While tens of thousands of Herero had perished in the desert thousands of Nama died in concentration camps. A certain number of Nama were actually deported as far as Togo and Cameroun where most of them died of unfamiliar tropical diseases. The German authorities were determined that the Nama and Herero 'nations' as such should cease to exist. The survivors of the rebellions were to be turned into a subordinate working class serving the interests of the white settlers. Cattle ownership by Nama or Herero was banned. Their few surviving cattle were confiscated. All forms of chieftainship were abolished. Traditional dress was banned and people were not even allowed to assemble in groups.

Within a few years virtually all Nama and Herero men were in full-time wage employment. In spite of this, however, colonists experienced a severe shortage of labour after the war. This was largely because of the effectiveness of von Trotha's extermination campaign. He had virtually killed off the territory's labour supply! The labour crisis became so acute that agents were sent to the eastern Cape and Transvaal to try and recruit labour for the colony. Small numbers were recruited, but Herero refugees whom they approached refused to return. It was thus during this period that greater German control was extended over the Ovambo in the north.

For some years traders had been operating in Ovamboland. As elsewhere, they had taken advantage of rinderpest and extended loans to impoverished Ovambo and then demanded their livestock in payment for the debts. Thus in the early 1900s the Ovambo were also becoming increasingly dependent on wage employment, especially at the Otavi copper mines. When Germany assumed control over Ovamboland in 1908, however, they were fearful of revolt and were careful not to seize land belonging to Ovambo. Missionaries were used to infiltrate Ovambo communities and act as labour recruiters for the German colonists further south.

In the period 1907 to 1914 several thousand German settlers poured into the colony and the white population rose from 8000 to 15 000. There was already a railway from the coast to Windhoek and a line was extended to the Otavi copper mines in the north. In 1907 a Land Settlement scheme was introduced to lend money to white settlers to encourage them to buy farms. By 1914 some 1300 farms of 10 000 hectares each had been sold to white settlers, mostly Germans. These German 'farmers' lived in relative luxury and treated their African workers with great brutality. Workers were frequently flogged and not even pregnant women were spared. Those that resisted such 'punishments' ran the risk of being killed. There were vigorous protests from local white settlers when the administration brought to trial a number of farmers who had beaten their workers to death. The regime in South West Africa was perhaps the most brutal in the whole of Africa.

The First World War and the transfer to South Africa

When war broke out in Europe in August 1914, the German and British colonies of Southern Africa found themselves on opposite sides. A number of Afrikaners (Boers) in the Union of South Africa were in favour of remaining neutral or even supporting their former German allies. But the Government of the Union, under the leadership of Generals Botha and Smuts, came out in clear support of the British Empire. As Botha prepared to invade South West Africa on behalf of the British, a number of Afrikaners rebelled against their Government and tried to promote a German invasion of the northern Cape.

By January 1915 the Afrikaner rebels had been overcome and Botha and Smuts led the successful invasion of South West Africa, helped by a British naval blockade of the coast. In July 1915 the final German garrison surrendered and the territory was brought under South African military occupation.

One of the first actions of the South African military government was to go to Ovamboland to 'persuade' the Ovambo chiefs to send more labourers to seek employment in the south of the colony. At the same time (1915) the Portuguese were engaged in a campaign of conquest against the Kwanyama Ovambo in southern Angola. Thousands were slaughtered as the Portuguese took no prisoners. Chief Mandume and surviving Kwanyama fled as refugees across the border into South West Africa. There they were allowed to remain provided they supplied labourers to the rest of the colony.

The League of Nations Mandate The First World War was brought to an end with the defeat of Germany in 1918. The Peace Treaty of Versailles (1919) forced Germany to give up all her African colonies. These now officially came under the charge of the League of Nations (the forerunner of the United Nations). Each former German colony was given to one of the victorious European allied powers (Britain, France or Belgium) who controlled a neighbouring colony. The power to rule these territories was called a League of Nations Mandate. In other words the European colonial powers ruled the territories on a temporary basis on behalf of the League of Nations. They were supposed to prepare the countries for self-rule and independence. In practice the mandated territories became the full colonies of the European power who got the Mandate. In the case of South West Africa, the Mandate was granted to the Union of South Africa which had conquered the territory. Although it was never officially joined to the Union, South West Africa was henceforth ruled by South Africa and according to South African laws.

Exercises

A. Think, discuss, understand and write

1 What developments in pre-colonial Namibian history assisted the early colonisation of the territory by the Germans?
2 Describe and discuss the main features of German colonising policy in South West Africa between 1884 and 1914.
3 Discuss the nature, successes and failures of African resistance to German colonisation between 1884 and 1900.
4 Discuss the causes and results of the Nama and Herero risings of 1904–07.

B. Imaginative writing

Towards the end of 1903 Samuel Maherero wrote to Witbooi urging a united rising, but the letter was intercepted by the Government. Write what you imagine might have been in that letter. If the letter had not been intercepted, what might Witbooi's reply have been? How do you think Namibian history might have been changed if the Nama and Herero had co-ordinated their risings in 1904?

C. Groupwork and class discussion

Make a short time-chart of events in this chapter. Compare the experience of the Namibian peoples in this period with that of other colonised peoples in Southern Africa. Do you think the League of Nations was right to give South Africa the Mandate for Namibia? What alternative action, if any, might have been possible under the circumstances of the time?

PART FOUR   THE TWENTIETH CENTURY CHALLENGE TO COLONIALISM

CHAPTER 15

The development of the South African state, 1910–40

The origins of African nationalism

One of the themes we have looked at so far in this book has been direct African resistance to colonial conquest. There came a time, however, when resisters had to accept that, whether they liked it or not, they had become part of a new colonial state. Once this was accepted, Africans expected and demanded to be allowed equal rights with whites within the state. But white colonists were reluctant to give up or even share their position of privilege, power and domination. Much of the history of twentieth-century Southern Africa, which is covered by the remainder of this book, is concerned with the struggle for equal rights by the African majority. They now looked beyond the boundaries of their old pre-colonial kingdoms. They saw themselves as part of a new African 'nation' within the colonial state. Their struggle gave birth to a new sense of 'African nationalism'.

The Ethiopian Church movement   The roots of African nationalism in Southern Africa are to be found among the early African converts to Christianity. They were the first to forsake traditional religious beliefs and chiefly authority. They accepted European culture: clothing, literacy and beliefs, and they sought to find a place in the new colonial society. They expected whites to live up to the Christian principles of equal rights for all. Unable to find equal acceptance, even by European missionaries, some outspoken African clergymen decided to form their own independent African Churches. Often the basis of the split concerned control over Church land or locally raised Church funds.

In the eastern Cape a breakaway 'Thembu National Church' was founded in 1884. Then in 1892 when a Wesleyan congress at Pretoria excluded

15.1 Tiyo Soga (1829–71), African missionary.

Blacks from its governing board, black ministers held an alternative meeting. Led by Mangena Mokone, a fiery preacher from Natal, they founded the independent 'Ethiopian Church'. (The name was chosen because in the Bible Africa is referred to as Ethiopia.) The Ethiopian Church grew rapidly and other independent African Churches in the region soon amalgamated with it. The movement drew inspiration from a similar movement among black Christians in America. In 1896 the Ethiopian Church became a branch of the African Methodist Episcopal Church (AMEC) of America.

But as a widespread national movement the Ethiopian Church was shortlived. It faced strong opposition from whites. Governments feared it would form a basis for black unity in the region and white missionaries found that it drew away their congregations. Around the turn of the century the Church was split by leadership rivalry and the movement fell apart. Mission Churches seized the opportunity to bring many black ministers once more under white supervision. Only a minority of the original 'Ethiopians' stayed loyal to Mokone and remained independent. But the desire by black Christians for freedom from white control has remained strong. Since the early 1900s an enormous number of independent African Churches have been formed all over Southern Africa. Most, however, have remained small and local in their appeal and so have not provided the basis for nation-wide black unity. Nevertheless churchmen and churchwomen have played an important part in the growth of the African nationalist movement.

Gandhi and 'passive resistance'   By the 1890s there were 80 000 Indians in Natal. Most worked on the sugar plantations but many who had finished their contracts chose not to return to India. They moved into shopkeeping and skilled as well as unskilled jobs. Whites began to fear that Indians would take over jobs that they felt should be reserved for them.

By the early 1900s a number of Indians had settled on the Witwatersrand. The Transvaal Government imposed a pass law on them and took steps to expel them back to Natal. In 1906 a mass meeting of Indians in Johannesburg swore an oath (known as *Satyagraha*) that they would use no violence but would refuse to obey the pass law. They were led in this policy of 'passive resistance' by Mohandas K. Gandhi, a recent immigrant who had qualified as a lawyer in England. Gandhi had already helped found the Natal Indian Congress. The struggle lasted several years. Gandhi and other Indian leaders were imprisoned, and Indians publically burnt their passes. The movement received worldwide publicity and eventually in 1913 the Union Government bowed to the pressure. The Indian pass law was abolished and the Government agreed to recognise non-Christian Indian marriages.

The example of Gandhi and the tactics of passive resistance was an important inspiration for the African nationalist movement. It was a tactic which Gandhi himself was to go on to use so successfully in the struggle for independence in India.

Newspapers and early political organisations   In the late nineteenth and early twentieth centuries, as literacy spread among the black population of Southern Africa, a number of regional African newspapers were founded. In 1884 *Imvo Zabantsundu* ('Native Opinion') was launched by John Tengo Jabavu, an eastern Cape journalist and lay preacher. It was published in Xhosa and English. Another Xhosa/English paper, A. K. Soga's *Izwi la Bantu* ('The Voice of the People') was published in 1897. In 1902 from the Barolong of Mafikeng came Solomon Plaatje's *Koranta ea Becoana* ('The Bechuana Gazette') in Setswana and English. And from Natal in 1906 came *Ilanga lase Natal* ('The Sun of Natal') published in Zulu and English by the Reverend John Dube, American-educated clergyman and founder (in 1889) of his own industrial and technical training school, the Ohlange Institute.

As the names of some of these papers suggest their aim was to provide a voice for African opinion, especially on political matters. Though moderate in tone they were used by their editors and contributors to express an African point of view, to criticise injustices and to comment on government policy. In particular they appealed to those mission-educated Africans who qualified to vote in Cape parliamentary elections.

On the whole these African newspaper editors supported those white liberal politicians whom they believed would best protect African interests. They were thus dismayed to find that blacks were totally excluded from the Bloemfontein National Convention of 1908 at which white politicans discussed the terms for the Act of Union. Jabavu, Dube and Rev. Walter Rubusana (author of *A History of South Africa from the Native Standpoint*) therefore summoned an alternative 'South African Native Convention' at Bloemfontein in 1909. There the sixty delegates protested at the proposed racial restrictions of the Union constitution: namely, the failure to extend the Cape's non-racial franchise to the other provinces of the Union and the ban on blacks becoming members of parliament. The Convention's protests were ignored in South Africa as was its delegation to England. The meeting's importance lies in the fact that it was the first attempt at black political organisation on a truly national scale in South Africa.

The founding of the South African Native National Congress

Following the Act of Union South African black leaders felt betrayed by their 'friends', the liberal

15.2 The South African Native National Congress delegation to England, June 1914. Left to right: Thomas Mapikela (Bloemfontein businessman, former member of a 1909 deputation to England to protest about the terms of the Act of Union and treasurer of SANNC); Rev Walter Rubusana (Congregational minister, the only elected African member of the Cape provincial council and vice-president of SANNC); Rev John Dube (American ordained missionary, newspaper editor, principal of his own school, Ohlange, in Natal, and president of SANNC); Saul Msane (prominent Transvaal member of SANNC); Sol Plaatje (newspaper editor, political spokesman, leading organiser of African opposition to the Natives' Land Act and general secretary of SANNC).

white politicians of the Cape. They saw the need to form their own political organisation on a national scale. A group of black lawyers led by Pixley Seme (recently qualified in America and England) summoned another meeting at Bloemfontein in January 1912. Educated Africans from every walk of life assembled from all over South Africa. Whites had excluded them from the politics of the Union of South Africa. They therefore came together, as Seme explained it, to form 'our national union for the purpose of creating national unity and defending our rights and privileges.' A number of local regional black political associations had already been formed. The delegates now set aside their regional differences to form the South African Native National Congress (SANNC). Dube was elected President General, Seme Treasurer and Plaatje Secretary General. The meeting opened and concluded with the first public singing of *Nkosi sikelel'i Afrika* ('God bless Africa'), composed by the Xhosa poet Enoch Sontonga.

The founders of Congress still believed in the merits of 'British justice'. Their aim therefore was to inform the white parliament of African grievances and wishes and to convince them that they spoke for the majority of blacks within the country. To give publicity to their views Seme founded a newspaper, *Abantu-Batho* ('The People'), with financial backing from the Swazi Queen Regent. Published in Zulu, Xhosa, Sotho, Tswana and English, it was the first attempt to found a truly national black South African newspaper.

Almost immediately Congress was put to the test. For some time blacks had been buying land from whites. The Government feared that if this trend continued blacks would in due course take over the bulk of the land in the country. At the same time white farmers feared black competition and wanted more pressure put on blacks to work for them as low-paid wage labourers rather than for themselves as peasant farmers. In 1913 therefore the Government passed the *Natives Land Act*. This banned all buying and selling of land between blacks and whites. Blacks were now restricted to the 'native reserves' which made up only 7 per cent of the land of the Union. Only blacks in the full-time employ of white farmers were allowed on white-owned land. The rest were liable to eviction though many remained as unofficial 'squatters' and tenants of white landowners.

As Africans were turned off the land in their thousands, Congress protested and petitioned the Government. But on this occasion they failed even to get the support of white liberals. When Dube, Plaatje and Rubusana took their pleas to England, their protests were similarly ignored. Britain was not prepared to interfere in the affairs of the self-governing Union. While in England Plaatje published his book *Native Life in South Africa* in which he publicised the dire effects and the suffering caused by the injustice of the Land Act. *Native Life* is still regarded as one of the great early works of African literature in English.

The mining industry, industrial unrest and the job 'colour bar', 1907–26

In the early years of South African gold mining experienced white miners from Europe, America and Australia had been able to dominate the skilled jobs in the industry. Black migrants, usually only on short contracts, did not stay long enough to develop the skills to rival white miners. When the Chinese were brought in on five-year contracts in 1903 whites feared they would have time to acquire their skills and so take away their jobs at lower wages. White

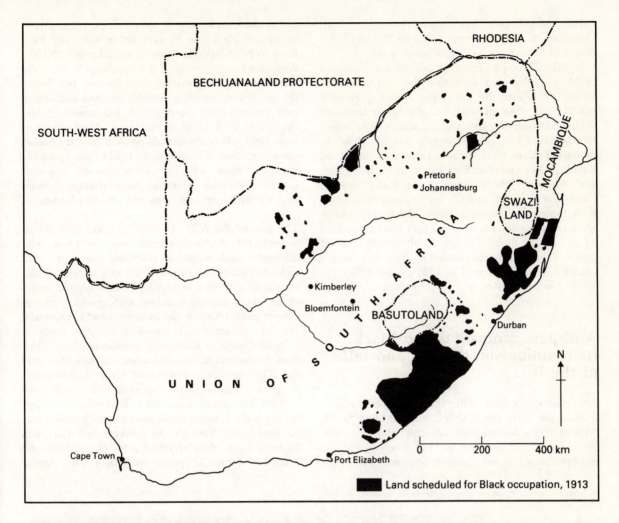

15.1 The South African 'Natives' Land Act, 1913

mineworkers therefore insisted that the Chinese were restricted to unskilled jobs. As the Chinese contracts drew to a close the white mineworkers tried to have this 'colour bar' extended to Africans. In 1907 they came out on strike in support of their demands. The mine-owners agreed to reserve the top skilled jobs for whites.

In 1911 the Union Government's *Mines and Works Act* legalised what was virtually a job colour bar. Skilled jobs required 'certificates of competency' and these were usually only ever given to whites. Strikes by white miners in 1913 and 1914 further strengthened their position. Though the strikes were brutally smashed by Government troops, they got recognition of a white trade union. In contrast, the black mineworkers' strike of 1913 against the colour bar and bad working conditions failed largely because they lacked unity and organisation. Thousands of

migrants were sacked and others were recruited in their place. In 1920 black mineworkers were better organised and 40 000 struck for higher wages. But they got no support from white mineworkers who joined with police in helping to break the strike.

The mine-owners, however, favoured opening more skilled jobs to blacks for then they could get the same work done for lower wages. Most blacks still worked in the urban areas on a temporary basis, leaving their families resident in the rural areas. Therefore, employers argued, they need only be paid a 'bachelor wage', for their wives and children would support themselves by peasant farming in the rural areas. But African access to land became ever more restricted, especially after the Land Act, and land in the reserves wore out through over use. Thus more and more families became totally dependent on wages earned in the mines and other industries. Despite this trend, however, both Government and employers still took the view that blacks only ever needed a 'bachelor' wage.

In 1921 the employers' organisation, the Chamber of Mines, attempted to reduce the cost of skilled labour by raising the job colour bar. Experienced blacks were thus allowed into the lower levels of skilled jobs hitherto reserved for whites. The white mineworkers reacted by coming out on strike in January 1922 in what became known as the 'Rand Revolt'. They paraded the streets in armed gangs and brought Johannesburg to a halt. Smuts's Government again brutally suppressed the strike with troops and heavy artillery. Some 200 whites were killed together with about fifty blacks, lynched by the striking mobs. Though the strike was crushed and its leaders were imprisoned or deported, the job colour bar was reinforced in 1926 by the *Mines and Works Amendment Act*.

Anti-pass campaigns and black trade unionism: the rise and fall of the ICU

Anti-pass campaigns   After the failure of its efforts against the Land Act SANNC tried tackling South African blacks' widest grievance, the hated pass law. An example had been set in 1913 when women in the Free State had led a passive resistance campaign

against women having to carry passes. Hundreds of women chose to go to gaol rather than pay their fines. When Charlotte Maxeke, founder of SANNC's Women's League, revived the campaign in 1920, the law requiring women to carry passes was withdrawn. In the meantime SANNC officials had organised an anti-pass campaign in Johannesburg and Pretoria in 1919. Mass meetings and demonstrations were held where thousands refused to carry passes knowing that Government could not possibly imprison them all. The Government, however, turned to violence. Mounted police charged demonstrators, broke up meetings and arrested leaders.

The rise of the ICU   In 1923 SANNC changed its name to the 'African National Congress' (ANC) and attempts were made to revitalise the party. But lack of positive achievement led to a temporary decline in its influence. In its place there emerged a movement which quickly acquired widespread working-class appeal. This was the Industrial and Commercial Workers Union (ICU), founded in Cape Town in 1919 by Clements Kadalie, a mission-educated clerk from Nyasaland (colonial Malawi). In December 1919 the ICU organised a strike of Cape dock-workers in protest against low wages and the high price of food. The workers refused to load food onto ships for export to Europe while food in South Africa was so expensive. Though the strikers failed to win higher wages, they received a lot of publicity and branches of the ICU sprang up all over South Africa.

15.3 Scene from anti-pass campaign, Johannesburg, 1920.

The 1920s was a period of great hardship for black workers both in town and countryside. As more and more blacks were driven off the land thousands of men and women crowded into the urban areas to find jobs in domestic service and in the expanding manufacturing industries. Wages were low and working and living conditions were very poor. The ICU rapidly became a mass movement demanding better working conditions and higher wages. By 1926 it had an estimated 100 000 members.

The Communist Party During this period also the Communist Party of South Africa (CPSA), originally active among white workers in the 'Rand Revolt', turned its attention to the black working class. The Communist Party's objective was the overthrow of the whole capitalist system. In the capitalist system land and industry, the 'means of production', is owned and controlled by private individuals and companies. They run these for their own profit at the expense of the workers who are paid the lowest possible wage. At times wages are raised, but usually only as a result of trade union struggle. In a country like South Africa, dominated by the capitalist system, the state supported the capitalist employers and helped them control their workers. The Communist Party aimed at the establishment of a revolutionary working-class state where there was no private property and the 'means of production' was returned to the workers. Though Communist Party membership remained small in South Africa, several black communists became active organisers of the ICU.

The decline of the ICU Despite its widespread support, however, the ICU achieved no real gains for its members and between 1928 and 1930 the union fell apart. There were a number of reasons for the ICU's failure. The most obvious ones were financial mismanagement and personal quarrels among the leadership. Kadalie was a great public speaker, but the union lacked sound organisational principles and as it grew in size the central committee lost overall central control. Each branch of the lCU, in the Cape, Natal or the Transvaal, pursued its own local grievances. Its widest membership in the mid-1920s was among rural squatters. But mere membership of the ICU could not save them from eviction. The union also made little attempt to attract the potentially most powerful group of black workers, the mineworkers of the Rand. Under pressure from white liberals Kadalie was persuaded to expel all communists from the ranks of the ICU and to steer the union away from taking actual strike action. But by taking no mass action the ICU was unable to produce any positive results and members simply stopped paying their subscriptions. In 1928 the Natal branch of the union broke away from Kadalie's ICU. This was followed by widespread splits throughout the country. The union rapidly ran out of funds and by 1930 the ICU had virtually ceased to function. Nevertheless, in spite of its ultimate failure, Kadalie's ICU had demonstrated a sense of black working class solidarity which future movements could build upon.

The rise of Afrikaner nationalism

The South African Party The white political party which had formed the first Government of the Union in 1910 was the South African Party (SAP), under the leadership of former commando generals Botha and Smuts. (Smuts took over as Prime Minister on the death of Botha in 1919). Their main support came from rural Afrikaner voters. But Smuts recognised that the main source of government taxation was a profitable gold-mining industry. He therefore supported the mine-owners in crushing the strikes on the Rand. But increasing numbers of poor rural Afrikaners had been moving onto the Rand in search of jobs. It was they who were at the heart of the 'colour-bar' strikes of 1913–22. Smuts's brutal crushing of the Rand Revolt did much to turn Afrikaner voters away from the SAP. Thereafter the SAP drew much of its support from the English-speaking mining and business community.

The National Party In 1913 the Afrikaner Free State politician, General J. B. M. Hertzog, was dropped from Botha's Government for being too anti-British. In January 1914 he founded the National Party devoted to the promotion of Afrikaner interests and the breaking of links with Britain. Hertzog's party benefitted from an upsurge of Afrikaner nationalist feeling prompted by the violent suppression of the Afrikaner rebellion of 1914 (see Chapter 14, p 146). A newspaper, *Die Burger* ('The Citizen'), was founded with finance from wealthy Afrikaner farmers of the western Cape. Insurance and investment organisations, SANLAM and SANTAM, were set up with Afrikaner capital to provide life insurance and small loans for Afrikaner farmers. In 1918 the Afrikaner *Broederbond* ('Brotherhood') was founded as a secret society to promote Afrikaans language and culture and to help fellow-members in business and employment.

Following the crushing of the Rand Revolt of 1922,

Smuts's SAP lost so much Afrikaner support that it was turned out of office in the general election of 1924. Hertzog became Prime Minister in a 'Pact' (alliance) between his National Party and the small, white working-class Labour Party.

The growth of racial segregation (separation) In an attempt to satisfy whites' demands and secure them in a dominant position in the economy, Smuts's SAP had already introduced some significant segregationist legislation. The *Natives Land Act* of 1913 (see above pp 150–1) was designed to maintain white domination in the rural areas. The *Natives Urban Areas Act* of 1923 strengthened the pass laws and prevented blacks from owning land in urban areas. The Act confined blacks to separate urban 'locations' where they were only allowed temporary residence. The *Industrial Conciliation Act* of 1924 recognised white trade unions but denied the same right to blacks and Indians.

Hertzog came to power in 1924 with a comprehensive list of segregationist legislation designed to protect the interests of rural and urban Afrikaners. The *Mines and Works Amendment Act* of 1926 spelt out the job colour-bar in clearer terms. All supervisory and skilled technical jobs in the mining industry were henceforth reserved for whites only. The *Native Administration Act* of 1927 brought blacks in the rural reserves under stricter control.

Hertzog's National Party government would have liked to have finally secured white supremacy by abolishing the Cape's non-racial franchise. In some Cape constituencies the increasing number of blacks and 'coloureds' who qualified to vote were in danger of forming the majority and overwhelming the white voters. But abolition of the Cape's non-racial franchise required a two-thirds parliamentary majority which Hertzog did not have. Instead he cancelled out the importance of the black and 'coloured' vote by extending the franchise to all white women in the Union thus effectively doubling the white electorate.

Economic crisis and further segregation, the 1930s

The Great Depression and the 'gold standard' crisis In 1929–33 South Africa felt the effects of the Great Depression which had hit the capitalist economies of Europe and America. In their attempts to recover from the depression European countries left the gold standard. Until then the value of their currencies had been fixed in relationship to a standard universal price for gold. By leaving the gold stan-dard they could devalue (reduce the value of) their currencies. This meant the prices of their goods abroad were much cheaper and so they could sell far more of them. This stimulated their manufacturing industry at home. Thus leaving the gold standard and devaluing their currencies helped European economies to recover from the depression.

South African industry and agriculture suffered particularly badly from the depression because Hertzog was determined not to take South Africa off the gold standard. He felt it was a sign of weakness to follow Europe in devaluing the South African currency. But this meant that the value of South African currency, and hence South African exports, was much higher than their European competitors. South African agricultural exports could not be sold abroad because they were too expensive. To make matters worse, South African bankers and industrialists simply removed their money from South Africa to Europe where it was now worth so much more. This left South African industry and agriculture very short of capital for investment.

Government investment in economic recovery Under pressure from all sides Hertzog finally took South Africa off the gold standard at the end of 1932. The result was an immediate boost to the South African economy and capital for investment flowed back into the country. The price of gold, no longer tied to the value of the currency, rose to great heights. The mining companies made huge profits which the Government was able to tax. In this way the Government's income increased and it had a lot more money to invest in agriculture and industry to help recover from the depression.

The 1930s was thus a period of huge Government investment in both the rural and the urban areas. Farmers had suffered particularly badly during the depression and the government was anxious to prevent 'poor whites' from drifting to the towns where there was little or no employment for them. The Government therefore invested heavily in irrigation schemes and loans to help struggling white farmers become established as capitalist employers of low-paid black wage labour. Similarly in urban areas Government made heavy investment in manufacturing industry to provide employment for the growing white urban population. Huge funds were poured into ISCOR, the state-owned Iron and Steel Corporation.

The 'Fusion' Government and racial segregation In order to tackle the economic crisis more effectively the National Party and SAP joined together to form the 'Fusion' Government in 1933. The merger was formalised the following year when the two parties combined to form the United Party, with Hertzog as Prime Minister. The 'fusion' gave Hertzog a huge overall parliamentary majority and he was now able to push through further segregationist legislation. The Government lost little time in abolishing the Cape's non-racial franchise by the *Representation of Natives Act* of 1936. The 11 000 or so blacks who had previously qualified to vote alongside whites were now removed onto a separate voters' register. Henceforth they were only allowed to elect three special white representatives to speak for them in parliament. A separate Natives Representative Council was set up to which twelve blacks were elected through local councils of chiefs and headmen. But its role was purely advisory.

The *Native Land and Trust Act* (1936) completed the work of the 1913 Land Act. Though it made more land available for adding to the 'reserves', it only increased blacks' share of the land to 13 per cent of the Union. More than 86 per cent of the land remained in white ownership. As Government invested in white capitalist agriculture stricter 'anti-squatting' regulations squeezed black peasant farmers off white-owned land. They were seen as dangerous competitors to white farmers. The Act had the desired effect of forcing more blacks to accept the very low wages offered by white farmers as the only way to stay on the land. But the Act also had the effect of pushing increasing numbers of former peasant farmers to seek employment in the urban areas. Meanwhile in the urban areas the *Native Laws Amendment Act* (1937) brought stricter enforcement of the pass laws.

Black political protest in the 1930s

The years of the depression threw many black workers out of work and the agricultural developments of the 1930s drove many peasant farmers from the land. African politicians, however, were unable to offer much effective opposition to the Government's increasingly repressive policies. The ICU had recently collapsed, unable to meet the high expectations of its members. In December 1930 Johannes Nkosi, an enthusiastic member of the Communist Party (CPSA), staged an anti-pass protest in Durban. 4000 attended a rally at which passes were publically burned. But police attacked the demonstrators and Nkosi was shot dead while speaking to the crowd. The following year the CPSA went through a leadership crisis which lost it much

African support. The ANC meanwhile was in a period of decline. In 1932 the ANC's newspaper, *Abantu-Batho*, was forced out of business by competition from the white-owned *Bantu World*.

In the mid-1930s political leaders from a number of organisations attempted to muster some united black opposition to Hertzog's proposed segregationist legislation of 1936–7 (see above). An important figure in the movement was Dr Abdul Abduraham, President of the African People's Organisation (APO), a political organisation mainly concerned with the 'coloured' community in and around Cape Town. Five hundred delegates from a range of African, Indian and 'coloured' organisations attended an All-African Convention at Bloemfontein in December 1935. But the leaders were reluctant to take decisive action and their protests as usual got them nowhere. They agreed to meet annually and Professor D. D. T. Jabavu of Fort Hare College was elected President with Dr James Moroka as Treasurer. Meetings such as these however lacked mass support and were not sufficiently in touch with the increasing mass of urban workers from among whom future protest movements were to emerge.

Afrikaner nationalism in the 1930s

Ardent Afrikaner nationalists had seen Hertzog's merger with Smuts's SAP to form the United Party as a betrayal of Afrikaner republicanism. A section of the National Party refused to follow Hertzog. They broke away under the leadership of Dr D. F. Malan to form the *Gesuiwerdes* ('Purified') National Party (GNP). It was strongly supported by the Afrikaner Broederbond which henceforth became an important policy-making body behind the scenes in the GNP. The centenary celebrations of the 'Great Trek' in 1935–38 provided the opportunity for a great revival in Afrikaner nationalism. In 1939 Hertzog resigned as Prime Minister and broke with Smuts over the issue of South Africa's entry into the Second World War. As Smuts led South Africa into the world conflict in support of Britain, Afrikaner nationalists reunited around Malan's National Party. During the War prominent Afrikaner nationalists openly expressed support for Hitler's Nazi Germany, among them two future Prime Ministers, B. J. Vorster and P. W. Botha. The GNP wanted to break all constitutional links with Britain and to introduce whatever laws were necessary to promote Afrikaner interests at the expense of blacks. The effects of their coming to power in 1948 will be examined in the following chapter.

Document 15.1 *Kadalie and the ICU. In January 1925 Clements Kadalie travelled by train from Cape Town to Johannesburg. On the way he stopped at Bloemfontein to address a huge gathering of African workers. In this extract from his autobiography Kadalie describes his speech and some of its effects:*

For two hours I held the huge audience spellbound. I attacked every form of oppression which the African endured. The Chamber of Mines came in for some severe censure. European churches also were rebuked for their practice of hypocrisy, for the ministers did not follow the teaching of the Master who sided with the poor and not with the rich. I also planned to test the English-speaking people by calling them hypocrites. I declared that 'I would not trust an Englishman, even if he and I were found in Hell together. I should watch him for fear he left me there while he found a way out for himself.' I told the people to make 'such a hell of noise that the white man cannot sleep', meaning, of course, the white capitalist. I also said that 'Parliament must tremble'.

The occasion was big, and I planned to exploit it to the full. I realized after I had spoken that some history had been made. On arriving at Germiston station at 7 a.m. the following day, I saw the *Rand Daily Mail*'s poster: 'Kadalie's outburst at Bloemfontein'. I bought a copy of the paper and read it casually as the train steamed in at Park Station. The paper also reported that I was on my way to Johannesburg. On arrival at the ICU office at 25 Fox Street, I took charge of the work. In the course of the day, a message came from Mr Taberer of the Chamber of Mines, asking me to call on him. I hesitated to accept the invitation, but, as a brave man, I went to see him.

Mr Taberer received me alone in his office and showed every kindness. He said that he had read with interest the speech in the *Rand Daily Mail* delivered in Bloemfontein, and that he was in sympathy with my aim to organize the Natives. He pointed out, however, that my attack on the Chamber of Mines was not justified, as the mining industry treated its African employees well, and much better than other employers. After eulogizing me, he finally asked me to withdraw the statement I had made against the mines in the course of my speech, and suggested I should send a statement to the press. I totally refused.

(Adapted from *My Life and the ICU* by Clements Kadalie, Humanities Press, New York and Frank Cass, London, 1970, pp 71–72.)

Exercises

A. Think, discuss, understand and write

1 Discuss the nature and tactics of the early African nationalist movement in South Africa up to 1923. Why did it so consistently fail to achieve most of its objectives?
2 Describe and discuss the land and labour policies of the South African Government between 1910 and 1940. How were South African blacks affected by these policies?
3 Account for the rise and fall of the ICU (Industrial and Commercial Workers' Union). Assess the importance of trade-union activity in general in South Africa before 1940.
4 What were the objectives of the Afrikaner National Party between 1914 and 1940? How far had they achieved those objectives by 1939?

B. Imaginative writing

Imagine you were present on one day of SANNC's anti-pass campaign in Johannesburg in 1919. You have been asked by the newspaper *Abantu-Batho* to write a report on what you saw on that day. Write your report in not more than 300 words. Be factually accurate, but at the same time be interesting and as informative as possible.

C. Groupwork and class discussion

Project: time-chart Draw up a time-chart of South African history for the period 1910–1940. Divide information into two vertical columns indicating: (1) black politics and trade-union activity and (2) economic developments, white trade-union activity and political parties and Government action. Discuss and compare developments as revealed by your chart.

Document study Read Document 15.1 and discuss the answers to the following questions:

1 What was the ICU?
2 What do you think was the main purpose of the speech which Kadalie describes in this extract?
3 Explain and expand Kadalie's reference to 'Englishmen' as hypocrites.
4 In this extract Kadalie presents himself as an outspoken critic of the Chamber of Mines. In practice to what extent were Kadalie and the ICU effective opponents of the mining employers?
5 From your reading of this extract, what conclusion can you draw about the character of Kadalie?

CHAPTER 16

The growth of the apartheid state, 1940–65

Economic developments in the 1940s

The period of the Second World War (1939–45) opened up important new job opportunities for blacks in South Africa. Firstly there was the War itself. Between 1940 and 1945 the South African Government sent some 220 000 whites and 100 000 blacks to fight with the Allies against Italians and Germans in Ethiopia and North Africa. Though the blacks were not allowed to carry arms, they played an important role as military labour especially in North Africa. The really significant impact of the war, however, occurred within South Africa itself.

Growth of manufacturing During the Second World War there was a rapid expansion in South Africa's manufacturing industries. This was partly because the war itself prevented imports from Europe. South Africa had to manufacture its own food, drink, clothing, textiles, chemicals, machinery and tools. But South African manufacturing also benefitted from the Allied armies' demand for arms and ammunition and the British navy's constant need for ship repairs. The port cities of Cape Town, Port Elizabeth, East London and Durban expanded rapidly during the period. Port Elizabeth became an important manufacturing region and there was rapid growth in the iron and steel manufacturing centre of Vereeniging south of Johannesburg. But the main industrial growth-centre remained Johannesburg and the surrounding urban areas of the Rand. By 1943 manufacturing had become more important than mining in terms of production and employment in the South African economy. In the late 1940s new rich gold deposits were discovered in the Orange Free State and this gave a further general boost to the South African economy.

Black employment and urbanisation The huge growth in manufacturing industry increased the number of jobs available in the urban areas. In an attempt to meet the increasing demand for industrial labour the Government temporarily suspended the pass laws during 1942–43. For some time the Land Acts of 1913 and 1936 had been combining with drought to bring increasing landlessness and poverty in the rural areas. Now with restrictions on their movements temporarily lifted blacks poured into the urban areas in search of work. By the mid-1940s the urban population of the Rand had reached $1\frac{1}{2}$ million, two-thirds of them black. For a short while during the war blacks were freer to move around in search of the best jobs and to bargain for higher wages and better working conditions. Small industrial strikes were widespread and many workers managed to improve their pay and working conditions. At the same time the absence of so many whites on military service enabled certain blacks to move into skilled and semi-skilled jobs which would otherwise have been reserved for whites. In spite of this however the general level of urban wages failed to keep pace with the rising price of food.

The rapid growth of black urbanisation soon far outstripped the demand for labour. Townships filled to overflowing and unemployment and urban poverty became widespread. Unemployed youths and criminal gangs preyed on black workers and the rich 'white' suburbs. Houses and rooms were let and sub-let but still there was not enough housing. Thousands turned to illegal 'squatting' and built their rent-free homes of scrap-iron, wood and card-board. One organised squatter township, founded south-west of Johannesburg in 1944, was eventually taken over by the municipality and became the basis for South-Western Township (Soweto). Urban poverty and the housing crisis was similar in other urban centres around the country.

The rise of Afrikaner power and the basis of apartheid

Afrikaner nationalists and the 1948 election From the mid-1940s there was a growing fear among whites in general of black domination of the towns as blacks poured into the urban areas in search of jobs. With memories of the unemployed 'poor whites' of the early 1930s Afrikaner nationalists viewed with alarm the growing pace of black urbanisation. They abhorred the relaxation of the pass laws during the war. The propaganda of the 'purified' National Party warned of the *swart gevaar* ('black peril') and the *oorstrooming* ('swamping') of the cities by blacks. It was on a programme to reverse this trend and to re-establish white (especially Afrikaner) supremacy that Malan's National Party fought and won the general election to the white parliament in 1948.

The year 1948, when the National Party won an overall majority in the white parliament, has often been seen as a turning point in South African history. The National Party came to power with a programme for what they called *apartheid* ('separateness'). In fact the *apartheid* laws which followed were a continuation of the segregationist laws which had discriminated against blacks ever since 1910 and even earlier. The difference after 1948 was that the overall aims of Government policy were more clearly formulated. And the National Party's parliamentary majority ensured that their legislation was pushed through with even more determination.

The theory of apartheid The National Party argued that for whites to survive (in their dominant position of power and privilege) it was essential to keep the races separate. Otherwise the far larger black population (8 million blacks compared with 2 million whites) would eventually take over economic as well as political power. *Apartheid* would ensure priority for whites in all jobs as well as urban housing. The basic way this was to be achieved was to classify the whole population according to race. The main racial divisions would be 'white' and 'non-white'. All 'non-whites' were divided into Indian, 'Coloured' and 'Native' (later changed to 'Bantu'). The latter were further sub-divided according to ethnic or 'tribal' origins. In this way the black majority was reduced to a series of separate 'tribal' minorities. Each black ethnic group was allocated certain rural

reserves or 'Homelands' (later called 'Bantustans') which together made up only 13 per cent of the country. These were the only places where they were legally allowed to be permanently resident. This applied even to those born and brought up in the 'white' cities or on white-owned farms and who had never set foot in their supposed 'homelands'. Blacks were only legally allowed in 'white' South Africa (86 per cent of the country) on a temporary basis in order to work for whites.

The system was controlled by the use of 'passes' which blacks had to carry at all times outside their designated 'Homelands'. The pass showed a person's ethnic group, his employer and his present address. A correctly stamped and up-to-date pass gave the holder the right to be present in a 'white' area on a temporary basis. Passes had to be renewed at specified pass offices every month. If a person lost his job his pass became invalid. Any black person who failed to produce a valid, up-to-date pass on demand by white police or government official was guilty of a criminal offence and was liable to fine or imprisonment. Every year tens of thousands were arrested for 'pass offences'. Police regularly went on 'pass raids' into black townships and used the system to intimidate urban blacks, especially trade-unionists and politicians.

The Suppression of Communism Act (1950) In order to give itself the legal powers to deal with opposition to *apartheid* the Government introduced the *Suppression of Communism Act* in 1950. The Act gave the Minister of Justice the power to 'ban' any person or organisation which he named as 'communist'. And 'communism' was interpreted freely to mean virtually any open opposition to *apartheid*. A banning order restricted a person's movements and prevented them from taking part in any organisation or talking to more than one person at a time. It was an effective silencing mechanism used against many Government opponents, black and white, in the decades to come. A person tried and found guilty of furthering the aims of any banned organisation was liable to be imprisoned for up to ten years.

The apartheid laws The main *apartheid* laws were as follows. The *Population Registration Act* (1950) and *Group Areas Act* (1950) classified the population according to race and indicated areas where each racial group was allowed or not allowed to live. The *Prohibition of Mixed Marriages Act* (1949) and the *Immorality Act* (1950) were designed to maintain the 'purity' of the white race. They prevented marriage or any sexual intercourse between whites and 'non-whites'. The *Abolition of Passes Act* (1952), despite its name, in fact made the pass system more efficient. It abolished the wide variety of employers' passes and introduced instead a single 'reference book'.

Other laws were introduced to tighten regulations against illegal 'squatters' in towns or on white-owned farms and to provide for the deportation of unemployed blacks from urban areas. The *Native Resettlement (Western Areas) Act* (1954) gave government the power to destroy a number of freehold black townships on the western edge of Johannesburg. Their residents were forced into the huge new municipal township of Soweto where they were brought under much stricter government control. In 1959 the *Promotion of Bantu Self-Government Act* allowed blacks limited political rights in their 'tribal homelands' but denied them any such rights in the rest of 'white' South Africa.

Another basic piece of *apartheid* legislation was the *Bantu Education Act* (1953) which was implemented in 1955. This separated blacks from the education system available to whites. It took away black education from the independent control of missionaries who had hitherto provided most of the schools for blacks. A new Bantu Education Department drew up separate syllabuses designed to emphasise the ethnic differences between blacks and show them that they really belonged in their separate 'Homelands'. The aim was to teach blacks no more than they needed to make them good workers for whites. It was deliberately intended as an inferior

form of education. In the words of one of the 'architects' of *apartheid*, Dr Hendrik Verwoerd, Minister of Native or Bantu Administration (1950–58) and later Prime Minister (1958–66), there was no place for blacks 'in the European community above the level of certain forms of labour'. To offer blacks the same education as whites, he argued, would 'mislead them by showing them the green pastures of European society in which they were not allowed to graze'!

The *apartheid* laws not only suited the racist views of Afrikaner nationalists; some of them also had specific advantages for capitalist employers. Blacks, who formed the bulk of the working class, were kept in a position of subordination. The *Native Labour Settlement of Disputes Act* (1953), for instance, made strikes by blacks a criminal offence. Denied the right to strike, blacks could be forced to accept low wages. The alternative was unemployment and the threat of removal to the poverty-striken rural reserves. Thus though many English-speaking white liberals vigorously opposed the open racism of *apartheid*, increasing numbers of English-speaking white businessmen came to support the Government. The National Party was returned to office with greatly increased majorities in the general elections of the 1950s and 60s. Despite this trend, however, a small but significant number of whites, Afrikaners as well as English, turned their backs on racist ideology and joined with blacks in trying to oppose the Government.

16.1 A scene from the Alexandra bus boycott: workers walking to work.

African nationalism: politics, protest and resistance, 1940–60

Meanwhile the so-called 'non-white' population of South Africa was not taking all this discriminatory legislation without considerable protest and resistance. The relaxation of the pass laws during the war had given a taste of freedom. Their reimposition in 1944 was even more bitterly resented. Black South Africans who had done military service in North Africa and Europe had served on the side of 'freedom and democracy'. They returned home after the war with great hopes of moves towards freedom and democracy in South Africa. Instead they were faced with even greater repression following the National Party victory in 1948.

Protest movements of the 1940s   Mass action on the Rand in the 1940s met with some initial measure of success and set the scene for the decade to come. The Alexandra bus boycotts of 1940–46 prevented the bus company from raising bus fares. Blacks demonstrated their economic power as thousands chose to walk the 20 kilometres to and from work in Johannesburg rather than pay the increased bus fares. The self-help squatter movement of 1944–47 got eventual municipal recognition of their unofficial squatter township south-west of Johannesburg. Mass action among mineworkers, however, met with tougher opposition. The wages of black mineworkers had remained static during the war despite the rise in prices. In 1946 the African Mineworkers Union led a strike of 70 000 miners in support of

16.1 South Africa: resistance to apartheid, 1948–65

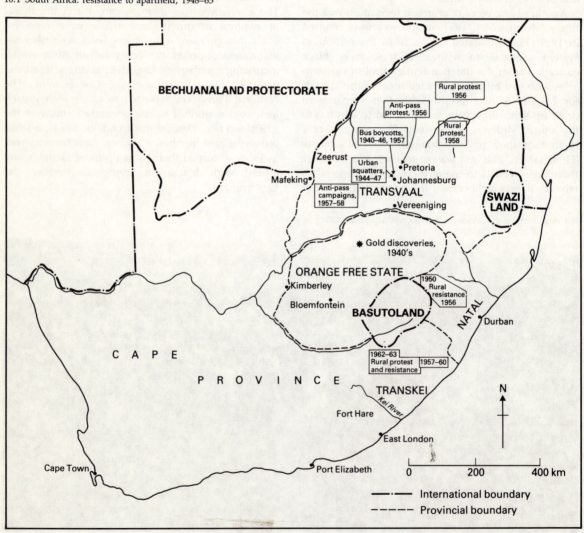

demands for a minimum wage and family housing. But police savagely suppressed the strike, arresting leaders, killing 12 and wounding 1200.

The ANC: Youth League and 'Programme of Action'

The national executive of the ANC had failed to take an active lead in the mass movements of the 1940s. This failure stimulated the growth of an important new movement within the ANC: the Youth League. Founded in 1944 by Anton Lembede the driving force behind the League were a number of young radicals expelled from Fort Hare College, among them two Johannesbureg lawyers, Nelson Mandela and Oliver Tambo. Unlike the old ANC leadership the Youth Leaguers were not afraid of mass action.

By 1949 a number of Youth Leaguers had been elected to the ANC's national executive, including Mandela, Tambo and Walter Sisulu, an active Johannesburg trade-unionist. Two other influential members of the executive were the prominent black communist trade-unionists, J. B. Marks and Moses Kotane. Dr James Moroka replaced Dr A. B. Xuma as President of the ANC and Sisulu became Secretary-General. With its new executive the ANC quickly re-emerged at the forefront of African politics and resistance. A 'Programme of Action' was drawn up: the aim was national freedom, political independence, the rejection of white leadership and the abolition of all segregationist laws. This was to be achieved through the mass action of boycotts, strikes and passive resistance.

The Defiance Campaign, 1952–3

A number of one-day strikes and demonstrations during 1950–51 led up to the ANC-sponsored 'Defiance Campaign' which began in June 1952. All over the country special volunteers deliberately defied petty *apartheid* restrictions. They courted arrest be sitting on 'white-only' park benches, using 'white' entrances to stations, post-offices and shops, crowding into 'white-only' first class railway carriages and refusing to carry passes. But there was still a reluctance among the leadership to exploit fully the real strengths of huge-scale mass action. The numbers making their defiant demonstrations were small, at most a few hundred at a time, while thousands looked on. There were those within the movement who felt that the Defiance Campaign had not gone far enough: wholesale defiance by thousands instead of hundreds would have choked the courts and prisons and brought the system to its knees. As it was by January 1953 eight thousand had been arrested, leaders were detained or banned and the campaign ground to a halt.

Women, protest and resistance in the 1950s

The economic depression felt by blacks during the 1950s fell particularly harshly on the rural areas, especially on women. The migrant labour system drew men away to the towns to earn 'bachelor wages' leaving women to bring up families on poor and inadequate land in the rural reserves. Poverty and attempts to pursue a normal family life drew many women to the urban areas where they fell victim to the newly extended pass law system.

In 1956 the Federation of South African Women, with prominent trade-unionist Lillian Ngoyi as President and Helen Joseph of the white Congress of Democrats as Secretary, organised a mass demonstration against the extension of passes to women. 20 000 women from all over the country converged on the central government buildings in Pretoria. There they handed in petitions and stood for 30 minutes in silent protest. It won them no material benefit but it was a moving demonstration which brought many more women actively into the political struggle. Women played a prominent part in a further (unsuccessful) bus boycott in Alexandra in 1957.

In the rural areas of northern and western Transvaal, Natal and Transkei, there was widespread resistance to Government policies in the late 1950s and early 1960s, much of it activated by women. Resistance was directed against *apartheid* laws, new 'Bantu Authorities' and Government inteference in agricultural practices. Fences and cattle-dipping tanks were destroyed in Natal. The Hurutshe reserve in the western Transvaal was prominent in the women's anti-pass campaign in 1957–58. Chief Abram Moilwa, who sympathised with the women, was deposed and Chief Lucas Mangope was installed in his place as the new Bantu Authority chief. In the Pondo district of Transkei resistance to new Bantu Authorities grew into more open revolt. A number of chiefs and headmen were killed and attempts were made to establish an alternative political authority. The revolt was crushed by heavy-handed police action and mass arrests. In further conflict in nearby Thembuland (1962–3) Chief Kaiser Matanzima rose in importance as a prominent supporter of the new Bantu Authorities.

The Congress Alliance, Freedom Charter and Treasons Trials

Following the suppression of the Defiance Campaign the ANC elected as its President-General Chief Albert Luthuli, a former teacher and chief of a minor Zulu clan. Almost immediately Luthuli was banned by the Government. Meanwhile the Communist Party (CPSA) had become a banned organisation under the *Suppression of Communism Act* (1950). It dissolved itself and secretly reformed as the SACP under the leadership of an Afrikaner lawyer, Bram Fischer. Former black CPSA members were already working actively within the ANC. A number of former white communists joined the new white radical political party, the Congress of Democrats. At the same time the Indian Congress (SAIC) began to associate itself more closely with the majority black population in their common struggle against *apartheid*. SAIC leaders played a prominent part in the Defiance Campaign.

In 1955 the main opponents of *apartheid* came together to form the Congress Alliance. This consisted of the ANC, the Indian Congress, the recently-formed Coloured People's Organisation, the non-racial South African Congress of Trade Unions (SACTU) and the radical white Congress of Democrats. The Congress Alliance drew up a 'Freedom Charter' which laid down the principles for a free and democratic South Africa. At a 'Congress of the People' held at Kliptown near Johannesburg on 25 and 26 June 1955 the articles of the Freedom Charter were read out and adopted. Of the 3000 delegates at Kliptown two-thirds were African and the remaining one-third was made up of Indians,

16.2 The founding of the 'Freedom Charter', Kliptown, 1955. Note the demands clearly stated on the posters.

16.3 A group photograph of the treason trialists, 1956. Standing just right of centre, third row from front is Nelson Mandela.

'coloureds' and whites. The Charter proposed a non-racial South Africa with equal rights and justice for all. The country's mineral wealth, banks and monopoly industry would be nationalised and 'The land shall be shared among those who work it'.

The Government reacted to the Congress Alliance and the growing pace of protest movements by arresting 156 of the country's leading opponents of *apartheid* and putting them on trial for treason. The 'Treason Trials' began in December 1956 and continued until the last thirty were finally acquitted in March 1960. The prosecution attempted to prove that the Freedom Charter was a 'communist' document. It failed to prove its case and all 156 were eventually acquitted. What the trials succeeded in doing was strengthening support for the ANC and other Alliance organisations.

The Africanists and the Pan-Africanist Congress

Within the ranks of the ANC not all were happy with the Freedom Charter or with the direction in which the movement seemed to be going. Among the most outspoken of these critics were the 'Africanists' who saw themselves as carrying on the spirit of the founder of the Youth League, Anton Lembede, who died in 1947. The Africanists believed that Africans should stand alone against the Government's racist laws. Africans should be proud of their own culture and reject white culture and foreign ideologies. For this reason they were suspicious of socialism and opposed co-operation with communists. They were critical of the ANC's close links with other racial groups who, they feared, were dominating the Congress Alliance. They opposed the socialist input in the Freedom Charter and tried to block its acceptance by the ANC.

The Africanists believed in the power of large-scale mass action and the need for black political leaders to identify more closely with the needs and grievances of the masses. One of the most important Africanists within the ANC was Robert Sobukwe, a lecturer in African languages and formerly a prominent early member of the Youth League. In November 1958 the Africanists left the ANC when the latter formally adopted the Freedom Charter as official Congress policy. In April 1959 the Africanists set up the 'Pan-Africanist Congress' with Sobukwe as President. By the end of the year PAC had 25 000 members. Many of these were rurally-based migrant workers, a group hitherto neglected by the ANC.

The Sharpeville massacre and its aftermath, 1960–65

As increasing numbers of political leaders were acquitted from the Treason Trials, the ANC and PAC laid plans for a renewal of mass defiance of *apartheid*. In December 1959 they announced plans for a massive anti-pass campaign in March 1960. The ANC proposed a single 'day of protest', 31 March, on which passes would be publically burned. In an attempt to win wider mass support the PAC deliberately chose ten days earlier, 21 March. And their action, unlike the single day of the ANC, was to be indefinite until the pass laws were removed. Blacks would march on police stations in their thousands and demand to be arrested. There would be so many 'pass offenders' that it would be impossible for police to arrest them all. It would demonstrate that the pass system could not be made to work if enough people were determined to defy it. Two things led to the failure of the PAC's plans. Firstly they did not have the mass organisation to get people out in sufficient numbers on the day. Secondly they had not counted on the violence of police reaction.

On 21 March the campaign began according to plan as Sobukwe and others marched to Orlando police station and were arrested. Some of the widest support for the campaign came from the Vereeniging suburbs of Sharpeville and Evaton where unemployment and poverty were acute. There was also strong support in the Cape Town suburbs of Langa and Nyanga where migrant workers from the eastern Cape were particularly affected by the restrictions of the pass laws. Between 3000 and 5000 people marched on Sharpeville police station and demanded to be arrested for not carrying their

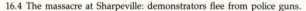

16.4 The massacre at Sharpeville: demonstrators flee from police guns.

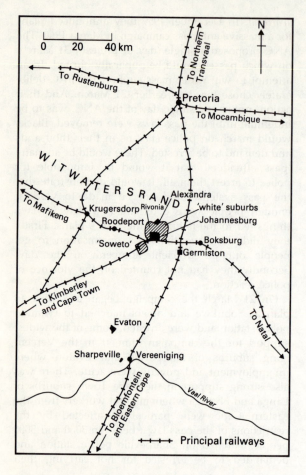

16.2 The Witwatersrand: South Africa's industrial heartland

passes. The police responded by opening fire on the crowd, killing 69 and wounding 180. Most of those killed were shot in the back as they fled. A further two demonstrators were shot dead by police in the Cape Town suburb of Langa.

The shock of the Sharpeville massacre reverberated around the world as nations everywhere condemned the South African Government's action and the *apartheid* system which had led to the conflict. For a few days even the South African Government itself was hesitant. In Cape Town local police suspended the pass laws in an attempt to defuse the situation. But then as multinational companies, fearing revolution, began to withdraw capital investment from South Africa, the Government finally reacted. On 30 March, the day before the scheduled ANC demonstration, the Government declared a 'State of Emergency' which gave them additional police powers. A week later the ANC and PAC were officially 'banned' and thousands of ANC

and PAC members were arrested.

Within the United Nations there were moves to isolate South Africa and thus force the Government to reverse its apartheid policies. But attempts to impose universal economic sanctions against South Africa were blocked by Britain and the United States. Faced with world-wide condemnation and criticism, the National Party turned its back firmly on the winds of freedom that were blowing across the rest of the continent. In 1961 Prime Minister Verwoerd broke the last constitutional links with Britain when he proclaimed the country a republic and withdrew South Africa from the Commonwealth. Meanwhile as a gesture of respect and support for the African nationalist struggle, the Norwegian Nobel committee awarded the world-renowned Nobel Prize for Peace (1961) to Albert Luthuli, President of the now-banned ANC.

Sabotage and guerrilla tactics With the banning of the ANC and PAC, African resistance was forced underground. The ANC sent Oliver Tambo to Bechuanaland (soon to become Botswana) to lead the struggle in exile. In June 1961 at a secret meeting of its national executive the ANC agreed to continue non-violent protest. But at the same time they founded a military wing, *Umkhonto we Sizwe* ('Spear of the Nation'), under the leadership of Nelson Mandela. Unlike the ANC *Umkhonto* allowed people of other races into its ranks and former Communist Party members played an important part in its planning and activities. *Umkhonto's* initial aim was to sabotage economic, political and communications targets like electricity pylons, railway lines and Bantu Administration offices. Injury to people was to be avoided wherever possible. It was hoped this policy would gain maximum world-wide publicity, sympathy and support. At the same time people were sent abroad to China and elsewhere for military training in case full-scale guerrilla warfare became inevitable. Sabotage attacks began in December 1961 and continued sporadically for the next eighteen months.

The PAC meanwhile had formed its own military wing, *Poqo* (meaning 'pure' or 'alone'). Its attacks were more widespread, aimed at people as well as installations. It targetted in particular Bantu Authorities' personnel in the Transkei. In 1963 *Poqo's* headquarters in Maseru (Basutoland) were raided by British colonial police who captured a membership list of 10 000 members. *Poqo's* South African network was then infiltrated by police informers and the movement's activities were more or less brought to a close by the mass arrest of 3000 *Poqo* suspects.

The 'Rivonia Trials' In 1962 Mandela, who had been in hiding for some time, went secretly abroad and travelled widely in Africa and Europe building up support for the ANC and *Umkhonto*. He was captured on his return to South Africa in August 1962 and imprisoned for inciting people to strike and for leaving the country without a valid passport. In July 1963 police raided a farm in the northern Johannesburg suburb of Rivonia. There they captured almost the whole of the *Umkhonto* 'High Command', among them Walter Sisulu and Govan Mbeki. In the subsequent trial, known as the 'Rivonia Trial' (December 1963 to July 1964) Mandela was brought out of prison to stand with the other eight defendants, five blacks, two whites and one Indian.

In a long speech to the court in his own defence Mandela traced the ANC's history of non-violent struggle. He showed how after all other means had been denied them, they had been reluctantly forced to turn to violence in their search for a free South Africa. He concluded in the now-famous words:

> During my lifetime I have dedicated myself to this struggle of the African people. I have fought against white domination, and I have fought against black domination. I have cherished the ideal of a democratic and free society in which all persons live together in harmony and with equal opportunities. It is an ideal which I hope to live for and to achieve. But if needs be it is an ideal for which I am prepared to die.

All the defendants except one white were convicted of sabotage and sentenced to life imprisonment. They were driven off to prison amid defiant shouts from the crowd outside: '*Amandla*! *Ngawethu*!' ('Power! To the People!').

The 'triumph' of apartheid During the early 1960s the Minister of Justice, B. J. Vorster, greatly strengthened the size and power of the police. The *General Laws Amendment Act* of 1963 gave police the power to detain people without charge and in solitary confinement for ninety days at a time. This was extended to 180 days in 1965. The widespread use of detentions and bannings in the 1960s effectively suppressed internal opposition and removed any new political leadership as soon as it emerged. At the same time trade-union activity was defined as 'economic sabotage' and mass arrests of SACTU officials virtually paralysed the trade-union movement. By the mid-1960s the South African Government could boast that it had, for the time being, firmly suppressed internal opposition and resistance. The danger of immediate revolution seemed to have been removed. Foreign investment capital flowed back into the country and the economy experienced an unexpected period of boom. In 1966 Verwoerd was assassinated by a deranged white parliamentary messenger and Vorster took over as Prime Minister.

Exercises

A. Think, discuss, understand and write

1 Describe and discuss the tactics of the ANC between 1912 and 1960. How and why were these tactics changed after 1960?
2 Describe the role of mass protest movements in South Africa between 1940 and 1960. Why did some succeed and others fail?
3 Assess the importance of the Youth League and the Freedom Charter to the black political struggle in South Africa. How do you account for the ANC/PAC split in 1958–59?
4 Assess the role of women in the struggle for freedom in South Africa between 1910 and 1965.
5 Explain the aims of the National Party's *apartheid* policy. How far had they achieved those aims by 1965?
6 How do you account for the growing white support for the National Party Government between 1948 and 1965? Why did South Africa become a republic and leave the Commonwealth in 1961?
7 What methods did the South African Government use to suppress opposition? How effective were their efforts?

B. Imaginative writing

In December 1959 the ANC and PAC both announced plans for a massive anti-pass campaign in March 1960. In fact they laid their plans separately and adopted different tactics. But *if there had been* a meeting between Luthuli and Sobukwe at this time, how might they have argued about their aims and the tactics they intended to adopt? Write a record of such a meeting.

C. Groupwork and class discussion

1. Project: time-chart Continue the time-chart recommended in Exercise C at the end of the previous chapter. Bring it up to 1965. Discuss and compare the information and developments as revealed in the chart.

2. Project: history of the 'pass law' 'As we have seen in earlier chapters, a system of passes had been in use in various forms for very many years'. Research earlier chapters in this book and discuss the history of the 'pass law' in South Africa.

Document 16.1 *Extract from a South African newspaper 1946:*

Document study Read Document 16.1 and discuss the answers to the following questions:

1 What evidence is offered in the report to suggest that the number of 50 000 strikers is an underestimate?
2 What did the striking miners hope to achieve?
3 What action according to this report was taken and by whom to try and defeat the strike?
4 What evidence is offered in this newspaper cutting that people other than miners supported the strike? What evidence is there to suggest the viewpoint of the newspaper itself?
5 Discuss the final outcome of the strike. How does the 1946 miners' strike compare with South African workers' strikes before or since?

GUARDIAN

Registered at the G.P.O. as a Newspaper.   THURSDAY, AUGUST 15, 1946   PRICE 1d.

GREATEST STRIKE IN S.A. HISTORY
MORE THAN 50,000 OUT

JOHANNESBURG — On Tuesday morning the African Mineworkers' Union office was raided by police. All documents, records of membership cards were seized. The police produced a search warrant, issued on suspicion that an "offence" had been committed.

On Wednesday morning the capitalist Press announced that "the first evidence" had been found connecting the Union with the strike! They ignored the fact that on August 4, at a meeting called by the Union and attended by delegates from most mines it was agreed to strike on August 12 unless the workers demands were met. THIS DECISION WAS WIDELY PUBLICISED BY THE UNION AND PUBLISHED IN THE PRESS CONTROLLED BY THE MINE-OWNERS AS WELL AS IN THE GUARDIAN.

The President of the Union, Mr. J. B. Marks (who is an African and not a Coloured man as the capitalist Press incorrectly reports), has been arrested. Another arrest is that of Mr. Ben Sischy, a prominent member of the Council for Asiatic Rights.

A committee of four Cabinet Ministers: Mines (Mr S. F. Waterson), Labour (Dr Colin Steyn), Justice (Mr. H. G. Lawrence), Native Affairs (Major P. van der Byl) has been appointed by the Prime Minister to deal with the strike.

THEIR JOB IS AN EASY ONE. LET THEM FORCE THE MINE-OWNERS TO NEGOTIATE WITH THE AFRICAN MINE-WORKERS' UNION, WHICH REPRESENTS THE WORKERS. THIS IS WHAT EVERY TRADE UNIONIST AND EVERY DEMOCRAT IN SOUTH AFRICA MUST DEMAND.

(African Mineworkers' Union Statement: Page five).

JOHANNESBURG. On Tuesday Morning, the police, bearing search warrants, raided the office of the African Mine Workers' Union and confiscated nearly all the documents, records and other papers. Mr. J. B. Marks, president of both the African Mine Workers' Union and the Transvaal Council of Non-European Trade Unions has been arrested on a charge under the Riotous Assemblies Act. Mr. F. B. Mofutsanyana, editor of "Inkululek," who was visiting the union office as a journalist, was taken to Marshall Square and kept there for five hours by the police for questioning, without any charge being made against him.

Despite unparalleled police violence and frantic propaganda efforts the whole week, between 45,000 and 50,000 African miners on the Witwatersrand struck work on Monday morning demanding 10s. a day minimum wage and improved conditions.

the strike was on.

The New Kleinfontein and Robinson Deep miners came out 100 per cent. All or part of the African labour force are now on strike at the following mines: Brakpan, State Mines Springs, West Springs, Van Dyk, City Deep, Marlevale Modder B, Nourse Mines, Van Ryn Estates, Vlakfontein, Simmer and Jack, Sub Nigel Witwatersrand Gold Mine.

At New Kleinfontein three men were arrested on Monday. Eight thousand workers marched to the Benoni police station demanding their release. A tense situation resulted with armed police standing at the gates of the police station with fixed bayonets refusing to allow the strikers to enter.

POLICE TERRORISM

There are reports of exceptional measures by the police at West Rand to prevent "strike" action. City Deep, Robinson deep and Randfontein report large forces of police were rushed from Johannesburg and serious violence was used against the workers.

It is stated in the capitalist press this police terrorism and baton charges against the strikers was on instructions from Pretoria.

The "Rand Daily Mail" on Monday, under the headline "Attempt to force Native Mine Strike", praised the action of the police and endeavoured to give its readers the reassuring impression that the strike was a total failure.

MORE THAN 50,000

African mine workers continue to join the strikers. The figures given by the capitalist press that 50,000 are on strike is underestimated. Many miners not mentioned in the "Star" and "Rand Daily Mail" press reports are out on strike. Sallies Brakpan, Witpoort are all mines which were on strike on Tuesday morning.

Despite all efforts, and intimidation, the spirit of the workers remains high.

Scores of workers and trade unionists assisting the union have been arrested on various charges.

SIX DEAD

AT SUB NIGEL MINE ON TUESDAY MORNING, THE POLICE OPENED FIRE ON THE WORKERS. SIX WERE SHOT DEAD AND OTHERS WOUNDED. THE REPORT OF THE SHOOTING OF THE SIX WORKERS WAS GRAVELY DISTORTED BY THE CAPITALIST PRESS WHICH TRIED TO MAKE OUT IT WAS THE WORKERS FAULT.

Telegram to Smuts

The following telegram has been sent to the Prime Minister by Mr. W. H. Andrews, the National Chairman of the S.A. Communist Party.

National Executive of Communist party condemns the use of police terrorism with resultant deaths to break strike of mine workers for the right to live stop. We demand your Government immediately end police intimidation and compel mine workers to negotiate with African Mine Workers' Union.

A news blackout was at first imposed by the capitalist press, but as the strike spread in response to the strike decision on the East Rand the newspapers were forced to admit

STRIKE FUNDS

The Passive Resistance Council of the Transvaal Indian Congress has passed a resolution pledging full support to the striking mine workers. The Johannesburg District Committee of the Communist Party has resolved to give all support. Other expressions of support have been received from the African National Congress. Cape, and Cape Town trade unions. £100 was collected towards strike funds at a Durban meeting held in Resistance Hall.

HELP THE BRAVE STRIKERS! Send donations NOW to: The African Mine Workers' Union. P.O. Box 6045, Johannesburg.

General Strike Called

A general strike of all African workers in Johannesburg, the Reef, Pretoria and Vereenuging has been called for Thursday, August 15, by a fully representative meeting of African trade unions under the auspices of the Transvaal Council of Non-European Trade Unions, held at Rosenberg Arcade on Tuesday evening. A resolution passed by a big majority, reads:

"After considering the implications arising out of the strike of African mine workers this meeting resolves to call a general strike of all African workers on the Reef, Johannesburg, Pretoria and Vereenuging, within 48 hours from now, in support of the miners and to implement a resolution for recognition of African unions and 10s. minimum daily wage arrived at by the Bloemfontein National Conference of Non-European trade unions in 1945."

INDIAN SUPPORT

JOHANNESBURG – The Executive Committee of the Passive Resistance Council of the Transvaal Indian Congress have pledged "full support" to the African Mineworkers' Union in their strike for a wage of ten shillings per day and for better conditions on the mines." The resolution adds that the African mineworker is the most oppressed of all South African Non-Europeans.

"The economic structure which allows the continuance of the present status of the Africans on the mines has been responsible to a very large extent for the policy of oppression which is being pursued against the African, Indian and Coloured people of South Africa. At a time when the Indian community is engaged in the passive resistance struggle, challenging the policy of segregation, this Council welcomes the action of the Africans who have opened another front against the policy of segregation which is responsible for their miserable conditions on the mines. The Passive Resistance Council wishes the African mine workers every success in their strike."

"QUIT INDIA"

JOHANNESBURG – "Indians in South Africa have every reason to be proud of the role they are playing in the history of this country in launching the present Passive Resistance Campaign. It is an inspiration to all sections which believe in a democratic South Africa," declared Councillor Hilda Watts, addressing a crowded meeting at the Gandhi Hall last Friday called by the Transvaal Indian Youth Volunteer Corps to demand that British Imperialism quit India.

CHAPTER 17

Colonial rule in the High Commission Territories and Namibia

South Africa and the High Commission Territories, 1910–60

The British colonial territories of the Bechuanaland Protectorate, Basutoland and Swaziland each came under the direct authority of the British High Commissioner for Southern Africa. They were thus known jointly by the British as the 'High Commission Territories'. It was assumed at the time of the Act of Union (1910) (see p 138), that all three would in due course become part of the Union of South Africa. They were seen by both British and South African governments as useful labour reserves for industrial South Africa. And as the Union's segregationist and *apartheid* system became more clearly developed the High Commission Territories were seen by South Africa as useful additional territory for blacks. If added to the Union they would increase the percentage of land for blacks from 13 per cent (1936) to almost 50 per cent. Much of this land was mountain (Basutoland) and desert (Bechuanaland) and therefore not required by whites while much of the worthwhile land in Swaziland was already in white South African ownership.

South African attempts to incorporate the High Commission Territories were particularly active during the premiership of Hertzog in the 1930s. Efforts were revived in the 1950s when Verwoerd proposed they form part of *apartheid's* self-governing 'Homeland' or 'Bantustan' system. By then the South African Government also wanted to bring them under closer political control in order to stop them becoming places of refuge for opponents of *apartheid*.

For most of the colonial period therefore the cloud of possible incorporation into South Africa hung heavily over the High Commission Territories. The

British Government saw them as economically part of a greater South Africa and thus saw no point in trying to develop them as economically viable units in their own right. Nevertheless Britain had taken over the 'protection' of Bechuanaland, Basutoland and Swaziland at the request or with the agreement of their African 'traditional' rulers. The British therefore promised them they would not be incorporated against their will. And throughout the colonial period the African 'traditional' leaders remained strongly opposed to any incorporation into the Union.

The Bechuanaland Protectorate, 1899–1966

The British began effective rule in Bechuanaland in 1899 when they marked out large 'reserves' for the principal Tswana chiefdoms and began collecting hut-tax. The Protectorate was administered by a 'Resident Commissioner' who was not in fact really 'resident' at all: his headquarters were across the South African border at Mafikeng. British interference in internal Tswana affairs was initially minimal. The chiefs still retained virtually full control over their own people and conducted their own courts. The British even used the chiefs to collect the hut-tax. To encourage them in this, the chiefs received a commission of 10 per cent on tax collected. To some extent this strengthened the power of the Tswana chiefs over their people. They were also recognised as legitimate rulers over non-Tswana groups within their 'reserves' such as the Kalanga in the north-east, the Mbukushi in the north-west and the Sarwa and Kgalagadi in the west and south-west.

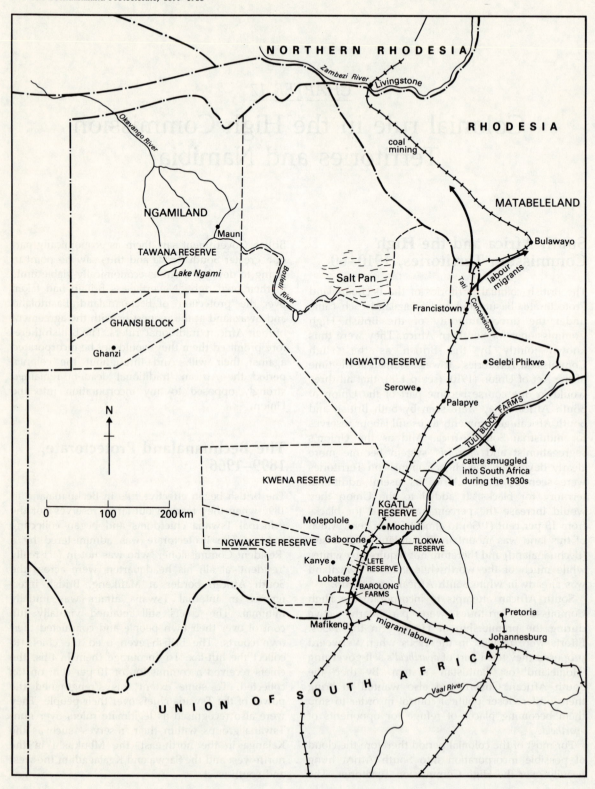

17.1 African community school in colonial Bechuanaland

In 1920 the British set up a Native Advisory Council (later changed to African Advisory Council). Its members were appointed by the main Tswana chiefs though it was boycotted by Khama of the Ngwato as he felt it implied a loss of chiefly authority and independence. The purpose of the council was to advise the Resident Commissioner on African affairs. But he was not obliged to take their advice and he normally used the occasion simply to inform the Tswana about government decisions.

Chiefly authority and British administration, the 1920s and 1930s In 1923 Khama III of the Ngwato died, aged nearly ninety. His son Sekgoma succeeded him for only two years before he too died leaving a four-year-old son, Seretse, as heir to the largest Tswana chiefdom. Seretse's twenty-one-year-old uncle Tshekedi left his studies at South Africa's Fort Hare College to become regent. British colonial officials unwisely assumed this young and inexperienced man could be easily 'advised' and manipulated. But Tshekedi was a highly intelligent, imaginative and capable ruler. He soon proved himself an outspoken and effective opponent of any who threatened the power and independence of the Ngwato chieftaincy.

In 1926 Tshekedi's rivals for the regency, the Ratshosa brothers, attempted to assassinate him. Tshekedi's firm action in confiscating their property, burning their houses and exiling them from Serowe aroused the concern of the colonial authorities. In 1933 Tshekedi again freely exercised 'customary law' in flogging a white resident of Serowe for assaulting an Ngwato woman. His 'high-handed' action on this occasion so outraged the Resident Commissioner,

Rey, that 200 British naval troops were sent up from Cape Town and Tshekedi was publically deposed in Serowe. But Rey's action provoked such united Tswana opposition that he was forced to back down and reinstate Tshekedi.

Rey was determined to curb the power of the Tswana chiefs, especially Tshekedi. In 1933–4 he issued proclamations which brought his administration into line with a form of 'indirect rule' devised by colonial officials in Nigeria and Tanganyika. In fact in the Bechuanaland case it enforced a more *direct* form of colonial rule. It effectively removed the independent authority of the chiefs and converted them into local government officials subject to the colonial resident magistrates. The village *kgotla*, where local courts were publically conducted and where the chief was answerable to his people for his actions, was abolished. It was replaced by special, government-controlled 'tribal councils'. Rey's proclamations aroused widespread Tswana opposition. Tshekedi and Bathoen of the Ngwaketse took the Government to court and challenged the legality of the proclamations on the grounds that they went against the 'protectorate' agreements of 1885 and 1895. But the case was overruled by the British Government which claimed the overall authority to issue whatever proclamations it chose. In the event a less dictatorial Resident Commissioner, Arden-Clarke, took over from Rey in 1937 and diplomatically persuaded the Tswana chiefs to accept a modified form of the proclamations which included the restoration of the *kgotla*.

Drought, depression and migrant labour, the 1930s The 1930s was a period of economic depression in the Bechuanaland Protectorate. The decade began with a prolonged drought: crops failed, grass withered and cattle died. The Tswana had suffered periods of drought before, but now to add to their difficulties were the annual demands of colonial tax collectors. At the same time the South African Government imposed a ban on the import of cattle from Bechuanaland in an attempt to protect Afrikaner farmers from Tswana competition. With little or no capital investment in the Protectorate there were few if any job opportunities within Bechuanaland. In the 1930s therefore levels of labour migrancy soared as thousands left their homes in search of wage employment on the farms and mines of South Africa and Southern Rhodesia. And during the Second World War 10 000 Tswana from the Protectorate volunteered for military service with the African Pioneer Corps in North Africa and southern Europe.

17.2 Seretse Khama and his wife Ruth (née Williams)

Tshekedi, Seretse and the 'marriage crisis'
In 1945 the Ngwato heir Seretse Khama went to England to study law. There in 1948 he married an English-woman, Ruth Williams. The marriage was vigor-ously opposed by Tshekedi and 'traditionalist' Ngwato who had not been consulted. Seretse returned to Serowe and in a series of *kgotla* meetings persuaded the Ngwato to accept his decision. But there had been bitter exchanges between supporters of Tshekedi and Seretse, Tshekedi being accused of trying to usurp the chieftaincy. Tshekedi resigned the regency and exiled himself to the neighbouring Kwena reserve.

Meanwhile the South African Government inter-vened. Seretse's marriage was a direct challenge to *apartheid* laws. With an eye to the future incorpor-ation of Bechuanaland into the Union, Prime Minister Malan insisted that the British Government prevent Seretse's installation as chief. Seretse was summoned to London and exiled from the Protectorate. There followed riots in Serowe as the Ngwato refused to elect an alternative chief. The problem was finally resolved in 1956 by both Tshekedi and Seretse resigning all personal claim to the Ngwato chief-taincy. The two were then reconciled and were allowed to return home to the Ngwato reserve.

Post-war developments in the Protectorate
In the years following the Second World War the move towards political independence gathered pace in the colonial territories of Africa. At the same time, with South Africa pursuing increasingly racist policies, incorporation of the High Commission Territories seemed increasingly unlikely. The British Govern-ment therefore finally turned its attention towards the economic and political development of its Southern African protectorates.

Britain's main contribution to economic develop-ment in the Bechuanaland Protectorate was the Commonwealth Development Corporation's funding of an abattoir at Lobatse which was opened in 1954. This provided a local market for the export of chilled and canned beef. Agricultural development mean-while suffered from lack of funds and poor rainfall. Much of the initiative for developments in cattle husbandry, crop cultivation and building of schools came from the Tswana themselves under the lead-ership of their chiefs. In the 1950s Tshekedi Khama, who had earlier distrusted mining concessions, now sought out a Northern Rhodesian copper mining company to develop copper mining within the Ngwato reserve. A concession was signed shortly before Tshekedi's death in 1959 and copper was found at Selebi Phikwe in 1965.

Meanwhile a new generation of educated Tswana, many with higher education from South Africa, were gaining administrative experience in the recon-stituted Tribal Councils. A Joint (African and Euro-pean) Advisory Council was formed in 1951 and from it came demands for a properly representative, elected Legislative Council which would decide the laws of the country.

African nationalism and Botswana Independence
Those who formed the early political parties in the High Commission Territories were strongly influ-enced by the African nationalist struggle in South Africa. Most had worked in that country or received their higher education there. The growing political crisis in South Africa during the late 1950s and early 1960s stimulated demands for independence in the neighbouring territories.

In the Bechuanaland Protectorate a short-lived Federal Party was formed in 1959 to be followed in 1960 by the Bechuanaland People's Party (BPP), a small but vigorous political party demanding immediate independence. Its founding leaders were K. T. Motsete, an educationist with political experi-ence in Nyasaland, Philip Matante, a former Johan-nesburg preacher with close links with the PAC, and Motsamai Mpho, a former 'treason trialist' in South Africa. In 1961 the BPP was weakened by a split and Mpho later founded the Botswana Independence Party, based in his home area of Ngamiland.

Meanwhile the British administration had agreed to the formation of a Legislative Council (Legco) with equal African and European representation. Its ten African members were drawn from the Tribal

Councils. A prominent member of the Legco was Seretse Khama, secretary of the Ngwato Council since 1956. In 1962 Khama and Quett Masire. a 'progressive' farmer from Kanye, formed the Bechuanaland Democratic Party (BDP). Another important and influential early member of the BDP was Chief Bathoen II of the Ngwaketse. Khama, as 'uncrowned king' of the Ngwato, and Bathoen were able to draw on the support of the more traditionalist Tswana who followed the lead of their chiefs and headmen. At the same time they belonged to the new generation of highly educated Tswana. The BDP leadership were careful to put forward a moderate image and to distance themselves from close alliance with South African political movements.

The BDP was in a powerful position with its members prominent in both Legco and Tribal Councils. The British accepted BDP's proposed timetable for independence and it was thus an unusually amicable transfer of power. Plans were made for moving the capital *into* the country from Mafikeng to Gaborone. In 1965 a new non-racial consititution led to the election of a new Legislative Council by universal adult franchise. The BDP won 28 of the 31 seats with the BPP taking the remaining three, and Seretse Khama became Prime Minister. The constitution was then slightly revised so that at independence on 30 September 1966 Seretse Khama became head of state and first President of the Republic of Botswana. Shortly before independence the British had honoured him with the title 'Sir' Seretse Khama.

Basutoland, 1900–1966

Rural poverty and migrant labour Rural poverty quickly became a major feature of colonial Basutoland. Only one-sixth of the land was arable: most of the rest was mountain, much of it not even suitable for grazing sheep. There was no surplus land for the expanding population. Even by the 1890s the overworked land was showing signs of exhaustion. And South Africa's land policies after Union progressively closed off Free State farms as places for Basotho to find alternative arable land. Migrant labour, especially to the South African mines, became firmly established from an early period. By the turn of the century 30 000 a year were seeking wage employment in South Africa. By the 1930s, when Basutoland's official population was well over half a million, 50 per cent of the country's adult men spent most of the year as migrant workers in South Africa. During the Second World War 20 000 volunteered for the African Pioneer Corps. We have already seen

in an earlier chapter how South African wages were deliberately kept below the level needed to support a family. This threw much of the burden of supporting the family on the women in the rural areas. In the case of Basutoland the severe shortage of land made this an ever more difficult task. The result was increasing rural poverty and disruption of Basotho family life.

Chieftaincy and the Basutoland National Council
As in the other High Commission Territories early British administration in Basutoland was kept to a minimum. A Government report in the 1930s referred to it as 'protection without control'. This was not strictly true. There certainly was control over the people as a whole, but it was applied indirectly, through the Basutoland chieftaincy. The heirs of Moshoeshoe were recognised as Paramount Chiefs: Lerotholi, 1891–1905; Letsie II, 1905–1913; and Griffith, 1913–1939. Internal Basotho affairs were left in the hands of the Paramount and his district chiefs who collected hut-tax, ran their own courts and controlled allocation of arable and grazing land. From 1910 a National Council was summoned annually. This further strengthened the power of the Paramount as he nominated ninety-four of the hundred members. Its role was purely advisory but, presided over by the Resident Commissioner, it was a demonstration of Government support for the authority of the Paramount. The effect of Government policy was to make the chiefs less answerable to their people. A number became autocratic and used court fines as their own personal wealth.

17.3 Mosotho horseman in Lesotho.

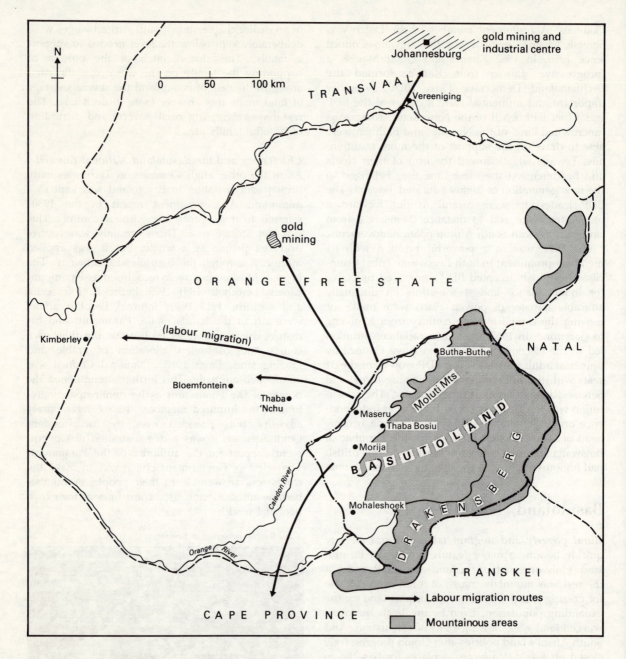

N

0   50   100 km

gold mining and
industrial centre
Johannesburg

Vereeniging

T R A N S V A A L

gold
mining

O R A N G E   F R E E   S T A T E

N A T A L

Butha-Buthe

Kimberley

(labour migration)

Moluti Mts

Bloemfontein

Thaba
'Nchu

B A S U T O L A N D

Maseru

Thaba Bosiu

D R A K E N S B E R G

Morija

Caledon River

Mohaleshoek

Orange River

T R A N S K E I

→ Labour migration routes

▨ Mountainous areas

C A P E   P R O V I N C E

17.2 Colonial Basutoland and South African neighbours

In pre-colonial times the various sons of a Sotho
clan chief would move off to fresh land to set up
their own villages. This practice continued during
the colonial period despite the shortage of land. The
fact that the chief's court ensured an income in fines
and dues encouraged the tendency. As a result by
the 1930s there were, in the words of a member of
the National Council, 'as many chiefs in Basutoland

as there are stars in the heavens.' In 1907 a group
of educated Basotho commoners had formed a
'Progressive Association' to voice their opposition to
the National Council and the abuse of power by the
chiefs. By 1920 they claimed a thousand members.
One of their more prominent spokesmen was Josiel
Lefela, a former Rand mineworker and close
supporter of South Africa's ANC. By the 1930s the

Basotho chieftaincy, so useful to the British in the early days of colonial administration, was coming under increasing Basotho criticism and badly needed reform.

Chiefly power and administrative reform   Between 1938 and 1946 the British Government introduced a series of administrative changes intended to reform the system. These 'reforms' reduced the power of the chiefs and brought internal Basotho affairs under more direct colonial control. This was made easier after 1939 by the death of Paramount Griffith and the succession dispute which followed. By 1941 Griffith's senior surviving widow, Mantsebo, had emerged as regent for the child-heir Seeiso, born in 1938. The Resident Commissioner took over from the Paramount the final say in the appointment and dismissal of chiefs. An official register of chiefs was drawn up and over the next few years the number of those entitled to hold their own courts was reduced from over 1300 to 122. By 1956 the number was down to 63. Registered chiefs became salaried government officials no longer dependant for their livelihood on fees and fines extracted in their local courts. Court fees were transferred to district 'National Treasuries' which also received a third of the district's hut-tax. The Treasuries' funds were expected to support health, educational and welfare services. However, since their income was drawn from the largely poverty-stricken people of the district, their funds were hopelessly inadequate for the task in hand. Furthermore grants from British development funds were too small to be effective.

Needless to say there was considerable resentment from chiefs who did not receive official recognition. The 1940s saw a revival of witchcraft and ritual killings in which a number of passed-over chiefs were believed to be involved. A further challenge to chiefly power came with the introduction of district councils in 1945. These were partly elected and were chaired by the colonial district commissioner. They were a means by which central government could bypass the local chief and hear the grievances and advice of commoners.

African nationalism and Lesotho independence
The first modern political party in Basutoland was the Basutoland African Congress (later renamed Basutoland Congress Party (BCP)). It was founded in 1952 by Ntsu Mokhehle, an early member of the ANC Youth League at Fort Hare and president of the Basutoland Teachers' Association. The large number of Basotho working in South Africa heightened Basotho awareness of the African political

struggle in that country. Many were active members of the ANC and there were close links between ANC and BCP. Many saw the BCP in Basutoland as an extension of the ANC's struggle in South Africa. Thus the rising political conflict of the 1950s in South Africa (see previous chapter) stimulated membership of the Congress Party in Basutoland.

Between 1955 and 1958 the Basutoland National Council, which consisted mostly of chiefs and headmen, pressed the British Government for constitutional changes. By 1959 a new constitution was agreed which converted the Council from an advisory to a legislative body. The new Legislative Council was to have eighty members, half nominated by the chiefs and Paramount and half nominated by specially-elected district councils.

But the chiefs and their supporters on the National Council feared the rising strength of the Congress Party in the forthcoming elections. So Chief Leabua Jonathan founded the Basutoland National Party (BNP) to fight the Congress Party (BCP) in the district council elections. He branded the BCP as a radical communist party and hoped for support from conservative, traditionally-minded Basotho. But the BCP had well-established support among Basotho commoners. Although it was weakened by splits over the future role of the Paramount Chief, in the elections of January 1960 the Congress Party won three-quarters of the district council seats. This gave them 29 of the 40 elected seats in the new Legislative Council. But Jonathan's National Party had the support of the chiefs and headmen who nominated 40 members to the Council. Together with the BNP's minority of 11 elected members, this gave Jonathan overall controll of Council. Thus in July 1960 Jonathan became Basutoland's first Prime Minister.

Basutoland now had control over its internal affairs, but the British High Commissioner was still in overall charge and in particular controlled the country's external affairs. In the years that followed the constitution was revised in preparation for independence and a wholly-elected legislative assembly.

Meanwhile Basotho refugees poured across the border from South Africa following the banning of the ANC and PAC. Mokhehle tried to distance the Congress Party from too close an alliance with ANC refugees. Nevertheless Jonathan was able to play on fears of conservative-minded Basotho about the consequences of open conflict with South Africa. He appealed particularly to the women who had not had the vote in 1960 and many of whom were dependent on the wages sent home by migrant workers in South Africa. Jonathan urged them to

17.4 Chief Johnathan, Prime Minister of Lesotho and H. F. Verwoerd, Prime Minister of South Africa.

'think of your stomachs' and support the BNP who would remain on good terms with South Africa. Jonathan's BNP narrowly won the General Election of 1965 with 31 out of the 60 seats in the new National Assembly. BCP won 25 seats and the remaining four went to a monarchist group, the Marema-Tlou Freedom Party. On 4 October 1966 Basutoland became independent from Britain as the Kingdom of Lesotho. The former Paramount Chief became nominal head of state as King Moshoeshoe II, but real power lay in the hands of the National Assembly and the Prime Minister, Leabua Jonathan.

Swaziland, 1907–1968

In 1906, when the Transvaal became a self-governing British colony, Swaziland, like Basutoland and Bechuanaland, was brought under the authority of the British High Commissioner. So far as the Swazi were concerned, the British followed a similar policy to that adopted in the other High Commission Territories. Internal Swazi affairs were left in the hands of the Swazi royal family. The only real contact between Swazi and British colonial officials was in the payment of hut-tax. The Swazi Queen Regent, Labotsibeni, who acted for the infant King Sobhuza II, ruled with the aid of a council of royal advisers, the *Liqoqo*. A general Swazi assembly, *Libandla*, was summoned once a year. The main Swazi concern, which dominated their policy throughout the colonial period, was the issue of reclaiming Swazi land.

The land issue As we saw in Chapter 12, whites had taken over two-thirds of the land in Swaziland during the concessions' scramble of the 1880s. Subsequent Swazi rulers, however, claimed that whites had only ever been granted the *use* of the land, not its ownership. On the expiry of the concession leases the land would revert to the Swazi. But British colonial authorities decided that Swaziland was desirable as a colony for white settlement. A British proclamation of 1907 recognised the concessions as absolute freehold ownership. In addition, land where the concession was in dispute reverted to the colonial government, for future sale to whites. This left the Swazi with only one-third of their country for use as communal land. The Swazi regent objected strongly to this injustice, but a Swazi protest delegation sent to London found no British sympathy for their cause.

The Swazi had hitherto been agriculturally self-sufficient and hardly any Swazi felt the need to work outside the country as migrant labourers. If they were not to be reduced to rural poverty on the scale of Basutoland, they clearly needed more land than the small reserves to which most Swazi were now confined. The Swazi regent therefore set up a national fund in 1912 to buy back land from the Government or from whites. Young Swazi men were sent on contracts to the South African mines to bring back money for the land fund. In this way the Swazi 'nation' managed to buy slightly more land for Swazi communal use in the 1920s and 30s. But during the same period most government land was sold to whites as private freehold land. During the 1940s and 50s the Swazi redoubled their efforts and increased the nation's portion of Swaziland to 45 per cent by 1945 and 55 per cent by the time of independence in 1968.

The system of Swaziland communal land ownership ensured that every married man had access to enough arable land to feed his immediate family. But land was limited, the population was growing and there was the constant demand to pay hut-tax as well as contribute to the land fund. Young unmarried Swazi in particular came under increasing family pressure to seek wage employment in South Africa or on white-owned farms and industries in Swaziland. In addition the great drought of 1929–34 forced many hitherto successful peasant farmers to leave the land in search of wage employment. By the late 1930s some 10 000 Swazi were working on regular contracts in the South African mines, and 4000 Swazi volunteered for the African Pioneer Corps in the Second World War.

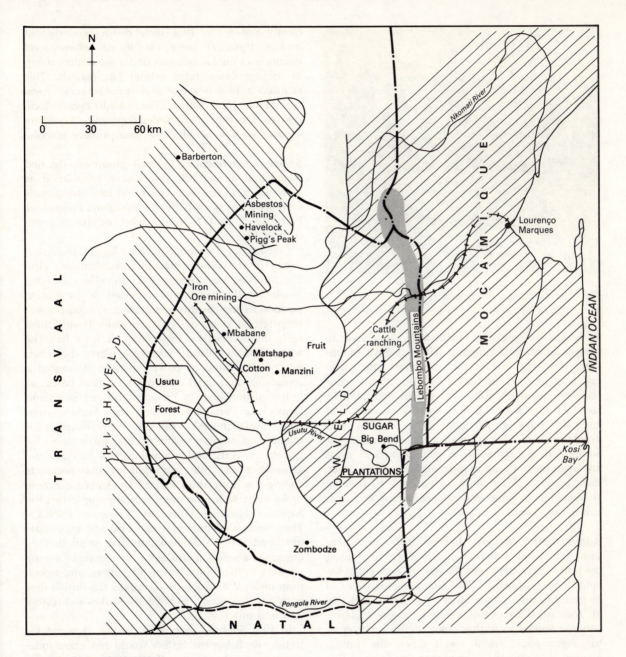

17.3 Colonial Swaziland, 1907–68

Colonial economic developments The colonial authorities were mainly interested in Swaziland as a place for white capitalist development. The Swazi were thus initially excluded from owning freehold property. In the 1940s and 50s there was heavy white investment in capitalist farming enterprises: beef ranches in the lowveld, irrigated sugar-cane plantations at Big Bend on the Usutu River and fruit farms in the middle veld. The Colonial (later

Commonwealth) Development Corporation invested in the planting of one of Africa's largest man-made forests, the Usutu Forest on the overgrazed slopes of the highveld. The Havelock asbestos mine near Pigg's Peak in the north of the country had been opened with South African capital in 1938. In the 1950s the Anglo-American Corporation of South Africa signed a contract with Japanese steel manufacturers to supply them with iron ore from Ngwenya.

17.5 Workers on a sugar plantation in Swaziland.

A special railway was built from Ngwenya to the sea in Mozambique and half Ngwenya mountain was cut away by the time the iron ore was finished in the 1970s. But these economic developments were on white-owned freehold land. All the Swazi got from them was some local low-paid wage employment. The benefits and profits went to white capitalist interests, mostly of South African origin. In an attempt to win royal favour in the build-up to independence in the 1960s the Swazi royal family were allowed to become shareholders in some of the major mining and agricultural industries.

Administrative changes In Swaziland the *Ngwenyama* (king) ruled over a much more centralised political system than was the case in either Basutoland or Bechuanaland. (The origins of this were to be found in pre-colonial times – see Chapters 4 and 5). The British use of this system for colonial administration tended to further strengthen the power of the *Ngwenyama*. As a result when the British attempted to reform the administration in the 1940s and 50s they were unable to deprive Sobhuza and the *Libandla* of the power to appoint local chiefs and headmen. Proclamations modelled on those of Basutoland set up National Treasuries and regularised local courts. But the overall control of the *Ngwenyama* was maintained. In Basutoland, as we saw, district councils became critical alternatives to the power of the chiefs. In Swaziland district villages were kept under more central control and there appears to have been much less abuse of local

chiefly power. In 1954 forty district government centres (*tinkudla*) were established where local members of the *Libandla* met under the chairmanship of an appointed royal official (an *induna*). This ensured a high level of widespread overall royal control over local districts. The tinkudla became local centres for the gradual development of welfare services such as health clinics and primary schools.

Swazi independence A small group of educated Swazi had formed the Progressive Association as early as 1929. This was converted into Swaziland's first modern political party, the Swaziland Progressive Party (SPP), by J. J. Nquku who became its president in 1945.

Constitutional negotiations for a legislative council began in 1960. Whites, who had had their own elective Advisory Council since 1921 and who controlled much of the economy, expected a prominent position in any constitutional reforms. Sobhuza was prepared to share a legislative council with them with the *Ngwenyama* appointing at least half the seats. The Swaziland Progressive Party, however, rejected this kind of power sharing. It wanted a completely non-racial elected government based on universal franchise. In 1962 a short-lived Swaziland Democratic Party was formed with backing from white 'Swazilanders'. It called for a non-racial parliamentary democracy with secure guarantees for private property and white business investments. Meanwhile the SPP was split by disagreements among the leadership. In 1963 Dr Ambrose Zwane broke away to form a more radical group called the Ngwane National Liberatory Congress (NNLC). They demanded universal franchise and immediate independence. To demonstrate their strength they organised a series of strikes for higher wages among workers in the mines, sugar plantations and wood-pulp mills. With Sobhuza's support the British flew in troops from Kenya to break the strikes and restore 'law and order'.

In 1964 Sobhuza, a political realist, changed his tactics. Realising the British would not grant independence without some form of elected government, he formed his own political party, the Imbokodvo National Movement. Years of benevolent royal rule, the gradual but steady success of the *Ngwenyama's* land policy and the high level of royal control in the countryside worked together in Sobhuza's favour. Imbokodvo received the overwhelming support of the electorate and won all 24 elected seats for the Legislative Council in 1965. The constitution was revised and in the pre-independence elections for the 'National Assembly' in 1967

17.6 *left* The 1923 Swazi delegation to London to protest against the loss of Swaziland to white freeholders from South Africa, with King Sobhuza II seated centre and Sol Plaatje (member of SANNC and unofficial observer/adviser) standing at rear right.

below Delegates to a Swazi constitutional conference in London, 1963. Note the deliberate wearing of 'traditional' dress, a conscious assertion of Swazi independent, non-British, culture. This is in sharp contrast to the delegation of forty years earlier when the delegates presented themselves as 'loyal British subjects' in the vain hope that this would win them fair treatment.

Imbokodvo again won all elected seats. Swaziland became independent from Britain on 6 September 1968 with King Sobhuza as head of state, and the leader of Imbokodvo, Prince Makhosini Dlamini, as Prime Minister. A small Senate, half elected by the National Assembly and half appointed by the *Ngwenyama*, had the power of veto over laws passed in the lower House. Ultimate control thus lay firmly with the King.

South West Africa (Namibia) under South African rule, 1919–1966

When South Africa took over the League of Nations Mandate for South West Africa in 1919 (see above, Chapter 14), it treated the territory like an extension of the Union. Although 6 000 out of 15 000 Germans were repatriated to Germany after the war, the South African Government used the country as cheap land to sell to Afrikaner farmers. Afrikaners from South Africa, and even a few Boer trekkers from Angola, poured into the territory in the 1920s. By 1930 there were 30 000 whites in South West Africa, double the number in 1915, and together they owned or controlled 60 per cent of the land. So white domination of the land was maintained and most of the 200 000 Africans were confined to reserves' in the northern third of the country. The Herero were allocated a desert 'reserve' in the northeast which was of little use to them. A number of small additional 'reserves' were set aside in the 'white' central and southern districts. Most of these were in the poor and undesirable parts of the country and they soon succumbed to overgrazing and soil erosion. The South African 'Administrator' appointed chiefs and headmen to the reserves but they had no independent power. Their only real purpose was to collect government taxes and help

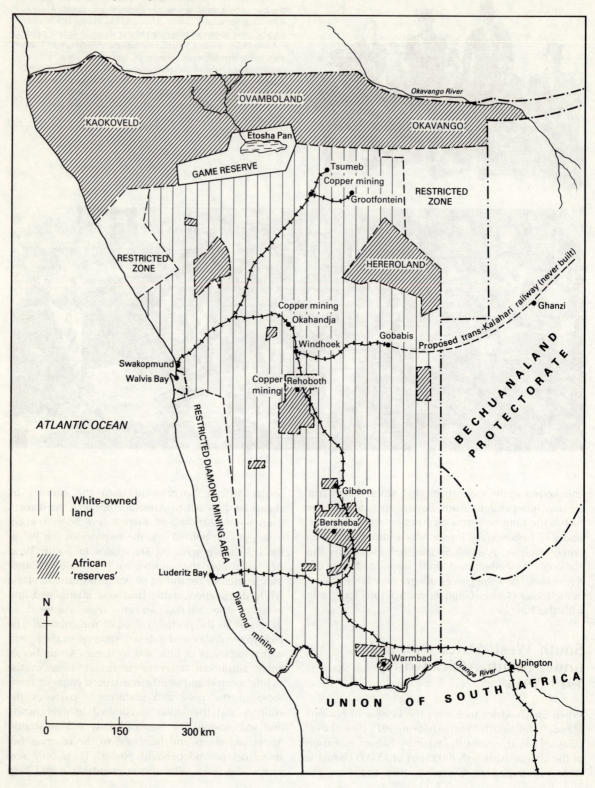

KAOKOVELD

OVAMBOLAND

Okavango River

OKAVANGO

Etosha Pan

GAME RESERVE

Tsumeb
Copper mining
Grootfontein

RESTRICTED
ZONE

RESTRICTED
ZONE

HEREROLAND

Ghanzi

Copper mining
Okahandja

Windhoek

Gobabis

Proposed trans-Kalahari railway (never built)

Swakopmund
Walvis Bay

Copper
mining

Rehoboth

BECHUANALAND PROTECTORATE

ATLANTIC OCEAN

RESTRICTED DIAMOND MINING AREA

Gibeon

Bersheba

| | | White-owned
land

Luderitz Bay

Diamond mining

African
'reserves'

N

0   150   300 km

Warmbad
Orange River
Upington

UNION   OF   SOUTH   AFRICA

recruit migrant workers. Basically the South African administration continued the German policy whereby Africans were primarily intended to work as labourers on white-owned farms, mines and other industries.

Most white settlers were involved in sheep and cattle ranching. Fisheries and canning factories soon became important industries at Lüderitz and Walvis Bay. But the biggest white capitalist developments were in mining, especially copper and diamonds. Copper mining had long been established at Tsumeb and Otavi in the north. Diamonds had been discovered near Lüderitz in 1907. After the war the German diamond mining companies were bought out by the South African-based Anglo-American Corporation which eventually amalgamated with De Beers. A huge tract of diamond-bearing desert coastland was closed off and declared a 'restricted area' (see Map 17.4). Most of the mine workers were hired on contract from the reserves by the employers' recruiting organisation, the South West Africa Native Labour Association (SWANLA). This ensured that workers were kept under tight control and on very low wages.

Early resistance to South African rule The first open African resistance to South African rule came from the Bondelswart Nama at Warmbad in the south. They had rebelled against the Germans in 1903–04 and had welcomed the South African invaders In 1915. But they soon found South African rule even worse than that of the Germans. In 1922 the 'dog tax' was increased from five shillings per dog to £1 for the first dog and £2 for a second one. To the Bondelswarts, who needed dogs for hunting, this was a heavy imposition. It was a clear attack on their ability to remain self-sufficient through hunting and they refused to pay the tax. Their former chiefs Abraham Morris and Jacob Christian returned from exile in South Africa to lead the Bondelswarts in their defiance of the Government. But they did not stand a chance against the ruthlessness of the Government. General Smuts sent in an armed force of 400 men, armed with machine-guns, and two aeroplanes to bomb the settlement. In this brutal crushing of a minor rebellion one hundred men, women and children were killed and many hundreds severely wounded.

Further north in 1924 the mixed-race community of Rehoboth refused to recognise South African rule and set up their own alternative Government. But their 'rebellion' was crushed in 1925 by a determined show of South African military force which included swooping low over the town in aeroplanes armed with machine-guns. This was followed by the mass arrest of over 600 'rebels'. At the same time the South Africans used the occasion to arrest a number of Herero in the region who had shown resistance to government authority.

South African defiance of United Nations 'trusteeship' After the Second World War South Africa refused to recognise the new 'trusteeship' of the United Nations (UN) which had replaced the mandates of its predecessor, the League of Nations. Other European powers accepted the UN principle of trusteeship and agreed to prepare their mandated territories for independence. But South Africa was moving in the opposite direction. It was determined not to give up 'South West Africa'. The territory contained valuable export minerals: uranium, lead and zinc as well as diamonds and copper. It also contained some valuable Afrikaner political supporters. When the National Party came to power in 1948 it in effect made 'South West Africa' a fifth province of the Union. Whites in the territory were granted the right to send six elected representatives to the South African Parliament. All six elected were National Party members: a valuable contribution at a time when the National Party still had only a narrow overall parliamentary majority.

South Africa had already extended its full range of segregationist legislation to Namibia: land restrictions, job colour-bars, pass laws and so on (see Chapters 15 and 16). There now followed a steady extension of *apartheid* laws to the territory. This included the Suppression of Communism Act and the familiar South African tactics of banning and detention to suppress opposition to its policies.

Resistance to South African rule For much of the 1950s the Namibian People's case against continuing South African occupation of their country was presented to the United Nations by an Anglican clergyman, Rev. Michael Scott. The South African authorities deliberately prevented Namibians themselves from travelling to the UN headquarters in New York. In 1958–59, as part of its implementation of the Group Areas Act, the Windhoek authorities forcibly removed 30 000 Africans from their Windhoek township to Katutura eight kilometres away. The Nama and Herero chiefs Samuel Witbooi and Hosea Kutako and the prominent Ovambo leader Sam Nujoma protested to the United Nations. But the UN was powerless to intervene. When the removals were physically resisted, heavy police action left thirteen dead and over fifty wounded.

In 1957 the Ovamboland People's Organisation

(OPO) was formed by Hermann Toivo Ja Toivo among Ovambo contract workers in Cape Town. In 1959 Ja Toivo, Jacob Kahange and Sam Nujoma launched the OPO in Windhoek and the following year widened it to become the South West Africa People's Organisation (SWAPO). Their aim was to unite Namibian workers against South African rule and to get the United Nations to take over the administration of the territory in preparation for independence. Meanwhile a largely Herero-based organisation, the South West Africa National Union (SWANU), was founded. It too opposed South African rule but criticised SWAPO for too great a reliance on outside help. As the South African Government banned African political protest in South Africa, SWAPO prepared for armed resistance. In August 1960 a small band of SWAPO guerrillas had their first clash with South African armed forces in the north of the country.

The United Nations and South Africa during the 1960s In the early 1960s there was mounting pressure within the UN from the increasing number of independent African states. In 1966 the UN General Assembly formally agreed to cancel South Africa's right to administer 'South West Africa'. The country's name was officially changed to 'Namibia' and the UN further agreed to recognise SWAPO as representative of the Namibian people. A UN 'Council for Namibia' was set up to look after Namibian affairs, but in the face of South Africa's continued refusal to withdraw it was unable to take over the administration of the territory. Furthermore, Europe and the United States were not prepared to take action against South Africa in case this upset their profitable business investments in the region.

Exercises

A. Think, discuss, understand and write

1 Compare the effects of colonial administrative changes on the rulers and peoples of Bechuanaland, Basutoland and Swaziland.
2 Assess the economic impact of colonial rule on either Botswana, Lesotho or Swaziland. In the light of this impact, what do you think should have been the main development priorities at independence?
3 Describe and compare the steps leading to the political independence of the three 'High Commission Territories'.
4 Discuss the relations between South Africa and the 'High Commission Territories' up to their independence. How did events in or relations with South Africa affect the development of African nationalism in any one of those territories?
5 Discuss the impact of South African rule on the peoples of Namibia. Why was South Africa so determined to hang on to Namibia?

B. Imaginative writing

Imagine you are the Rev. Michael Scott representing the case of the Namibian peoples to the United Nations in the 1950s. Write a five-minute speech presenting their case to the UN General Assembly.

C. Mapwork, groupwork and class discussion

Imagine that South Africa had succeeded in incorporating the High Commission Territories and Namibia into the Union of South Africa. Draw a map to represent this 'greater South Africa', including railways, the main industrial centres and labour migration routes. Discuss the thinking behind South Africa's desire to achieve this incorporation. Why did the other countries concerned resist these proposals? What might have been the situation today if the South African Government had achieved its aims?

CHAPTER 18

Southern Africa since the 1960s

Apartheid and the 'Bantustans'

The logic of *apartheid*, as outlined in Chapter 16, was to remove from 'white' areas all blacks except those needed for employment by whites. They were to be moved into 'tribal homelands', the old rural 'reserves' soon to be renamed 'Bantustans' which made up a mere 13 per cent of the land of South Africa (see Map 18.1). As a Government Commission reported in 1956 the 'homelands' were too small and too overcrowded on poor land to support even half of the black population. Nevertheless when Verwoerd became Prime Minister in 1958 he was determined to press ahead with the complete separation of blacks into self-governing 'independent' Bantustans. Economically it gave Government stricter control over the recruiting and movement of labour. Wages could be kept down and blacks could be prevented from organising effective trade-union activity. At the same time it was hoped that Bantustan self-government would defuse growing African nationalist demands for full political rights in South Africa. Blacks would be offered limited political 'freedom' in the government of 'their own homeland'. Such a system would also have the effect of breaking up South Africa's overwhelming black majority and disperse it into a series of separate 'tribal' minorities. This, it was hoped, would weaken black political opposition.

Not surprisingly there was widespread black opposition to Bantustan 'independence', especially among blacks in urban areas. More than half the official population of the various Bantustans lived permanently outside their appointed 'homelands'. Many had never even been to their so-called 'homelands'. But if their 'homeland' became politically 'independent', they would lose their South African citizenship and become 'foreigners' in the country of their birth.

Nevertheless the Government found some support for their policies from within the Bantustans, especially among Government-appointed chiefly authorities. They took the view that the limited gains of local self-government were better than no gains at all. In 1976 the Transkei became South Africa's first 'independent' Bantustan with Paramount Chief Kaiser Matanzima as Prime Minister. Next came Bophuthatswana in 1977 with Chief Lucas Mangope as Prime Minister. Then followed Venda in 1979 and Ciskei in 1981. Kwa-Zulu's Chief Minister, Gatsha Buthelezi, refused 'independence' unless he could have the whole of historic 'Zululand', that is the whole of Natal, instead of just a mass of scattered 'reserves'.

The Bantustan policy was accompanied by massive forced removals of population. Isolated black 'reserves' were closed and people forced into the main blocks of the Bantustans, often onto dry, barren and overcrowded land. Hundreds of thousands of 'illegal squatters' were driven off white-owned farms and from the squatter townships surrounding the main urban centres of employment. The Bantustans were used as dumping grounds for South Africa's unemployed, elderly and very young. Literally millions of people were affected: uprooted from their homes. In Qwa-Qwa, the tiny Sotho 'homeland' on the northern edge of Lesotho, for example, the population rose from 24 000 in 1970 to 300 000 by 1980 with numbers still rising. Most of them were forced in from outside the territory onto land that is barren, into settlements that have poor sanitation and where there is no local employment. The result was terrible hardship: overcrowding, poverty, malnutrition and disease.

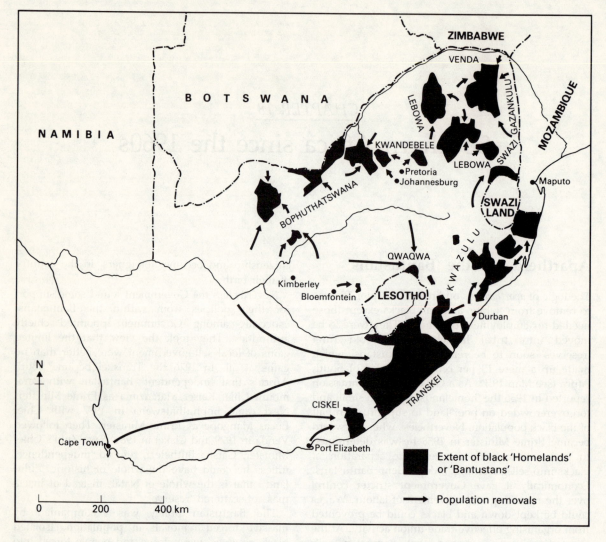

18.1 South Africa: 'Bantustans' and population removals

Opposition to apartheid since 1965

The mass arrests and bannings of the mid-1960s temporarily silenced black political opposition within South Africa itself. Umkhonto's sabotage campaign went into decline as the leaders in exile adjusted to their new position. They were dependent now on help from friendly countries and on funds raised in Scandinavia, Eastern Europe and the Soviet Union. The ANC's main military training camp was established at Morogoro in Tanzania. Until 1975, however, the white-controlled territories of Mozambique and Rhodesia formed an effective barrier against the penetration of Umkhonto guerrillas into South Africa. This situation was dramatically changed by the collapse of the Portuguese colonial empire and the independence of Mozambique in 1975.

Trade unionism and 'Black Consciousness', the early 1970s The early 1970s saw a rise in black self-confidence and political opposition within South Africa. This was promoted by the success of trade union activity and the spread of the 'Black Consciousness' movement. The apparent industrial calm in South Africa was shattered by a series of successful strikes by black factory workers in and around Durban in early 1973. Workers defied the law and struck for higher wages in the face of rising prices. Employers, anxious to avoid revolution, were prepared to meet their demands. The success of the early strikes encouraged others. The result was a revival of trade union activity throughout the country during the 1970s and the Government was forced to allow the official recognition of registered black trade unions. Though a large number of black and non-racial trade unions registered, many preferred to remain unofficial and so less restricted in their activities.

Meanwhile black students at the new segregated 'homeland' universities formed the South African Students Organisation (SASO) as a rival to the non-racial National Union of South African Students (NUSAS). The latter was dominated by white liberals at the four main English-speaking white universities. Students of SASO formed a 'Black Consciousness' movement in the early 1970s. They were the successors to the Africanists who in an earlier generation had broken away from the multi-racial policies of the ANC. They were dedicated to promoting black self-confidence and the belief that black people would liberate themselves without help from liberal whites. They rejected the Government's racial classification of 'non-white' and were prepared to accept Indians and 'coloureds' as well as Africans as 'blacks'. The main Black Consciousness leader was Steve Biko, a former medical student at the University of Natal. Biko was soon banned by the Government and in 1977 he died as a result of police assaults while in police detention. Between 1963 and 1986 something like a hundred people died while in police detention, some driven to commit suicide, many others dying from injuries received during 'interrogation'.

The Soweto uprising, 1976–77

On 16 June 1976 Soweto's secondary school students rose in revolt and the Government faced its most defiant challenge ever to *apartheid*. The students had begun protesting against the compulsory imposition of Afrikaans as the language of instruction for mathematics and social studies. Afrikaans was the language of the Government, their oppressors. Their rejection of Afrikaans symbolised the rejection of the whole inferior system of 'Bantu Education'. Apart from being compelled to teach 'inferior' syllabuses, black schools were starved of funds. They received per head of population only one-tenth of the amount of money allocated to white education. In many black schools classrooms were overcrowded and poorly equipped, teachers were poorly trained and there were few if any textbooks.

The revolt was sparked off by the over-reaction of police who tear-gassed and shot at a protest march of 15 000 school children. The initial clash with police left two children shot dead and many more injured. Within hours the whole township was ablaze in riot as cars were destroyed and administration buildings and beer halls were burnt to the ground. In the days that followed, the revolt spread to the rest of the Rand, to Natal and by August to Cape Town. Workers struck in sympathy. Defiant students challenged police with stones for weapons and dustbin lids for shields. The police replied with tear gas and live ammunition.

Although the revolt had largely subsided by the end of the year, school boycotts, riots and clashes with police continued on and off during 1977, especially on the first anniversary of the uprising. Altogether the revolt left 600 dead and 3000 wounded, most of them shot by police. By then compulsory Afrikaans had been dropped and the Government hoped to stem further urban unrest with promises of reform. But these were hollow promises as population removals, the Bantustans and *apartheid* continued. Meanwhile thousands of youths expelled from school had fled into exile, many to join the ANC.

South Africa in the 1980s

During the early 1980s the tempo of political events in South Africa rapidly gathered pace. Following 'Soweto' Umkhonto's sabotage attacks steadily increased. The Sasolburg oil refinery was set on fire in June 1980, and eastern Transvaal power stations were bombed in July 1981. But Umkhonto's campaign took a new turn in May 1983 when a bomb blast outside air force headquarters in a busy Pretoria street left 19 dead and 188 wounded

In 1983 the United Democratic Front (UDF) was formed as a non-racial political federation of anti-

18.1 Students in Soweto defy police armoured 'hippo', 1976.

apartheid organisations in South Africa. The UDF was widely seen as the internal political front of the banned and exiled ANC. One of its most strident calls was for the release of Nelson Mandela (imprisoned since 1962) and the unbanning of the ANC. Leading UDF figures frequently faced banning and detention. Nelson's wife, Winnie Mandela, defied banning orders and police harassment to become an outspoken opponent of *apartheid* and an inspiring leader in her own right. Meanwhile on a smaller but significant scale and more in the Africanist tradition of the Black Consciousness movement was the Azanian People's Organisation (AZAPO). Founded in 1978 AZAPO had tentative links with the exiled remnants of the PAC. And in opposition to both AZAPO and the UDF was Inkatha, a Zulu cultural organisation revived by Buthelezi in the mid-1970s. Though officially a broad-based political organisation, Inkatha remained primarily Zulu in composition. It claimed the support of at least half the country's six million Zulu. Inkatha members dominated the Kwa-Zulu Legislative Assembly and most prominent black members of the Zulu civil service also belong to Inkatha. Buthelezi appeared to be using Inkatha as a power base to win a prominent Zulu voice in any future South African political settlement.

In 1985 the then Anglican Bishop of Johannesburg, Desmond Tutu, became the second black South African to receive the Nobel Prize for Peace. Tutu used his position as a prominent churchman to appeal to South African whites to heed moderate black demands and dismantle *apartheid* before the country was torn apart by violent revolution. A number of significant Afrikaner intellectuals and even many Dutch Reformed Church ministers came to openly condemn the principles of *apartheid*. But still the majority of whites continued to support the Government's attempts to suppress opposition and

18.3 Aerial view of black workers on strike in Namibia, December 1971.

introduce 'reform' in the belief that this would prevent a black revolution.

The National Party Government introduced certain constitutional changes in the name of 'reform'. In 1984 Indians and 'coloureds' were brought into the parliamentary system though in a subordinate position. But the majority black population was still excluded from power and most Indians and 'coloureds' boycotted their parliamentary elections. P. W. Botha, who had succeeded Vorster as Prime Minister in 1978, became State President with vastly increased powers. Botha's 'reform' of *apartheid* included the abolition of the Immorality Act in 1985. But the main principles of the racially-based economic and political system of *apartheid* remained intact. In 1986 Botha announced the abolition of the hated 'pass laws'. But the Population Registration Act (which defined people according to race) and the Group Areas Act still remained in force. While the Government still pursued its policy of 'independent Bantustans' (now renamed 'Nation States'), the 'pass laws' which were expensive to administer, were no longer relevant. With most blacks officially belonging to an 'independent Nation State', the Government could argue that they were 'foreigners' in 'white' South Africa, subject to immigration control and obliged to carry

18.2 Funeral of the victims of the police 'state of emergency', South Africa, 1986. Note coffins draped in ANC flags.

a 'passport'. Opponents of *apartheid* maintained that the system could not be reformed, it could only be abolished.

During 1985 and 1986 Botha's Government found itself under attack from both sides of the political divide. A significant minority of Afrikaner nationalists criticized the Government for being too 'soft' with black opposition. They broke away from the National Party to form their own extreme opposition parties. One of these, the 'Afrikaner Resistance Movement' (*Afrikaner Weerstandsbeweging*) or AWB, was modelled on Hitler's Nazi party. It was pledged to use violence to uphold the 'purity' of Verwoerd's apartheid dream. On the other hand the main white political opposition in parliament, the Progressive Federal Party (PFP) came to accept the principle of black majority rule. Even some of the controllers of leading white capitalist industries such as the mining companies were beginning to favour a rapid and peaceful change to black majority rule. They felt this might be less damaging to their business interests than the alternative: a long drawn out and violent revolution. With this in mind some of the most powerful white businessmen in the country travelled to Zambia in 1985 to talk with exiled ANC leaders.

Beginning in September 1984 South Africa found itself in a near constant state of simmering revolution. There were massive strikes and school boycotts. Radical young blacks attacked and killed a number of black councillors, black policemen and suspected police informers in an attempt to expel all Government agents from urban townships. The aim of the 'Comrades' as they called themselves was to take over complete control of the townships. They showed their economic muscle by staging black boycotts of white-owned shops in the towns and cities, forcing a number out of business. Govern-

18.4 Reed dance in Swaziland.

ment security forces attempted to break the power of the Comrades by encouraging conservative groups of black 'vigilantes' to attack the Comrades and burn the houses of their supporters. This happened in particular in the Crossroads 'squatter' township near Cape Town. At the same time many hundreds of blacks, including school children, were shot dead by police in their attempts to reassert Government control in the townships. But blacks had a new-found confidence in their eventual victory. They no longer fled the country as refugees, but remained to pursue the struggle at home where they fought with arms smuggled in by the ANC from abroad.

The struggle for Namibian independence

During the 1960s small-scale guerrilla warfare continued in northern Namibia between SWAPO and South African security forces. In 1967 the South African Government tried to break SWAPO's political organisation by putting thirty-seven prominent SWAPO members on trial for treason in Pretoria. Ja Toivo among others was sentenced to twenty years imprisonment on Robben Island. Meanwhile the enforcement of *apartheid* continued. As in South Africa itself, there were large-scale population removals. Blacks were forced from small reserves and from white-owned land and pushed into dry, infertile, overcrowded 'Bantustans'.

As we saw in Chapter 17 most wage labour in Namibia was hired on contract by the recruiting agency SWANLA. Under the contract system men were separated from their families and were prevented from changing jobs in search of better pay and conditions. This high level of labour control enabled employers to pay very low wages. In December 1971 a series of strikes against the contract system brought the country's mines and other industries to a standstill. The strikers succeeded in getting SWANLA abolished, but they soon found that little else was changed. Freedom of movement was still restricted and wages and working conditions were just as bad.

Meanwhile the Government pushed ahead with its 'Bantustan' system. In 1973 'Ovamboland' was granted its 'independence'. But the people's rejection of the system was shown by the fact that less than three per cent of Ovambo voted in the elections. The new 'Bantu Authorities', however, were useful allies of the South African Government. They suppressed political opposition in the rural reserves

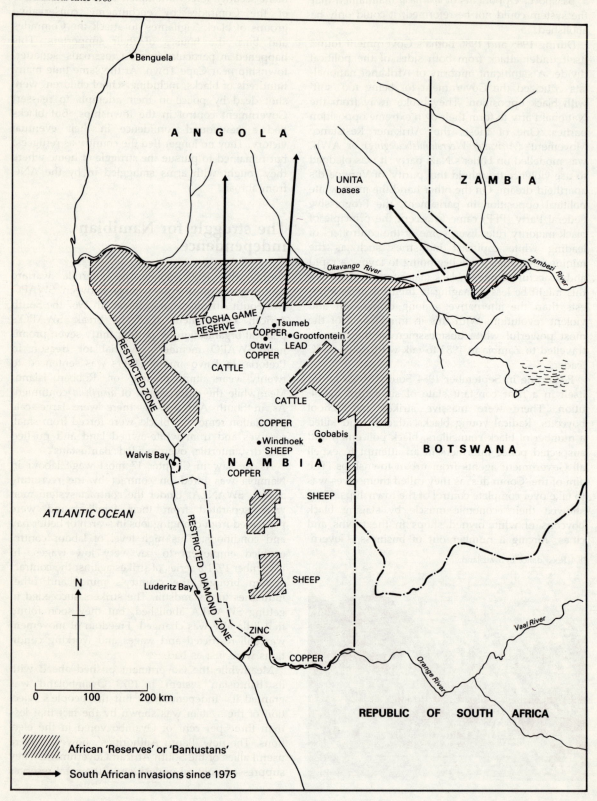

African 'Reserves' or 'Bantustans'

South African invasions since 1975

and many known members of SWAPO were brutally flogged.

The collapse of Portuguese rule in Angola in 1974–75 encouraged Namibians that the end of white rule in their own country might be drawing near. Many SWAPO supporters went into exile as refugees in Angola and neighbouring Zambia. The UN Commissioner for Namibia set up the Namibian Institute in Lusaka to educate the refugees and train them for government.

South Africa meanwhile saw the independence of Angola as a direct threat to its own position in Namibia. As the Soviet-supported MPLA prepared to take control of Angola at independence in November 1975, South African troops invaded the country from Namibia. South Africa hoped to replace the MPLA with Jonas Savimbi's rebel UNITA movement. This would provide the South Africans with a friendly neighbour who would prevent SWAPO using Angola as a base to attack them in Namibia. But the MPLA called in the assistance of several thousand Cuban troops to repell the South African invasion. South Africa withdrew but continued to keep its forces in the border region and to make periodic further invasions of Angola in support of UNITA and against SWAPO.

Within Namibia itself South Africa had been trying to bypass the United Nations and establish an independent Namibia under its own terms. Its aim was to set up a government which would exclude SWAPO, be friendly towards South Africa and maintain white domination of the economy. In 1978 white politicians in Namibia formed the 'Turnhalle Democratic Alliance' with 'Bantu Authorities' and other internal black leaders who were prepared to come to terms with South Africa. The United Nations, however, continued to insist that an independent Namibia based on South African-sponsored elections would not receive international recognition. South Africa must first end its illegal occupation by withdrawing its troops from the territory. Only then could 'free and fair' elections be held under direct UN supervision. But even in the face of world-wide condemnation South Africa continued to stall. From November 1984 the South African Government insisted that it would only withdraw its own troops from Namibia after Cuban troops were withdrawn from Angola. The majority of UN member states pressed for economic sanctions against South Africa to force it to withdraw from Namibia. But this was blocked by Britain and the United States who feared it would disrupt the country's valuable mineral exports, especially Namibia's uranium needed for their nuclear fuel. By the end of 1986 South Africa was still in full control of Namibia.

Lesotho since independence

Lesotho's history following political independence from Britain was dominated by heavy economic dependence upon South Africa. In fact the number of Basotho migrant labourers employed in South African mines doubled from 70 000 at independence in 1966 to 140 000 in the early 1980s. Within Lesotho itself opportunities for employment were very limited. As the population rose to 1.5 million, fewer and fewer families were able to support themselves from the worn out land.

When it became clear that the ruling BNP was losing the general election of January 1970, Prime Minister Jonathan cancelled the election and suspended the constitution. A major reason for Jonathan's increasing unpopularity had been his policy of co-operation with South Africa. Jonathan now reversed this policy, became an ardent supporter of the ANC and a strident critic of *apartheid*. His South African links had brought him no particular economic advantages. Lesotho had got very little aid and practically no economic investment from South Africa. Moreover, the South African Government had scornfully rejected appeals to discuss the return to Lesotho of the fertile 'Conquered Territory', taken in wars with the Orange Free State in the 1850s and 60s. Jonathan's new policy brought him greater international aid. But foreign aid was often mismanaged or wasted and dependence on South Africa for employment in fact increased. Though Jonathan's new hostility to South Africa won him back some popular support, this was soon undermined by his harsh suppression of political opposition.

Within South Africa opposition to *apartheid* was gathering pace. The Pretoria Government blamed the increasing internal unrest on the exiled ANC. It was therefore determined to force its neighbours to give up their support for the ANC and to expel South African refugees from their territories. In December 1982 a South African raid into Lesotho killed 42 people, twelve of them Lesotho nationals, the rest South African refugees or visitors. This was followed in 1983 by a partial blockade of Lesotho's borders, disrupting the regular flow of people and goods between the two countries. To relieve the pressure the ANC withdrew many of its refugees from Lesotho. But South Africa was still not satisfied.

In January 1986 South Africa mounted a complete blockade of Lesotho's borders. With food and petrol supplies running low and Jonathan becoming increasingly unpopular, the army took action. On 20 January a 'Military Council' took over power in Lesotho. Within ten days sixty ANC refugees had been forced to leave the country and the borders were reopened. But Lesotho's major economic problem of heavy dependence on South Africa remained. Yet at the same time the South African Government was cutting back on the employment of Lesotho nationals in order to help solve its own huge black unemployment problem. The future for Lesotho did not look bright, even if there were a change of government in South Africa.

Swaziland since independence

In contrast to Lesotho, Swaziland managed to maintain a fair degree of economic self-sufficiency. By the 1980s the extent of Swazi national land had been increased to sixty per cent of the country. Despite the increase in population to some 600 000, virtually every married Swazi man still had access to arable land. On this land families were able to grow enough food for basic survival but not much more than that. Most families had one or more members in full-time paid employment. Much of this employment was now to be found within Swaziland itself: in professional, clerical and administrative jobs, or in mining, forestry, sugar plantations or commercial

18.3 Lesotho since independence

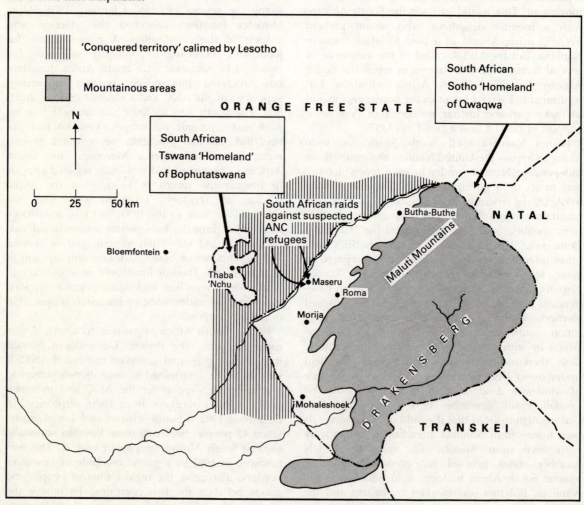

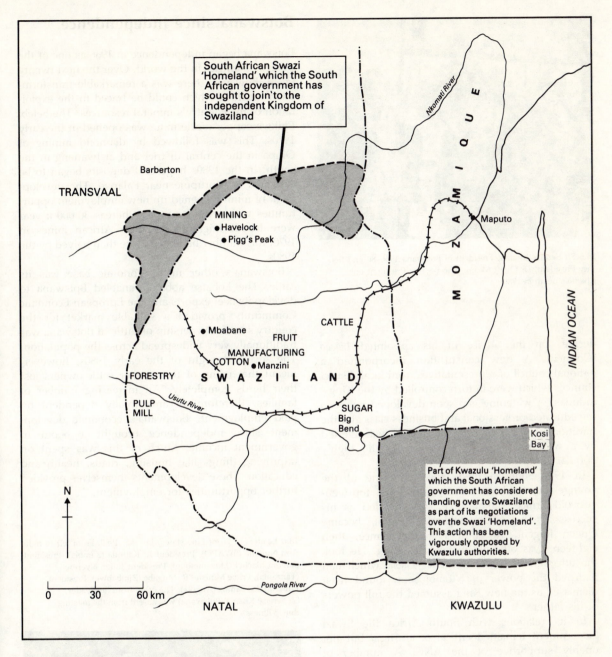

South African Swazi 'Homeland' which the South African government has sought to join to the independent Kingdom of Swaziland

Barberton

TRANSVAAL

MINING
● Havelock
● Pigg's Peak

Nkomati River

M O Z A M B I Q U E

● Maputo

CATTLE

● Mbabane

FRUIT
MANUFACTURING
COTTON ● Manzini

FORESTRY

S W A Z I L A N D

INDIAN OCEAN

Usutu River

PULP
MILL

SUGAR
Big
Bend ●

Kosi
Bay

Part of Kwazulu 'Homeland' which the South African government has considered handing over to Swaziland as part of its negotiations over the Swazi 'Homeland'. This action has been vigorously opposed by Kwazulu authorities.

N

0   30   60 km

Pongola River

NATAL

KWAZULU

18.4 Swaziland since independence

farming. Most of the major capitalist industries were financed by South African capital though the Swazi royal family owned twenty-five to forty per cent of the shares in many of these concerns. Royal profits from these investments were regarded as national rather than personal income.

Politically the monarchy maintained its dominance of Swazi national life. In the years immediately following independence in 1968 the power of the King was increasingly challenged by young educated Swazi, especially in the civil service. In the 1972 general election Dr Zwane's Ngwane National Liberatory Congress (NNLC) won three of the twenty-four elected seats. Soon afterwards, in 1973, Sobhuza abolished parliament and banned political parties. When Zwane protested, he was put in detention. But there was little further open opposition to Sobhuza's move. The King now ruled by

189

18.5 Sir Seretse Khama, President of Botswana 1966–80 and his Vice-President, Dr Quett Masire who became President on Khama's death in 1980.

Botswana since independence

Botswana began independence in 1966 as one of the poorest countries in the world. Over the next twenty years, however, there was a remarkable transformation much of which could be traced to the exploitation of the country's mineral resources. The Selebi Phikwe copper-nickle mine was opened in the early 1970s. This was followed by diamond mining at Orapa in the central district and at Jwaneng in the south. In the 1980s huge coal deposits began to be exploited at Morupule near Palapye. The development of mining opened up new employment opportunities within the country. Whereas 30 000 a year were labour migrants to South African mines in 1970, this number had been more than halved by the 1980s.

Botswana's other main economic base was its cattle. The Lobatse abbatoir enabled Botswana to develop its beef exports and the European Economic Community provided a valuable market for the country's beef. Ownership of cattle in Botswana was traditionally very widespread across the population. The severe drought of the early 1980s, however, meant that many of the smaller cattle-owners lost their herds completely. An increasing number of families, therefore, became totally dependent on paid employment. Botswana's economic development since independence brought a boom in government income. Much of this was spent on improving things like housing, roads, health and education. These developments themselves provided further opportunities for employment.

decree, on the advice of his appointed *Liqoqo* (Council). A new constitution incorporated a national council of representatives from local district councils which were in turn controlled by the King's indunas. A widening gap soon developed between the educated professional and business class and the traditional Swazi heirarchy. But a clash was averted by a widespread sense of loyalty to the highly popular King.

In 1982 Sobhuza died, aged 83. One of the youngest of Sobhuza's sixty-eight sons, fourteen-year-old Prince Makhosetive, was selected as his successor. The senior widow, Ntombi, became Queen Regent. In April 1986 the Prince, then eighteen, was officially installed as King. He took the title Mswati III. The regency *Liqoqo* which had usurped the power of Ntombi soon found itself dismissed as the new King assumed the full powers of his father.

In its relations with South Africa the Swazi Government remained critical of *apartheid* but not openly supportive of the ANC. A number of suspected ANC activists were arrested in Swaziland in the late 1970s, and in 1983 the Swazi regency signed a secret 'non-aggression pact' with South Africa. This guaranteed that Swaziland would not allow the ANC to operate from its territory. In spite of this assurance South African security forces flouted Swazi independence. Towards the end of 1986 they raided across the Swazi border and killed or kidnapped a number of people whom they alleged had connections with the ANC.

18.6 Leaders of Front Line states, Lusaka, 1980. From left to right Sam Nujoma (SWAPO), President K. Kaunda (Zambia), President Samora Machel (Mozambique), President Julius Nyerere (Tanzania), Prime Minister R. Mugabe (Zimbabwe), President Eduardo dos Santos (Angola). The other front line leader, Sir Seretse Khama (Botswana) was absent from the meeting due to illness.

Politicaly Botswana managed to achieve a remarkable level of stability. By the end of 1986 it remained the only country in Africa that had maintained an unbroken record of multiparty parliamentary democracy since independence. Botswana's first President, Sir Seretse Khama, was a confirmed believer in the value of a system which officially recognised and tolerated a parliamentary opposition.

18.5 Botswana since independence

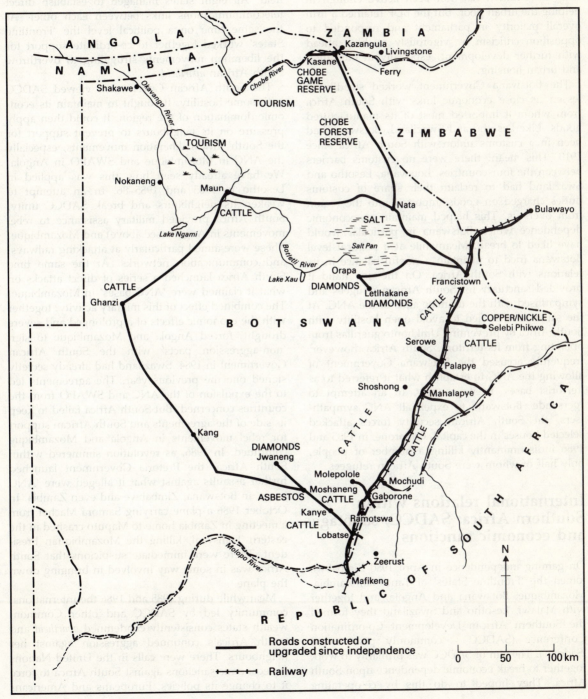

On Khama's death in 1982 he was succeeded as President by his deputy, Quett Masire, who continued the democratic tradition. At the general election of 1984 the Botswana National Front (BNF) gained a number of seats in urban areas where unemployment was high. The BNF argued that the BDP Government had not been active enough in helping the urban poor. But the BDP retained a firm overall majority in parliament and responded to opposition criticism by vigorously pushing ahead with further development, especially in education and urban housing.

The Botswana Government worked steadily to lessen its close economic links with South Africa from whom it imported most of its manufactured goods. Like Lesotho and Swaziland, Botswana had been in a customs union with South Africa since 1910. This meant there were no customs barriers between the four countries. Botswana, Lesotho and Swaziland had to reclaim their share of customs duties charged on goods imported into the region from overseas. This helped maintain an economic dependence which Botswana in particular would have liked to break. Meanwhile at a political level Botswana tried to maintain a careful balance in its relations with South Africa. On the one hand it provided sanctuary for South African refugees and sympathised with the ultimate aims of the ANC. At the same time it tried to avoid open hostility with South Africa by preventing Umkhonto guerillas from operating from its territory. South Africa, however, frequently accused the Botswana Government of allowing the ANC to establish what it referred to as 'terrorist bases' in its country. In an attempt to 'persuade' Botswana to expel all ANC sympathisers, the South African security forces attacked selected houses in the capital, Gaborone, in 1985 and 1986 indiscriminantly killing a number of people, only half of whom were South African refugees.

International relations within Southern Africa: SADCC, sabotage and economic sanctions

On gaining independence in April 1980 Zimbabwe joined the 'Frontline States' of Tanzania, Zambia, Mozambique, Botswana and Angola, and together with Malawi, Lesotho and Swaziland they formed the Southern African Development Co-ordination Conference (SADCC – commonly pronounced 'Saddac'). The aim of SADCC was primarily to work together to break economic dependence upon South Africa. They hoped to do this by co-operating between themselves on economic, transport and communications matters. The Conference held annual meetings to discuss problems and promote co-operation. Though regional economic and transport developments were difficult and slow, there was considerable success in the communications field. All eight states managed to establish direct telecommunications links between each other. At the same time on a political level the 'Frontline States' worked together to co-ordinate support for the liberation movements struggling to overthrow South African *apartheid*.

The South African Government viewed SADCC with some hostility. It sought to maintain its economic domination of the region. It could then apply pressure on its neighbours to prevent support for the South African liberation movements, especially the ANC in Mozambique and SWAPO in Angola. We have already seen how this was applied in Lesotho in 1983 and 1985–86. In an attempt to weaken its neighbours and break SADCC unity, South Africa provided military assistance to rebel movements in Angola (see above) and Mozambique. These were aimed particularly at attacking railways, and communication networks. At the same time South Africa launched a series of direct attacks on what it claimed were 'ANC bases' in Mozambique. The combined effect of this military activity, together with the economic effects of a prolonged and severe drought, forced Angola and Mozambique to sign 'non-aggression pacts' with the South African Government in 1984. Swaziland had already secretly signed one the previous year. The agreements led to the expulsion of the ANC and SWAPO from the countries concerned. But South Africa failed to keep its side of the agreements and South African support for rebel movements in Angola and Mozambique continued. In 1986, as revolution simmered within South Africa, the Pretoria Government launched further assaults against what it alleged were 'ANC bases' in Botswana, Zimbabwe and even Zambia. In October 1986 a plane carrying Samora Machel from a meeting in Zambia home to Maputo crashed in the eastern Transvaal, killing the Mozambiquan President. There were immediate suspicions that South Africa was in some way involved in bringing down the plane.

Meanwhile during 1985 and 1986 the international community led by SADCC and other Commonwealth states consistently condemned *apartheid* and South Africa's continued aggression against her neighbours. There were calls in the United Nations for economic sanctions against South Africa to force it to change its policies. Europeans and Americans with heavy capital investment in South Africa, however, were reluctant to agree to economic sanctions. And without their wholehearted support, sanctions were unlikely to be very successful.

Within Southern Africa at the beginning of 1987, history is very much 'in the making'. Every decade, every year even, major changes seem to be taking place. As we have seen in the final part of this book, events in South Africa itself have continued to dominate the region. The longer the liberation

18.6 Southern Africa in the 1980s: regional organisations and transport

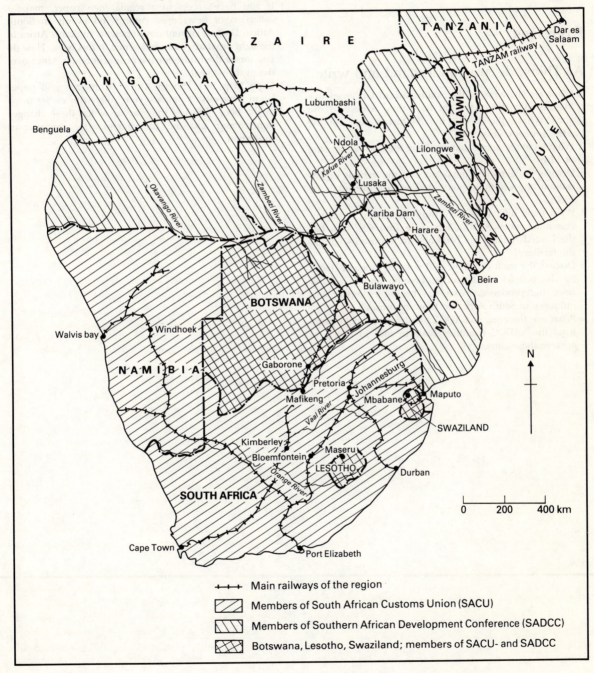

Main railways of the region

Members of South African Customs Union (SACU)

Members of Southern African Development Conference (SADCC)

Botswana, Lesotho, Swaziland; members of SACU- and SADCC

struggle in that country continues, the more complex and violent it becomes. And this violence cannot help but spill over to affect the whole region. We can seldom be sure of much in the future, but one thing is certain: many more people will suffer and many more lives will be tragically lost in the struggle for a freer and more just society for all the peoples of Southern Africa.

Exercises

A. Think, discuss, understand and write

1 What are the aims of the South African Government's 'Bantustan' policy? How far have they achieved these aims? What is the effect of the 'Bantustan' policy on the African people concerned?
2 What were the causes and results of the Soweto uprising of 1976?
3 Discuss the aims and importance of the various organisations opposed to the South African Government in the 1980s.
4 What main difficulties have those struggling for Namibian independence had to face since the 1960s? Why has the United Nations not been able to impose its will on the territory?
5 Discuss the main economic and political problems faced by the peoples of Botswana, Lesotho and Swaziland since independence. What has been the impact and influence of South Africa on those countries?
6 What are the aims of SADCC? Discuss the main problems the SADCC countries have to face in trying to achieve those aims.

B. Imaginative writing

Imagine you were present in Soweto on 16 June 1976. In not more than 300 words write a report for a newspaper on the events you witnessed on that day.

C. Mapwork, groupwork and class discussion

1 If you have access to a regular newspaper, make a collection of newspaper cuttings on events in South Africa. Discuss current developments in South Africa in the light of what you have learned in this book. How do you forsee the future for the people of South Africa over the next few years?
2 Copy Map 18.1, 'South Africa: Bantustans and population removals'. Compare your copy with earlier maps in the book. Discuss the way in which these changes came about and the consequences for the peoples concerned.

Recommended further reading

Unless otherwise stated, all books listed are available in paperback.

Suitable for School Certificate ('O level') students:

Benson, M., *The Struggle for a Birthright* (IDAF, London, 1985)

Callinicos, L., *Gold and Workers, 1886–1924* 'A People's History of South Africa Vol I', (Ravan, Johannesburg, 1981)

Callinicos, L., *Working Life, 1886–1940* 'A People's History of South Africa Vol II', (Ravan, Johannesburg, 1987)

Cameron, T. and Spies, S. B. (eds.), *An Illustrated History of South Africa* (Jonathan Ball, Johannesburg, 1986. Hardback)

Children under Apartheid: in photographs and text (IDAF, London, 1980)

Dachs, A. J., *Khama of Botswana* (Heinemann, London, 1971. Pamphlet)

Frederikse, J., *South Africa: a different kind of war* (James Currey, London, 1986)

Kallaway, P. and Pearson, P., *Johannesburg: Images and Continuities, 1885–1935* (Ravan, Johannesburg, 1986)

Luthuli, A., *Let My People Go: an autobiography* (Fontana Books, 1963)

Mandela, N., *No Easy Walk to Freedom* (Heinemann, London, 1973)

Mandela, N., *The Struggle is My Life* (IDAF, London, 1986)

Parsons, N., *A New History of Southern Africa* (Macmillan, London, 1982)

Parsons, N., *The Word of Khama* (Neczam, Lusaka, 1978. Pamphlet)

Plaatje, S. T., *Mhudi: an historical novel* (Heinemann, London, 1978)

Rasmussen, R. K., *Mzilikazi of the Ndebele* (Heinemann, London, 1977. Pamphlet)

Ritter, E. A., *Shaka Zulu* (Allen Lane, London, 1976)

Sanders, P., *Moshweshwe of Lesotho* (Heinemann, London, 1971. Pamphlet)

Saunders, C., (ed.), *Black leaders in Southern African History* (Heinemann, London, 1979)

Tlou, T. and Campbell, A., *History of Botswana* (Macmillan, Gaborone, 1984) *Unity in Action: a photographic history of the African National Congress* (ANC, London, 1982)

Warwick, P., (ed.), *The South African War* (Longman, London, 1980. Hardback)

Women under Apartheid: in photographs and text (IDAF, London, 1981)

Suitable for the general reader, teachers and more advanced students:

General;

The Cambridge History of Africa, 8 Volumes, each volume containing at least one chapter on Southern Africa (Cambridge University Press, 1977–86. Hardback)

Davenport, T. R., *South Africa, A Modern History*, 2nd Edition (Ravan, Johannesburg, 1986)

Denoon, D., and Nyeko, B., *Southern Africa since 1800*, 2nd Edition (Longman, London, 1984)

Matsebula, J. S. M., *A History of Swaziland*, 2nd Edition (Longman, London, 1976)

Maylam, P., *A History of the African People of South Africa* (St Martin's Press, New York, 1986. Hardback)

Omer-Cooper, J. D., *History of Southern Africa* (James Currey, London, 1987)

Wilson, M., and Thompson, L. (eds.), *The Oxford History of South Africa* 2 Vols (Oxford, 1969, 1975. Hardback. Vol. I, Paperback Edition, David Philip, Cape Town, 1981)

Part I: Before 1800:

Elphick, R., *Khoikhoi and the founding of White South Africa* (Ravan, Johannesburg, 1985)

Elphick, R. and Giliomee, H., (eds.), *The Shaping of South African Society* (Longman, London, 1979)

Inskeep, R. R., *The Peopling of Southern Africa* (David Philip, Cape Town, 1978)

Lewis-Williams, J. D., *The Rock Art of Southern Africa* (Cambridge University Press, 1983. Hardback)

Phillipson, D. W., *The Later Prehistory of Eastern and Southern Africa* (Heinemann, London, 1977)

Thompson, L., (ed.) *African Societies in southern Africa* (Heinemann, London, 1969)

Part II: 1800–1870:

Lye, W. and Murray, C., *Transformations on the Highveld* (David Philip, Cape Town, 1980)

Marks, S. and Atmore, A., (eds.), *Economy and Society in Pre-Industrial South Africa* (Longman, London, 1980)

Morris, D. R., *The Washing of the Spears* (Sphere Books, London, 1966)

Omer-Copper, J. D., *The Zulu Aftermath* (Longman, London, 1966)

Peires, J. B., *The House of Phalo* (Ravan, Johannesburg, 1981)

Peires, J. B. (ed.), *Before and After Shaka: papers in Nguni history* (Rhodes University, Grahamstown, 1981)

Rasmussen, R. K., *Migrant Kingdom: Mzilikazi's Ndebele in South Africa* (David Philip, Cape Town, 1978)

Sanders, P., *Moshoeshoe, Chief of the Sotho* (Heinemann, London, 1975. Hardback)

Thompson, L., *Survival in Two Worlds: Moshoeshoe of Lesotho* (Oxford, 1976. Hardback)

Part III: 1870–1910:

Beinart, W., *The Political Economy of Pondoland, 1860–1930* (Cambridge University Press, and Ravan, Johannesburg, 1982)

Bley, H., *South-West Africa under German Rule, 1894–1914* (Heinemann, London, 1971. Hardback)

Bonner, P., *Kings, Commoners and Concessionaires: the evolution and dissolution of the nineteenth-century Swazi state* (Cambridge University Press, and Ravan, Johannesburg, 1983)

Bonner, P. (ed.), *Working Papers in Southern African Studies* (Ravan, Johannesburg, 1981)

Bundy, C., *The Rise and Fall of the South African Peasantry* (Heinemann, London, 1979)

Delius, P., *The Land Belongs to Us: the Pedi polity, the Boers and the British in nineteenth-century Transvaal* (Heinemann, London, and Ravan, Johannesburg, 1983)

Duminey, A. and Ballard, C. (eds.), *The Anglo-Zulu War: New Perspectives* (University of Natal, Pietermaritzburg, 1981)

Guy, J., *The Destruction of the Zulu Kingdom* (Longman, London, 1979)

Katjavivi, P., *Namibia: A History of Resistance* (James Currey, London, 1988)

Marks, S. and Rathbone, R. (eds.), *Industrialisation and Social Change in South Africa* (Longman, London, 1982)

Pakenham, T., *The Boer War* (Futura, London, 1982)

Palmer, R. and Parsons, N. (eds.), *The Roots of Rural Poverty, in Central and Southern Africa* (Heinemann, London, 1977)

Shillington, K., *The Colonisation of the Southern Tswana* (Ravan, Johannesburg, 1985)

Tlou, T., *A History of Ngamiland, 1750–1906* (Macmillan, Gaborone, 1985)

van Onselen, C., *Studies in the Social and Economic History of the Witwatersrand, 1886–1914, I New Babylon, II New Nineveh* (Longman, London, and Ravan, Johannesburg, 1982)

Warwick, P., *Black People and the South African War* (Cambridge University Press, and Ravan, Johannesburg, 1983)

Webster, E. (ed.), *Essays in Southern African Labour History* (Ravan, Johannesburg, 1978)

Part IV:

Benson, M., *Nelson Mandela* (Penguin Books, Harmondsworth, 1986)

Bozzoli, B. (ed.), *Labour, Townships and Protest: studies in the social history of the Witwatersrand* 'History Workshop 1' (Ravan, Johannesburg, 1979)

Bozzoli, B. (ed.), *Town and Countryside in the Transvaal: capitalist penetration and popular response* 'History Workshop 2' (Ravan, Johannesburg, 1983)

Bozzoli, B. (ed.), *Class, Community and Conflict* 'History Workshop 3' (Ravan, Johannesburg, 1987)

Halpern, J., *South Africa's Hostages: Basutoland, Bechuanaland and Swaziland* (Penguin, Harmondsworth, 1965)

Hanlon, J., *Beggar Your Neighbours; apartheid power in Southern Africa* (James Currey, London, 1986)

Hirson, B., *Year of Fire, Year of Ash. The Soweto Revolt: Roots of a Revolution?* (Zed, London, 1979)

Kane-Berman, J., *Soweto: Black Revolt, White Reaction* (Ravan, Johannesburg, 1978)

Kuper, H., *Sobhuza II: Ngwenyama and King of Swaziland* (Duckworth, London, 1978)

Lacey, M., *Working for Boroko: the origins of a coercive labour system in South Africa* (Ravan, Johannesburg, 1983)

Lodge, T., *Black Politics in South Africa since 1945* (Longman, London, and Ravan, Johannesburg, 1983)

O'Meara, D., *Volkskapitalisme: class, capital and ideology in the development of Afrikaner Nationalism, 1934–1948* (Cambridge University Press, and Ravan, Johannesburg, 1983)

Plaatje, S. T., *Native Life in South Africa* (Ravan, Johannesburg, 1982, and Longman, London, 1987)

Roux, E., *Time Longer than Rope* (Wisconsin, 1964)

Simons, J. and R., *Class and Colour in South Africa* (Reprint, IDAF, London, 1983)

Willan, B., *Sol Plaatje, South African Nationalist* (Heinemann, London, and Ravan, Johannesburg, 1984)

Index